D0202832

When Public Housing Was Paradise

When Public Housing Was Paradise

Building Community in Chicago

J. S. Fuerst

with the assistance of D. Bradford Hunt

PRAEGER

Westport, Connecticut
London

Library of Congress Cataloging-in-Publication Data

When public housing was paradise : building community in Chicago / [compiled and edited by] J. S. Fuerst ; with the assistance of D. Bradford Hunt.
p. cm.
Includes bibliographical references and index.
ISBN 0–275–97497–9 (alk. paper)
1. Public housing—Illinois—Chicago—History. 2. Chicago Housing Authority—History. 3. African Americans—Housing—Illinois—Chicago—Interviews. 4. Community development—Illinois—Chicago—History. I. Title: Building community in Chicago. II. Fuerst, J. S. III. Hunt, D. Bradford, 1968–
HD7288.78.U52C478 2003
363.5′85′0977311—dc21 2002037058

British Library Cataloguing in Publication Data is available.

Library of Congress Catalog Card Number: 2002037058
ISBN: 0–275–97497–9

First published in 2003

Praeger Publishers, 88 Post Road West, Westport, CT 06881
An imprint of Greenwood Publishing Group, Inc.
www.praeger.com

Printed in the United States of America

The paper used in this book complies with the Permanent Paper Standard issued by the National Information Standards Organization (Z39.48–1984).

10 9 8 7 6 5 4 3 2 1

To Dorothy,
without whom this book would never have been written,
and to Elizabeth Wood,
without whom the public housing program would not have flourished

Contents

Acknowledgments xi

Foreword by John Hope Franklin xiii

Preface xv

Introduction **1**

Chapter 1 The Vision and Its Implementers: The Staff of the CHA **9**

Oscar C. Brown, Sr. 10
John Ducey 12
Ed Holmgren 15
Ruth Sable 16
Emil Hirsch 19
Tom McDade 22
Ted Greenhalgh 24
Winston Kennedy 26
Daisy Brumfield 29
Muriel Chadwick 32
Patricia McArthur Harris 34
Beverly Shepherd 35
Phyllis Offord 37

Chapter 2 Laboratories for Leadership **41**

Cordell Reed 42
Bennie L. Crane 44
Bertrand Ellis 47
Leon Hamilton 52

Andrew Greenlee 57
Jerry Butler 60
Melvin Wilson 63
Joseph Berrios 66
Nelvia Brady 68
James Fletcher 70
Wilson Frost 72

Chapter 3 Gateway to the American Dream 75
Erman and Dorothy Sing 76
Edgar Johnson 79
John Wilson 83
Acey Harris 86
Margaret Austin 89
Charlotte Young Moore 92
Troy L. Yates, Jr. 94
Henry and Elouise Messiah 97

Chapter 4 Reflections on Integration, Segregation, and Choice 101
Sidney and Bernice Bild 103
Gwendolyn Duncan Alexander 105
Stephen Pugh 106
Andrew Thompson 108
Phillip and Jeffery Roberts 110
William Shaw 114
Adolph Slaughter 116
Angela Willuweit 119
Deborah Gilliam Mayes 121
David Doran 122

Chapter 5 Investments in the Mind: The Importance of Education 125
Eugene Farmer 125
Rita Lewis-Perry 128
Winifred DeLoache 130
Abdul Alkalimat 133
Maude Davis 137
Mary Robinson 138
Ananias Samuel, Jr. 140
Vonsell Ashford 144
Joe Thompson 146
Hortense Irwin Bright 147

Chapter 6 The Building of Character: Religion, Sports, and Music **151**
Claude and Addie Wyatt 152
Alvin Lewis 155
Everett Jackson 156
Roscoe King 159
Bill "Butterball" Crane 161
Walter Blocker 163
Ramsey Lewis 166
Barbara Jones Slater and Leon Jones 168
Alyce Holden and Loretta Martin 171
Richard Townsell 172
Arnold Weddington 174
Sam Mendenhall 176

Chapter 7 And the Band Played On and On . . . and Then Off Key: Residents Who Stayed in CHA **179**
Hattie Calvin 180
Hallie Amey 182
Helen Preston 183
Margaret Wilson 185
Rosita Henry 187
Edna McNeal 189
Hazel Johnson 189
Myrtle Morrison 190

Conclusion: The Rebirth of Public Housing **193**
Design and Size 195
Race and Location 197
Community Building, Religion, and Sports 198
Quality of Staff and Regulations 199
Tenant Selection 200
The Real Solution: A Return to the Policies of Yesterday 203

Afterword 205

Notes 211

Further Reading 215

Index 217

Photo Essay follows page 124

Acknowledgments

During ten years of research and writing, this book involved countless hours of interviewing, editing, and reviewing. I owe a great debt to the many people who opened themselves up to me and who took the time to share their life stories. Their friendship has been a valuable enhancement to my life.

The ideas in the conclusion are my own, distilled from evidence in the interviews and supplemented by my years of experience with public housing. From 1946 to 1953, I served as Director of Research and Statistics for the Chicago Housing Authority, and since that time I have written extensively on public housing and social welfare. However, several current experts in the field have read the conclusion and provided important suggestions and additions. These include Gordon Cavanaugh, General Counsel to the Council of Large Public Housing Authorities and the former head of the Philadelphia Housing Authority; Daniel J. Wuenschel, longtime Executive Director of the Cambridge (Massachusetts) Housing Authority; and Joseph Shuldiner, most recently Executive Director of the Chicago Housing Authority but previously in top positions with the U.S. Department of Housing and Urban Development, the Los Angeles Housing Authority, and the Housing Department of New York City.

Many individuals were invaluable in helping this project reach fruition. Several of the interviews were conducted by Kathleen McCourt, a thoughtful oral historian at Loyola University in Chicago. Nearly all the interviews had to be considerably shortened and condensed into readable form without sacrificing the essence of the respondent's views. The first round of this task was painstakingly performed by Jim McNeill, to whom I am grateful. Most of the interviews were transcribed from tapes by Natalie Hector, who did an efficient and conscientious job. Jane Sims provided encouragement and essential organizational support during the final stages of this project.

I am especially grateful for the patience of my daughter Ruth Fuerst, my son Dan Schauben-Fuerst, his wife Ronna Schauben, and my son-in law Jim Block, who each read the entire manuscript and made many valuable contributions. Their love and guidance have sustained this book to its completion. Others who read the work-in-progress and were helpful include my friends Robert Glass, Miles Shapiro, Jane Hunt (Brad Hunt's mother), and the late Bill Newmann. Bill's support was an important encouragement, and his passing in 2002 was a great loss. Finally, Sydney Lewis, who has worked on several of Studs Terkel's oral history projects, graciously proofread the manuscript, making enriching suggestions.

Many other friends were great supporters of this endeavor. Ethel Shufro, whose husband, Milton (Mick) Shufro, brought me to the Chicago Housing Authority in 1945, was an important catalytic agent in the initiation of this book. Others whose support was invaluable include Charles O'Reilly, Eugene Simonoff, Rado Mijanovic, Eugene and Sylvia Cotton, the late Leon and Van Bobrow, Jack and Audrey Sullivan, Ernie and Priscilla Leazer, Geri and John Macsai, Sarah and the late Robert Busch, Hy and Pearl Hirschfield, Dan and Fay Levin, Murray Gruber, Dorothy Gans, Sophie Bloom, and Tiny Jackson.

In 1998, I had the great fortune of meeting Brad Hunt, then working on his dissertation on the history of the Chicago Housing Authority at the University of California at Berkeley. Brad agreed to take on the bulk of editing and organizing this book, seeing it through to the end. We spent many pleasurable hours together discussing the interviews, debating the conclusions, and reviewing the numerous details involved in completing a manuscript. His extraordinary patience, help, and friendship have been most rewarding.

Finally, my grandchildren Sarah, Matthew, and Jessie have brightened my spirits when I needed it. Up to the time of her death in October 1998, my beloved wife, Dorothy Fuerst, was a constant guiding spirit without whose cooperation, understanding, and forbearance I could never have completed this work.

J. S. Fuerst, Chicago, IL

Foreword

Jimmy Fuerst has given us something remarkable in this book. It is a journey of recovery that unearths forgotten truths about the past. In contrast to the usual image of gang-dominated, rat-infested, unattractive "projects," Fuerst offers another view, carrying us back to a time when low-rent public housing meant healthy and attractive communities that were well-designed and well-managed. He allows recent inhabitants and former residents of Chicago's developments to share their stories—engaging and inspiring vignettes seldom heard or read. Their narratives deserve telling, and I can think of no one whose experience and interest provide greater preparation than Jim Fuerst.

The interviews here capture the lives of working, middle, and higher-income individuals that were influenced in unique and particular ways as a result of their experiences in and with public housing. Most are African Americans who took advantage of New Deal policies and, against numerous odds, found their way out of poverty. There are role models, quiet leaders, and even a few heroes in this volume, but what each testimony highlights and reinforces is a genuine respect for public housing and the sense of community it once inspired.

As the voices here suggest, the participants in this nuanced and intriguing past were politically aware, socially conscious, motivated, and disciplined. Their individual and collective success can, in part, be attributed to housing policies that included careful tenant selection, efficient management, and an informed leadership dedicated to the concept that public housing was both necessary and worthwhile.

The histories contained herein represent a starting point for further study—insisting that a reformed and robust public housing program did, at one time, adequately serve the social and economic needs of its dwellers.

Hopefully, today's policymakers will hear and listen to the voices of these former residents and begin the process of rejuvenating programs and policies that will once again inspire continuity and community in Chicago's public housing.

John Hope Franklin
James B. Duke Professor History Emeritus and
Chairman of the Advisory Board to "One America in
the 21st Century," former President William
Jefferson Clinton's Initiative on Race

Preface

In the last two decades of the twentieth century, American politicians turned away from the idea that government can play a constructive role in addressing social problems. The turn to the right began with President Ronald Reagan and continued through the 1990s with House Speaker Newt Gingrich, but it engulfed much of the Democratic Party as well. President Bill Clinton in 1996 declared to the nation that "the era of big government is over," and signed a welfare reform bill that repealed long-held entitlements to government assistance. In the 1990s, "privatization" became a buzzword and then public policy for institutions such as prisons, utilities, and schools. Today the Social Security program, the hallmark of President Franklin Roosevelt's New Deal, is threatened by similar trends. Government at all levels has retreated from its previous commitment to protecting and improving the lives of its citizens.

Americans seem to believe that ameliorating the weaknesses of the market should be attempted only indirectly, through a minimal regulatory state and not an activist one. Whether in health care, the environment, education, or housing, the idea that government can solve social problems is on shaky ground in American political life. The New Deal—a period of great advancement in social welfare programs—is today portrayed as a necessary evil, needed only to save capitalism from itself. Meanwhile, Western European nations have long accepted the need for a well-managed and relatively generous safety net for education, health, housing, and welfare. Residents in these countries demand government programs and pay progressive taxes to finance them, even if they do not directly benefit.

Although conservatives often trumpet "individualism," American society also has deep roots in a social contract that emphasizes community and togetherness. New Deal programs have successfully aided this social contract in several areas, one of which is public housing—or at least it was during its first two decades. The story of how these efforts have positively affected the lives of people and communities has never been fully told. Public housing—wisely implemented and supportive of citizen aspirations in its early years—facilitated the building of community and the achievement of the American Dream.

Most studies of community-building rarely mention the constructive role of the federal government in the past, nor do high-level studies of government housing ever examine concrete examples of successful outcomes. No book has described the contributions of public housing to Chicago's working class. The result is a dangerous lack of understanding of how government made positive gains in the past, the nature of its decline, and how it can succeed in the future.

This book looks at community-building at the local level, through the original voices of seventy-nine individuals from Chicago who lived or worked in public housing when it was paradise. On the city's South Side, poor but striving families benefited from federal and local government programs wisely administered by a caring bureaucracy with a strong sense of mission. The resulting accomplishments of these families is nothing short of remarkable, and their voices deserve to be heard. This book is the story of these families—their hopes and dreams and achievements. Their stories are told in their own words, in a series of interviews with those who were there.

The future role of government in community-building remains an open debate. But the story of the advancements begun in the New Deal and carried out by dedicated individuals demonstrates that national resolve is capable of providing a path toward positive advancement for millions of families. It is vital to recognize that just as there were thousands of poor but worthy families in the 1940s and 1950s, so there remain today tens of thousands of similar families struggling to meet the rent in less-than-adequate buildings. They are in great need of solid, affordable housing. We need a renewed public sector commitment to help make the American dream a reality for these families, now denied the chance. This book stands as a testament to the fact that government action created strong, positive communities in the past and can do so in the future.

Introduction

> "There he is again, Bigger!" the woman screamed, and the tiny, one-room apartment galvanized into violent action. The rat leaped and turned and ran in a narrow circle, looking for a place to hide and leaped again past Bigger and scurried on its rasping feet to one side of the box and then to the other, searching for the hole. Then it turned and reared upon its hind legs.
>
> —Richard Wright, *Native Son*

In the spring of 1940, when Richard Wright's *Native Son* was first published, Bennie Crane was four years old and living with his parents and two brothers in a small, run-down, rat-infested apartment on Chicago's South Side. Like the fictional Bigger Thomas, Bennie Crane and his family resided in the heart of the Black Belt, where more than 90 percent of Chicago's African-American community was crowded into some of the city's most dilapidated and dangerous housing. Again and again, ancient furnaces and faulty hot plates sparked fires that tore through the area's notorious "kitchenette" apartments in buildings subdivided to accommodate the enormous influx of black migrants from the South after World War I. The Cranes lived in a typical Black Belt tenement designed to house four families but filled with a dozen. In a scene straight out of *Native Son*, Crane remembers sitting up nights "to chase the mice away from my younger brothers." Though his father had a good job in the nearby stockyards, it was extremely difficult for any but the wealthier African-American families to find adequate housing in the Black Belt. The combination of white hostility and racist real estate codes made it extremely risky for black families to go looking for housing anywhere else in Chicago.

Despite these obstacles, Bennie Crane's family would soon be living at one of the addresses most sought after by African Americans in the city. In early 1941, the Chicago Housing Authority (CHA) opened the Ida B. Wells Homes, a handsome, well-planned 1,600-unit public housing consisting of two-, three-, and four-story brick apartment buildings. More than 18,000 families applied to live in Wells, and the Cranes made the cut. In a city starved for new housing, the opening of Wells was a major media event. The Chicago *Defender*, the legendary African-American daily, printed a twenty-page special section to mark the occasion. The Chicago *Herald American* ran a photo essay celebrating one family's move "from hovel to haven." More than fifty years later, Crane still remembers the novelty of having his own living room and kitchen. "It was just nice and spacious, clean and well-lit. And it was home." Something a kitchenette apartment could never be.

Ida B. Wells proved to be a remarkable incubator for the young Bennie Crane. The first in his family to attend college, Crane would go on to become deputy chief of the Chicago Fire Department. Crane's story is hardly unique and is repeated by many of the individuals who come to life in this book. Cordell Reed, a neighbor of Crane's whose father also worked in the stockyards, went on from Wells to become an engineer and eventually a senior vice president with Illinois's largest electric utility. Bertrand Ellis, another child of Wells, grew up to be a vice president of Chicago's Northern Trust Bank. Thousands of CHA residents from this generation rose from equally humble circumstances to become teachers, police officers, attorneys, and executives.

Public housing once served as an engine for upward mobility and as an incubator of the middle-class, a fact largely ignored today. Early Chicago Housing Authority projects like Ida B. Wells, Altgeld Gardens, Dearborn Homes, Cabrini Homes, and Leclaire Courts, to name a few, helped thousands of Chicagoans escape slum housing conditions and enter a world that offered first-rate housing, a close-knit community, and the positive pride that comes from a shared experience. In short, public housing and the CHA once worked—spectacularly well.

Today, when people talk about public housing, the discussion is almost entirely negative, an understandable reaction for those unfamiliar with public housing's first twenty years.[1] Media coverage of periodic horror stories and best-selling books on life in "the projects" have formed the basis of the public's image. Alex Kotlowitz's *There Are No Children Here* is a grim chronicle of two brothers growing up in a CHA high-rise project in the mid-1980s, and Nicholas Lemann's *The Promised Land* describes the multi-generational descent of one family into the underclass in Chicago's Robert Taylor Homes. Movies such as Frederick Wiseman's *Public Housing*, a 1997 documentary centered on the Ida B. Wells Homes in the early 1990s, offer no historical context and no recognition that Wells was once a highly desirable, thriving, maturing community.[2] Bleak tales like these have caused us to forget how well public housing once worked and have convinced most Americans that it can never work again.

This book retrieves the almost bucolic world of public housing in the 1940s and 1950s that was the norm—not the exception—for people like Bennie Crane. The residents in this book have hundreds of different stories to tell, but almost always they return to one central idea: the CHA's complexes were more than mere housing complexes; they were, in the words of several residents, more like "extended families." In its first twenty years the CHA fostered an environment that created a strong sense of community—these projects were true "villages" raising children. CHA-sponsored sports teams, clubs, parades, and flower contests inspired residents to invest all sorts of energy in improving their projects. Frequently, interviewees brought up specific attributes that, while small, were vital elements of project life. Flowers were a constant source of pride. Tenants remembered with a touch of fear the fact that if they so much as walked on certain grass areas, they risked a fine. Numerous interviews recall in almost reverent terms the responsibilities for cleaning hallways and porches and other common areas. Many traced the decline of their developments in the 1960s not merely to the arrival of gangs but also to management's laxity in enforcing its own rules and to the disappearance of flowers.

The interviews in this book challenge several myths. It is commonly assumed that throughout its history public housing has been a curse on black Chicagoans. Yet for many years public housing was cherished by the black community. A second myth is that public housing has always been designed as housing for the poorest of the poor. The early residents were in fact upwardly mobile. Finally, few remember that CHA projects were efficiently managed; the former tenants interviewed here speak highly of the CHA's early management and the standards they upheld. That public housing once worked in Chicago is a fact that cannot be repeated enough because it is so contrary to today's perceptions.

Why did the early Chicago Housing Authority work so well? To understand the initial success of the CHA, one must start with its talented leadership. Elizabeth Wood served as CHA Executive Director for its first seventeen years and led the CHA with vision and integrity. Born to missionary parents in Japan, Wood was a rare mix of crusader and pragmatist. She taught poetry at Vassar College before moving to Chicago in the early 1930s to work for one of Chicago's private welfare agencies. She quickly grew frustrated with its methods. In an interview with Studs Terkel for his book *Hard Times*, she explained her social work colleagues' tendency to "sit, be passive, and let your client tell you what's wrong." Searching for some tangible way to improve the lives of her clients, she turned to housing. With one particularly troubled family—an alcoholic father, his despairing wife, and their nine children—she found that moving them from a cramped three-room apartment to a sunny apartment with plenty of room did far more for their disposition than any other kind of service. "I saw the magic that house performed," Wood told Terkel. "The family bloomed. I learned my first lesson about the meaning of a house."[3]

In 1934 Wood was appointed director of the Metropolitan Housing Council, a prominent housing reform group, and in 1937, Mayor Edward Kelly chose her as the Executive Secretary of the newly chartered Chicago Housing Authority. Wood proved remarkably adept early on at negotiating Chicago's treacherous political terrain. Kelly, a shrewd machine politician, was no patrician reformer. But Wood's deputy, Milton Shufro, convinced Kelly that he could help his politically tarnished image by making the CHA an incorruptible housing authority.[4] As a result, the CHA remained free from patronage under Wood's tenure. Several members of the early staff are interviewed in Chapter 1.

Residents also had to meet standards. The CHA carefully screened incoming tenants and swiftly evicted destructive ones. Former residents interviewed here talk repeatedly—and approvingly—about the strict rules of the early CHA. If residents lived in row houses, they were expected to tend the lawn outside their apartment. If they lived in high-rises, they made sure the hall outside their door was spotless. If they did not, the on-site manager levied fines. Such a regimen may sound draconian, but tenants appreciated the careful attention to their community.

The CHA also worked closely with outside agencies to provide a variety of social services. Oscar Brown, the first manager of Ida B. Wells [see interview], arranged with the city's health department to bring dentists and doctors to the development—services hard to come by in the privately owned kitchenette buildings surrounding the complex. As Brown remembers it, residents began referring to the development as "Well Town," insisting that their children's health improved dramatically after moving in. At Leclaire Courts, a Southwest Side development opened in 1950, manager Winston Kennedy (see interview) worked with the local public school to provide afterschool activities for children with working parents, one of many such programs fostered by the CHA. And, as mentioned earlier, Wood held flower competitions to beautify projects, inspiring residents to invest energy in improving the CHA grounds.

Even as the CHA was winning national recognition for its accomplishments, its political support in Chicago eroded after World War II. Not surprisingly, race was at the core of the conflict. Wood and the CHA Board of Commissioners (headed by African American Robert R. Taylor from 1943 to 1950) believed that the CHA should not discriminate on the basis of race. During the war, the CHA constructed and then integrated the Francis Cabrini Homes (now part of the Cabrini-Green complex). Its opening drew an outcry from the neighboring Italian-American community. Given Chicago's notoriously tense race relations, some expected a racial explosion at Cabrini. It never came, and the CHA fostered an unusual racial harmony.

Angela Willuweit, who is white (see interview), lived in the Cabrini Homes from 1943 to 1953. "With an integrated project we were all one big happy family," Willuweit says. "It was a real village."

In 1946 and 1947, however, the CHA tried to integrate projects for veterans located in outlying white neighborhoods, triggering a violent white backlash. At Airport Homes near Midway Airport, whites overturned cars and hurled rocks at the apartments occupied by black veterans. In 1947, the move-in of black veterans to Fernwood Homes on the Southwest Side generated even greater levels of white violence. The CHA persisted, however, and succeeded in integrating most veterans' projects. The city's white aldermen soon sought to restrict the CHA's activities, using their power over site selection as powerful leverage. In 1948 and again in 1950, the City Council blocked nearly all the CHA's requested sites in white areas and forced the CHA to build nearly all its housing in black neighborhoods. This pattern was repeated in the late 1950s under Mayor Richard J. Daley's rule.[5] As a result, nearly all postwar public housing in Chicago was built in African-American neighborhoods.

The City Council's war against the CHA extended beyond site decisions. Any CHA staff members deemed too radical—especially those who most publicly advocated integration—were subjected to constant political and personal attack. In 1948 City Council leaders targeted two of Wood's closest aides, Shufro and Planning Director John Ducey (see interview), after they personally criticized the Council. Several City Council leaders responded that they would obstruct the normal operations of the CHA until Shufro and Ducey were gone, and by the end of 1948, both men had tendered their resignations. It was a major blow. In a speech delivered after their forced departure, Wood fired back:

> Chicago is in a most violent though invisible state of war on the question of race; and every public servant must decide on which side he will enlist, whose enmity he will incur. Though he may seek with all his mind the safe way to play it, there really is no safe way. . . . [There is] a great overflow of Negroes out of their ghettos in all parts of the city. Because this overflow is against the official will it takes place with desperation and illegality; and new slums are being created daily. The exploiters are having a field day; and the next generation will have to cure this generation's blindness.[6]

Wood had the support of the CHA Board in the 1940s, but in 1950, the resignations of Chairman Taylor and Commissioner Claude Benjamin tipped the scales against her. The loss of Benjamin was a particular blow; he had been Wood's strongest backer and the CHA Board's most eloquent voice for racial justice. Mayor Martin Kennelly replaced Taylor and Benjamin with members less friendly to Wood's agenda, and the increasing hostility between Wood and the Board undermined her power. Still, she continued to fight for integration and racial justice, especially after a particularly fierce race riot broke out at Trumbull Park Homes in the summer of 1953 when a black couple moved into the previously all-white project.[7] Violence and controversy raged for a year until Kennelly and the CHA Board pushed through a "reorganization" of the CHA in 1954 that resulted in Wood's ouster.

The public housing communities developed during the early period did not crumble overnight. Though there was some turnover in the upper ranks of the CHA after she departed, many dedicated managers remained in the developments, and a sizable proportion of working families continued to live there. In 1964, ten years after Wood's removal, only a third of the CHA's apartments were occupied by single-parent families on public assistance. (Today, the figure is close to 80 percent). But a more politicized board of directors and an increasingly mediocre leadership paved the way for decline. During the 1960s and 1970s, Wood's successors virtually eliminated screening, failed to enforce rules, and neglected basic maintenance, attributing this neglect to the lack of federal funds. Working-class families with options fled in the early 1970s, triggering a budget crisis that brought about a further deterioration of conditions. A highly predictable downward spiral ensued, and the CHA's ineffective leadership made little effort to stem the bleeding. Public housing was allowed—through poor leadership and neglect—to become the city's housing of last resort.

This book began as a modest research project, one initiated in 1988 as a series of interviews with CHA managers who had worked during public housing's heyday in the 1940s and 1950s. Loyola University's School of Social Work provided generous support for the research, which soon grew beyond this limited scope after an enlightening interview with Daisy Brumfield, one of the CHA's first female African-American managers. Brumfield suggested that the most inspiring stories about the CHA's early years were likely to come not from the staff but from the residents. Over the next ten years, interviews were conducted across the city. Several grapevines proved especially fruitful, including Lady T's barbershop on 35th Street, the Vernon Park Church of God, and the University of Illinois Dental School. All told, 140 interviews were conducted between 1988 and 1997.

Most interviewees lived in CHA projects between 1940 and 1965, though several remain there after 2000. The selection process for these interviews was not random; often, one former tenant would recommend several others. But the selection of interviewees neither sought out the elite nor excluded those who appeared less promising. There was no weeding out of those with negative views. On the whole, the residents interviewed constitute a reasonable cross-section of the population of the early projects. What was notable, however, was that virtually every resident talked about the profoundly positive effect that public housing had on his or her life.

The interviews in this book are organized into chapters centered on several themes. Chapter 1 profiles the CHA staff, including many from the Elizabeth Wood era as well as several from later administrations. Chapter 2 selects several inspiring stories of personal achievement, while those interviewed in Chapter 3 present more "salt of the earth" characters. The personalities in Chapter 4 share their experiences with race and integration. Chapter 5 includes the stories of those who cited education as well as public housing as an important factor in their lives. Sports, religion, and music provided alternative paths for those interviewed in Chapter 6. The voices of those who chose to remain in public housing through its decline are heard in Chapter 7. Finally, the conclusion to this book offers a discussion of how the lessons of the past can be used to revitalize public housing and return it to the positive force it once was.

These interviews—which have been abridged for readability—ranged widely and sometimes far from the topic of life in public housing. Childhood, school, and work histories are all included here, as are more recent concerns about the subsequent decline in project life, the state of schools, trends in race relations, and affirmative action—even the value of the Million Man March. Others talked about their families with great pride. These digressions document the rise of a successful, thoughtful, but too often ignored African-American middle class, supported and nurtured in part by public housing. Their testimonies provide an eloquent explanation for the problems of public housing's past and the path to a positive future. What follows, then, are the voices of those who left and the voices of some who stayed. In their words lies a blueprint for what could again allow public housing to flourish.

Chapter 1

The Vision and Its Implementers: The Staff of the CHA

The former residents interviewed for this book consistently remember their public housing developments as clean and well run, with vigilantly made repairs and enthusiastically provided tenant services. Moreover, they attribute these conditions to the high quality of the CHA staff, at least during its first twenty years.

The leadership for this dedicated management came from Elizabeth Wood, CHA Executive Director from its founding in 1937 until 1954. For seventeen years she provided inspirational guidance to CHA staff and residents. Those who knew her speak universally of her energy, dedication, and toughness. She was compassionate yet demanding, sympathetic yet unyielding. She held strongly progressive views and believed fervently in the ability of public housing to provide a stepping-stone to a better life for low-income families. Under Wood the CHA had a reputation as one of the best-run public housing authorities in the country.

Wood assembled a top-flight staff of like-minded progressives from among the ranks of the country's social workers, architects, and managers. The quality of the CHA's early staff is evidenced in part by their impressive later careers. Ed Fruchtman, CHA Counsel from 1947 to 1953, became a prominent Chicago labor lawyer. Martin Meyerson, former Director of Planning, went on to a distinguished academic career as President of the University of Pennsylvania, and Herbert Gans of the Planning Department became a preeminent sociologist at Columbia University. John Ducey, Wood's top aide through much of the 1940s, left in 1948 and later became Executive Director of the National Association of Housing and Redevelopment Officials and Director of Rent Control in the federal Office of Price Administration. Ducey is interviewed here.

In 1954, however, the CHA Board of Commissioners fired Wood for her outspoken views on integration. She believed strongly in equality for all, and she sought to introduce black families into CHA projects in traditionally white neighborhoods. Her efforts in 1953 to integrate the CHA's Trumbull Park Homes on the far South Side led to vicious rioting by whites and racist attacks on those few brave black families willing to challenge the residential segregation that deeply divided Chicago in the 1950s. Ted Greenhalgh, Trumbull Park's manager at the time, is interviewed here. Mayor Kennelly and the CHA's increasingly conservative commissioners rejected Wood's agenda and forced her from the job on the spurious charge of management inefficiency.[8]

After Wood's dismissal, the CHA's top management lost the passion and commitment to the public housing cause so essential to its success. Her top aides drifted off after 1954, and the CHA staff and management grew increasingly more bureaucratic. Engineers replaced social workers, and bureaucrats replaced managers. Mayor Richard J. Daley further contributed to the loss of direction by appointing commissioners and executive directors known for their loyalty to him rather than for their housing knowledge or commitment to public housing.

Despite the deterioration in the expertise and overall quality of the CHA staff, a few administrators and a number of former managers in the 1950s and 1960s embraced their work with the dedication reminiscent of the earlier years. Several are interviewed here. They share a tough-mindedness, a certain tenacity, and a willingness to fight through (or even sidestep) the bureaucratic obstacles they saw as inhibiting successful management.

OSCAR C. BROWN, SR.

At age ninety-five, Oscar Brown still went to work every day at his real estate office, smartly dressed in a three-piece suit. "I was from Edwards, Mississippi. In Mississippi they wouldn't let you do anything. It was a white situation and the blacks had no rights whatsoever. The grade school [for African Americans] ran for only six grades, and they [white leaders] offered no high school because they wanted nothing to interfere with the cotton. The cotton, that was the thing. As we grew up, we had to get out of there."

After serving in the Army during World War I, Brown earned a law degree from Howard University in 1922 and started a private real estate firm in Chicago. In 1941, after an extensive search, the CHA hired Brown to be the first manager of the Ida B. Wells Homes. He subsequently managed Altgeld Gardens when it opened in 1944. In 1983, he published a memoir, titled By a Thread. *Oscar Brown passed away in 1997.*

Ida B. Wells worked. It worked 100 percent. I hadn't been to any social work school, but I had ideas about how it should be. The social work people thought that we should take each tenant separately and tell them how to behave. I said, "I won't do it that way. I'll take the tenants from each building and have a conference with all of them and say, 'Here's what we are supposed to do.'" I asked them, "Are you agreeable that we're going to make this thing work?" And they all said yes. So I said, "You've contracted among yourselves that we will make a success of this thing." That's how I did it.

It wasn't a social services operation, it was a commonsense operation and, of course, it worked. I have a theory that if you praise people, they'll do. Down at Ida B. Wells, if I'd see a man out shining his windowsills, you know what I'd do? I'd send out a letter to the whole project congratulating him for shining his windowsills. Do you know what would happen the next day? Everybody was out shining their windowsills. And then I'd see a man out rolling his baby. I'd send a letter out congratulating him. Next week, I'd see a lot of men rolling their babies. Praise gets a lot of things done.

We made them think that flowers were something fine. So all of them wanted to plant flowers. The place had flowers everywhere. Wherever there was a vacant space, they'd say, "Mr. Brown, can I have this space to plant my flowers?" They had flowers in the windows, flowers everyplace. So much so that the people outside Wells who had thought it was going to deteriorate their neighborhood said after two or three years, "You've improved the neighborhood." I didn't do it. They did it. They planted the flowers, washed the windows, rolled the babies.

And I told people to take advantage of all the health facilities available. We brought medical services into Ida B. Wells. We brought them in, and instead of calling it Ida B. Wells Town, we called it the "Well Town" because we had a better health record at Ida B. Wells than anywhere else.

There were a number of widowed women out there [at Wells] who had boys. I called the boys in and said, "You don't have a papa now. I'm your papa. I'm your father, and if there's anything that plagues you, come in and let's talk about it." I said another thing: "I don't want you to stay out late at night because you'll worry your mother to death if she doesn't know where you are at ten or eleven o'clock at night. So you go home." I also wanted to tell the girls how to keep clean and how to do this and do that, but I just didn't know how. Well, at that time, they had a switchboard operation right there in Ida B. Wells. And so I started a switchboard operator school for the girls. In order to get the switchboard job, you have to be that kind of a person. I didn't care whether they got a switchboard job or not, but I wanted them to be that kind of person.

We didn't select the highest income of the poor people. We had eighteen thousand applicants for sixteen hundred units, and we took the poorest of those. That's why I'm proud of Ida B. Wells—because we poor folks did it. The fact that they had low income didn't mean that they didn't have the determination to be somebody. In our first year, we had all sixteen hundred tenants pay their rent—without a single missed payment. That's inconceivable because even in the highest plateau of income you're not going to find 100 percent. In fact, there were three or four who hadn't paid, but the rest of the tenants went around and said, "Well, on Oscar Brown's birthday, we're going to give him a present of 100 percent collection." So they went out and collected more than the deficit that we had for three tenants.

That's why the Vice President of the United States [Henry Wallace] came out there. Milt Shufro [CHA Associate Director] put this out on a national radio broadcast, and Franklin Roosevelt sent his Vice President out to see what was happening. You see, you can do good things, but if nobody tells about it, nobody knows about it, and Mick Shufro told about it.

Ida B. Wells was the first housing development that was actually built by the CHA under Elizabeth Wood. Trumbull Park, Jane Addams, and Julia Lathrop Homes were built by the federal government. As a director, Elizabeth Wood was perfect. There are people who get things done, and she was that kind of person. I think that when God made people, he made a superior person in woman. And if they have an opportunity, they'll do things. You'd have a better world if the men would get off and go on and sit down somewhere.

Well, in 1944 they built Altgeld Gardens to house workers in the armament plants out in that area, and so I went out to manage Altgeld Gardens until the war ended. Altgeld Gardens was patterned after Ida B. Wells. But I couldn't have as much control over them as I could at Ida B. Wells because that was a different project with a different objective. At Wells we were first interested in low-rent housing for needy people. But at Altgeld, those were not all necessarily needy people; they were people who contributed to the production of armaments. I tried to get them to follow the pattern that we had established at Ida B. Wells for keeping neat homes, clean homes, the lawns, the flowers, and all that type of thing. And they did it. Somebody came in one day and said, "Mr. Brown, down there the man is cutting his lawn with scissors."

The most remarkable thing is that here we had a sample of public housing developments that succeeded, so why didn't anybody ever want to follow it? Instead, they began to build those high-rise buildings. When they built those, they had something in mind besides public housing.

JOHN DUCEY

John Ducey was CHA Director of Planning from 1941 to 1948. He was harshly criticized by aldermen who opposed the CHA's attempts to build integrated developments in white neighborhoods. With the City Council threatening to disrupt CHA operations and the Board of Commissioners unwilling to mount a fight, Ducey resigned in 1948. He later became Vice President of the Real Estate Research Corporation, one of the most prestigious private real estate research firms in the country. Later he became Executive Director of the National Association of Housing and Redevelopment Officials in Washington, and then the head of the national rent control program.

The CHA always tried to do more for the city and more for its tenants than it was legally or contractually required to do. To me, that was a very fine attitude. Elizabeth Wood inspired people with a kind of trust that went both ways. It was a two-way loyalty. She inspired people all the way down the line—at least as long as I was there. Now, after I left, there were some people who were spies for the City Hall group that wanted to get her kicked out.

But she was just a superb manager. Whether she had run a foundry, or a university, or a housing authority, she would have had superb support. I think the real test of management is making certain tough decisions. If she asked you to do something that you couldn't see was reasonable, you would do it anyway because you knew that in the long run she was right.

Let me give you an example. After the war, we had this money to build some relatively small projects. Elizabeth brought me into her office one day and said, "John, I want you to set up a system for selecting architects for these five projects."

I said, "I'm not an architect. I'm not even a good architectural critic."

She said, "Well, I know enough about your talent for evaluating alternatives. I'm going to trust you with this. We want to select five good architectural firms and have them vie for excellence against one another."

She hoped this would improve the standard of architecture in public housing throughout the country. I came up with a list of recommendations, one of which was to use Harry Weese. The biggest thing he had ever designed was a church, which probably cost $150,000 to build. But I knew Harry Weese was a great architect. Now don't ask me to explain how I knew, but I knew.

I went into Elizabeth with the recommendations, and she said, "John, I don't think I can sell Harry Weese to the commissioners because he hasn't had enough experience with big projects. And I'm getting some pretty intense pressure from the commissioners to go with Lowenberg and Lowenberg"—whom I'd left off the list. "Why don't you see if you can work out a marriage between Lowenberg and Lowenberg and Harry Weese?"

I went back to Lowenberg and Lowenberg. These are two nice brothers, but they didn't even know what design was. I said, "Look, here's a factory that you've done. Nice-looking factory. Here's an apartment building that you've done. Nice-looking factory. What you need is a real good designer. Why don't you call up Harry Weese and see if you can come in jointly on a design?" The project they did together—Loomis Courts—won a prize from *Progressive Architecture* magazine. Subsequently, Harry became internationally famous. Now, that's management.

Elizabeth saw the deleterious influence of federal control forcing localities into architectural straitjackets. She had a big fight with [federal officials] once about the diameter of curtain rods, believe it or not. They said you don't have to have half-inch curtain rods. A three-eighth-inch diameter curtain rod is adequate. Can you imagine a federal agency saying this? And this was a pall not just on Chicago and New York, big cities, but on Peoria and Decatur and so on.

CHA management worked differently. When Dearborn Homes was in the planning stage, one of the people in the Planning Department, Reinhart Lesser, came up to me and said, "John, I am hesitant to mention it, but Loebl, Schlossman and Bennett came up with a horrible site plan for the project."

I said, "Tell me about this. I don't see anything wrong with it."

"Well, they've lined up their buildings like soldiers on parade. The angle to the sun is all wrong."

It didn't mean anything to me. But he explained it. And in addition to that, the architects had used up too much of the site. This project was in the center of a slum area that didn't have enough school facilities or park facilities. He thought we could accommodate a school and a small park on the site if we just rearranged the buildings. So he drew me a site plan, and there were eight acres left over that we could make available for school and park use.

I said, "Reinhart, eight acres is all right for a school, it's all right for a park, but I don't think it's enough for both of them."

He said, "Well, you'll have to get the school board to agree to let the Park District use the school buildings for park activities."

I said, "Do you know the Park District and the school board staff have not spoken to one another in twenty years?"

He said, "Maybe this will be a chance to break that pattern."

So I went in to Elizabeth with this, and she was enthusiastic about the idea. She said, "John, you haven't got much of a chance of doing this, but go over and talk to them anyway."

I had a friend at the park district who was in charge of park development. I said, "We've got seven or eight acres here. We need a school and we need a park. We'll give you the land. Just pay us a dollar for it. But the school will also have to have access to the land."

He said, "I'm 100 percent in, count on me, but the school board is never going to listen to me."

So I went over to the school board and I sold them on it. I am not a good salesman. I mean, if I had worked selling cars, I would have been a flop. But somehow or other I was infected with the idea that this was something that would be a feather not in my cap, but in Elizabeth Wood's cap. Two municipal agencies that were not on speaking terms got together, and the Housing Authority was the catalytic agent. At any rate, the park district and the school board both agreed to it. And our commissioners agreed to it.

We did our damnedest to make Dearborn Homes an integrated project. We went to every white family we could think of who would move in. And that included Quakers. It included people of the extreme left. Anybody who was white and had kids, we would say, please move into Dearborn Homes. And that lasted for about a year. And then because of the school situation and all other things, the white families gradually moved out, and it became an all-black project.

Well, anyway, this is the sort of thing that Elizabeth believed in. She believed in public agencies being catalytic agents outside of the narrow field of their assigned jobs. And to some people that was radical. But what it really involved was good planning and engineering: government planning and engineering. But that's the kind of thing that passes for socialism or left-wing do-goodism, or whatever you want to call it.

Elizabeth knew when to compromise. She was a realist to the extent that she knew you couldn't have just purists, like me or Mick Shufro or Ed Fruchtman or people like that. Elizabeth used to say to me, "John, you've got to have a certain number of sonofabitches if you want to run an operation."

ED HOLMGREN

Ed Holmgren was the CHA Director of Tenant Selection from 1947 to 1954. He remained with the CHA until he was "fired" by Elizabeth Wood's successor, former General William B. Kean.

In 1950, a large bond issue was approved by the state legislature which created the funding for a number of projects, the so-called city-state projects. It was during the site fight for the city-state projects that the conflict between the Council and the Authority really emerged. With the passage of this new act, we had a lot of new housing coming in. The Authority commissioned a vacant land survey, and this revealed that on the outskirts of the city there was a hell of a lot of vacant land which would be available for public housing.

Elizabeth Wood and the commissioners pushed for building on the vacant land, on the very obvious principle that this would require less demolition and displacement. Displacement—mostly of black families—was a very large issue in those days. You had displacement for the Eisenhower Expressway, which was the first one, and then the Dan Ryan, which was later, and for Michael Reese Hospital and Lake Meadows. So with all this displacement going on, we tried to opt for a vacant land program.

This is where the battle raged, because most of these [vacant land] sites were in all-white areas, especially the Southwest and near Northwest Sides. It developed into a kind of charade, really. The City Council had the right to approve sites, so the Council went on a series of bus rides to check out these sites. This is where the farce comes in. As a result of these bus rides, they nixed practically all of the sites in the West Side wards and dumped most of them in the wards of the two aldermen who were the most supportive of these kinds of site selections. One was Bob Merriam in the 5th Ward, in Hyde Park, and the other one was Ben Becker in the 40th Ward, on the Northwest Side [a largely Jewish area]. There was great furor over that. It wasn't a matter of the Council trying to put one or two sites in those wards, but all of them. Well, this site fight went on for well over a year, and it was finally resolved with the decision, essentially, to contain the black community. So we lost—the Housing Authority lost that battle. The result is what you have today.

As an aside, I would say that the politicization of these institutions has only occurred in the last twenty years. Daley completely politicized both the Housing Authority and the school board. In any case, in the early days the CHA was independent, and that's why the Council was so angry—because they couldn't get at Wood as easily as they can get at the CHA these days.

I stayed on after Elizabeth left in 1954. The others who were close to Elizabeth resigned as soon as she was canned. Keane had asked for my resignation at first, and I asked, "Why?" He said, "I don't have to give you a reason." [Laughs] So I said, "No, I won't resign." So I was about the only one that was fired. I think one of the reasons for my firing was some of that stuff with the [Chicago Police Department's] Red Squad. I had been a radical at the University of Chicago, and I was still active with the NAACP, which was becoming very aggressive at that time.

You know, Elizabeth herself wasn't radical. A number of us used to talk about it, and we thought of her as kind of left-of-center populist. It wasn't noblesse oblige that drove her. She wasn't out to enhance the noble savage. I think it was something more than that. Her politics, I think, were formed by the Depression and the New Deal, which simply involved doing something for the people who were temporarily down on their luck. Then she fell into the job of Director of the Metropolitan Housing and Planning Association, which was a new organization created out of some kind of civic goodwill in the early 1930s. Then she got the Housing Authority job because she was the only one who seemed fitted for it when the CHA was created in 1937. She grew in the job. But I don't think that she ever thought very much about radical politics.

RUTH SABLE

Ruth Sable worked as a secretary for Milton (Mick) Shufro, the CHA Public Relations Director and later its Deputy Executive Director. She also worked for Shufro's successor. In 1954, she resigned from the CHA in protest of the unjust removal of Elizabeth Wood.

I started in with the Chicago Housing Authority as a stenographer in 1943. It was a very small agency at the time. And there was a lady and a man that kept running through—they never walked, they always were running. And I was told that the lady was Elizabeth Wood. And the man that was always running from one place to the other was Milton Shufro. He was the public relations chief. Wood was Executive Director. And so whenever they'd come running through the halls, I'd stand on the side. I understood they were very busy; that's about all I knew.

As we began to enlarge the agency, I worked for several divisions, which gave me a background in housing and the way it was built. Then one day, Shufro approached me and asked me if I'd like to be his secretary. It was then that I began to be very much aware of what the situation was. There were people who were opposing all of public housing on the basis of discrimination. People would call. Eventually, the girls from the switchboard would transfer calls to me. And these people were ugly in their abuse. And I had to talk with them. I just resented the fact that they could be such vicious people. It reminded me of the Nazis.

I remember Edward Murrow came in with a photographer to do a story for CBS. And I remember that specifically because Murrow told me I had a beautiful carriage as I was sitting there typing. [Laughs] Murrow's photographer didn't care about the riots one way or the other. So he went out to Trumbull Park [in 1953] and started taking pictures. Some of the mob got after him and broke his camera. Suddenly, this man became a socially conscious creature—How dare they do this to my camera, and how dare they beat up on people, and how dare they riot? There is no excuse for people rioting.

I was sent out to the projects a few times during the riots to lend support to the people who were in there. One time—I don't remember which riot it was—I was turned over in a car. Another time I remember running down a street; some man lifted a garbage can lid and said get in. And I didn't think twice, I jumped in because these people were chasing us. And thank God he came back to get me. I was more hysterical inside the garbage can than I was in the mob. [Laughs]

There was just not enough time for all the things that were happening. There was no such thing as nine to five at the CHA. I would come in at 8:30 and work late, maybe 6:30 or 7. I was usually asked to come in on Saturdays, occasionally on Sundays. But I didn't work till midnight, as they did.

And always, every day, I worked with Elizabeth Wood. There was no division there between Wood and Shufro. She was either in Shufro's office, or he was in her office. And it was extremely crucial for both of them to have people they could trust. You were dealing with citizens, you were dealing with politicians, you were dealing with the press. It was a most unique job.

Shufro was a dynamo. He had fifty-five things going at the same time. He was a brilliant man. Very sharp, very intuitive, and very forgetful about his personal things. So I'd always have to call his wife to find out if there was a note in his sock or in his handbag. But I'm grateful I had the opportunity to work for him. No boss could throw me after that.

People would come into the office looking for housing, and they'd sit at the receptionist's desk to be sent to another office to be processed. I remember one lady came in, and she had to go the ladies' room, and she left an eight-month-old baby with a lady sitting in the chair right at the door. And that lady in the chair happened to be Elizabeth Wood. The baby was hungry, and the mother had given Wood the bottle. And there sat this great Elizabeth Wood feeding the baby, and a newspaper reporter walked in. He walked right past her, and he said he was going to see Elizabeth Wood. And he walked past her again. And he's out in the hallway, and he did a double take, and he came back in. I've never forgotten this.

I wouldn't say that everyone who worked in the Housing Authority agreed with Elizabeth Wood's principles, but their jobs weren't jeopardized because of that. It was really a very democratic office. However, if you expected a political patronage job, you didn't get in. And that's where she ran into trouble with Richard J. Daley. He tried to place his second cousin with the Housing Authority.[9] The man wasn't qualified. And Wood wouldn't allow it.

Now, if you're not allowing any patronage jobs, and if you're not allowing any politicians to get their hands on the funds, you become anathema to the rotten, corrupt politicians. And the only way they can get their hands on the money would be to get rid of the people. And they had to do this in such a manner that they couldn't be accused of doing it. And so they—and I'm now talking of the mayor, the City Council, and the real estate groups—made use of McCarthy.

Shufro was very strong, and Wood was strengthened by him. He wasn't taking any guff from the politicians. But they started to use the McCarthy technique of red-baiting. There was nothing to dredge up with Wood. This was a straitlaced lady, who came from a conservative background, who happened to have a heart of a gold, and who happened to have compassion for people. So they began by chipping away at Mick. They went after his background as a liberal reporter. He was with the New York papers. They went after his consistency about having fairness in housing. And there was anti-Semitism involved; it was always covert, but the innuendoes were there. Had his name been O'Flaherty, they might have had a little more difficulty in doing away with him. But if you were Jewish and if you were a liberal, then you were being red-baited and tainted and all the people around you the same way. Really, when you look back, this was the first attempt to start weeding out those people who were around her—the strongest people, like Eddie Fruchtman and Eddie Holmgren. And this was very deliberately done.

It was a blow to Elizabeth. She didn't want Mick to leave. And yet she knew that she had to keep on fighting for the right things. I was still so young, and as far as I was concerned, the world was still going to go on. But I was becoming aware of how a dirty battle is fought. You remove the people around the person you want to get to. And it was always very subtly done.

The commissioners, the CHA's Board of Commissioners, appointed by the mayor of Chicago, decided on a tactic. They decided to take the fingerprints of all the employees, ostensibly to protect the women and children of the housing projects against rape by the maintenance men. That's what they said. But all the people who were hired at the Housing Authority were very thoroughly investigated, and so we understood what was going on. We were not accused of a crime. But with McCarthyism, if you said anything about not being fingerprinted, you became suspect.

But we had enough employees who had a lot of moxie to them. They were very progressive, liberal-minded people. And they said, "Forget you! We're taking you to court." We were the first group of employees in the entire country to do this. We had people who called in and red-baited us to hell. Nevertheless, we found a couple of attorneys who were willing to take the case, and we managed to get an injunction for two years. But we didn't have enough money to go up to the Supreme Court, and the injunction didn't hold. It took two years for those bums to try and do us in. When they finally did do the fingerprinting, the one who had a record, and the one who was a bastard, turned out to be a commissioner. And the commissioners were very upset because everybody else had a clean record. We had always been under the impression that the commissioners were definitely interested in good public housing for the people. And it never occurred to us, truly, that these were political appointees and that somehow, down the line, they would sell out.

I remember the last day that I was there, there was a *Tribune* reporter, Tom Buck, who said to me about Elizabeth—and I think you should quote this—"She's the last decent, honest public servant to go." I've never forgotten that. Ninety percent of the reporters had tremendous respect for her. Sometimes they didn't exactly agree with the way certain things were done, but they had tremendous respect for her.

After I left the Housing Authority, Elizabeth Wood kept in touch with me. And I was very touched by it because I idolized her. She became a mother figure to me, but also a role model. I never have ever seen any woman as dedicated to the interest of every human being. All I know is that in my lifetime there'll never be another Elizabeth Wood.

EMIL HIRSCH

Emil Hirsch joined the CHA in 1942 as an assistant to Mick Shufro, then the Director of Public Relations. When Shufro moved up to Associate Director, Hirsch took over the PR job. He resigned in 1955, soon after Elizabeth Wood was forced out of the CHA.

Very early on, Elizabeth was asked to put somebody on the payroll or give a contract to somebody. It was a politically inspired thing and it disturbed everybody. So Mick Shufro got an audience with Mayor Kelly. When he came back, he told us what had happened. It was really amazing. Shufro pointed out to Kelly that around the country his administration had a reputation of corruption, and he told the mayor that this agency was something he could point to with pride. If anybody criticized the city, he could say, "Look, we've got an honest, noncorrupt CHA." And the mayor caught on to that, and from that moment on, anytime Elizabeth or anybody else had a request from some politician to do something, all we had to do was let Mr. Kelly know, and if it wasn't a warranted thing, that would be the end of it.

Kelly really became enthusiastic for the program, and when requests were made for additional funds, for additional units, he was always behind it. Later on, years later, after he was no longer mayor, the Public Housing Association had a fund-raising dinner at the Sheraton downtown, and Ed Kelly came in and stepped up.[10] He contributed a thousand dollars from his own pocket to the program. To his dying day, I understand, he was sincerely interested in the program.

After Mayor Martin Kennelly [1947–1955] came in, the main change that we could perceive was that instead of dealing directly with the mayor, we had to get approval for projects from the City Council leaders. In Kennelly's regime it was obvious that the mayor was not the decision-maker. And the City Council was not supportive. At one point they had hearings and asked us all kinds of things. They tried to imply that, among other things, we were part of some terrible Communist plot to put black families in every neighborhood in Chicago. It was the most ridiculous thing.

We had to house families, and the majority of the people who were coming to us were black families. If anything, the Authority was forced, more or less, into the forefront of the integration fight. When I first came to the Housing Authority, we had a vast majority of white applicants and white tenants. Then the picture began to change. With the veterans' program, maybe a fifth of the applicants were black and four-fifths were white. And all of the veterans' projects were in white neighborhoods, almost without exception. So those projects had to be integrated. There was just no way out of it. Then we had the redevelopment and slum clearance program where we were taking displaced families from the waiting list, and an overwhelming number came from the black community, and the whole picture changed.

Being a progressive program in the McCarthy era, public housing was opposed by many who hated subsidized things of any kind. Yeah, I very well remember the fingerprinting and loyalty oaths. To me it was a completely phony thing. But it was the McCarthy era, and everybody was being asked to swear on a stack of Bibles that they were faithful to the government of the United States and its institutions and everything else. There may have been some subversive people around, but I'm sure that 99 percent of any agency—whether it was the Housing Authority, the schools, or whatever—were perfectly loyal Americans.

We had an open policy at the Authority. Anybody could come in and ask any questions of us, and we'd answer. People would come in to investigate our books, and we'd open them up. There wasn't anything that was hidden. I had heard that that there were FBI people checking on things and that the police department's famous "Red Squad" had people around. I remember seeing an undercover officer at a couple of citizens' meetings on housing. He was there taking notes, and it was pointed out to me that that's who he was. [Laughs] Yeah, they knew who he was, and to me it was amusing, but it isn't so amusing when you stop to think about it.

It's kind of crazy: government people using taxpayers' funds to spy on these civic movements. There may be people who try to infiltrate these movements and get them to do things in accordance with either fascist or Communist theory. But 99 percent of the people in those movements are there because they're in favor of whatever it is that the movement actually promotes.

Elizabeth had ongoing communication with the people in citizens' organizations and church groups that had an interest in or—as she felt—should have an interest in the whole public housing program. She constantly built on that. Actually, after Mick Shufro left the Authority, he was very active with those groups. And there was very strong and constant communication between Elizabeth and Mick and the other people in the citizens' movement. There were groups aggressively pushing for public housing on vacant land outside of the black-occupied areas. They pushed as hard as they could in the face of tremendous opposition. But you know, if a referendum were taken at that particular point in time—maybe even today—75 percent or more of the people would have said no. And they were actively saying this through their aldermen.

I think the powers that be felt the situation had gotten to an impasse and that there was no further pushing that could be done—by Elizabeth or anybody else. I think the city fathers, as part of a compromise with the people who were opposed to the whole program, must have made a deal and said, "We'll get rid of Elizabeth Wood and the people supporting her if you won't kill the whole program."

Here's the way they got Elizabeth out of the agency. In the spring or early summer of 1954, she was quite seriously ill. She was in Presbyterian Hospital for six weeks with bronchitis; she couldn't even talk. We used to go out to the hospital and see her. She was on a medical leave, and in the meantime the commissioners had hired this outfit to do a survey of the Authority. This was a sham thing if there ever was one. Anyway, she got back and this report came out encouraging her to leave. The people responsible for her ouster thought they were making a deal to benefit the future of the city by getting something versus nothing. That was their argument. But right or wrong, it was a tragedy, because in the process they threw the baby out with the bathwater. The people who were really concerned about the welfare of the tenants were replaced by a staff that saw this as a nine-to-five job.

We had tried to maintain some sort of integration of the projects in the face of a mounting black application list. When her successor, Kean, was confronted with this huge buildup of black applications, he handled it just the way an army general would. He simply said, "We can't do this anymore. It's got to be a first-come, first-served thing." And that's what happened, exactly. Under Ed Holmgren, who had been Director of Tenant Selection, there was a lot of careful screening of the people who were going into some of these situations. I gather that this was completely dropped about the time I left the Authority.

You no longer had a director and a staff who were aware of the changes in the tenancy of the projects. You had many residents coming in who had no background, or very little background, in urban living. You had a higher percentage of welfare cases and broken homes—the kinds of things that resulted in juveniles going out and starting the gangs and all that.

If the staff under Elizabeth had been there when this thing started to happen, there would have been a conscious effort to try to do something about it. Whether it would have succeeded or not, I don't know. But she would have done her damnedest to get community agencies in to help. Whether it was organizing teenage activities to get the kids away from gang stuff or whatever, she would have been out there in the forefront with the other people on the staff, saying, "Look, we've got to do this, because if we don't, the result is going to be a disaster."

Under Elizabeth, the CHA wasn't just a brick-and-mortar thing. While the Housing Authority had no funds for social programs, we could call in people to help improve the atmosphere in these developments. When we were forced to build high-rises, she tried to get the design set up in such a way that these projects would have play areas upstairs so the kids didn't have to go down in the elevators to the play lot. It wasn't the ideal life for families in the high-rises, but she was very concerned that if they had to build them that way, they'd be set up so the thing could work.

TOM McDADE

From 1947 to 1949, Tom McDade, an honors graduate of the University of North Carolina, managed Ashburn Homes. A racially integrated project for veterans on the Southwest Side, Ashburn was built as a "temporary" project to handle the immediate postwar housing crisis. It was torn down in 1955. After leaving the CHA in 1952, McDade spent many years as the general manager of Park Forest, a planned and racially integrated "new town" community southwest of Chicago. Park Forest was developed by Philip Klutznick, who later went on to serve as Secretary of Commerce under President Jimmy Carter.

Before me, the first person who managed [at Ashburn] walked around with a pistol on his hip. I guess good Elizabeth Wood had to hit him on the head with something heavier than a pistol to get some blacks in there. But even then he put them all in one section of the development. It was my hope to truly integrate the community. But I was also highly selective of the candidates.

Well, what I did was scatter them. What gave me a kick was when I'd take a visitor—I had many visitors—and we'd come to one of the dwellings that would be particularly attractive, and people would remark on it without my saying anything. And I'd say, "Yes, that's one of our black families, you know." Any time a black family came in, Sally Rotecki [a tenant] would always arrange to visit with the family and have the neighbors come in for refreshments and help them in their adjustment.

We lived in Ashburn; many of the managers lived in the developments at the time. I remember one day—my wife told me of this—when my son came in from play, and he'd been playing with this other little boy who was black. As he sat down to lunch, he said that everything with Johnny was dirty.

My wife said, "No, Johnny is not dirty." She told him that was Johnny's actual color, and that he was definitely clean and not dirty.

"But he was dirty, he fell in the mud puddle." [Laughs] That was early integration.

The kids could be rather rough on the school grounds, but I played the heavy boss man in that respect. I wanted orderly conduct over there, and I didn't want them to disturb their neighbors. And I walked my project. I just wonder how things would be if CHA managers walked their projects at all times of day and night. But in 1949, I left Ashburn. And why? Because of that stupid edict that CHA employees could not live in CHA housing. Then I went into tenant selection at the downtown office.

We were there primarily to evaluate applicants relocating from what is now Lake Meadows.[11] We set up procedures so that every family would be interviewed and there would be a home visit. We endeavored to be quite selective. In a home visit you checked under the bed, and you'd expect that there might be today's or yesterday's debris under there, but if it was last week's, we didn't want them. Ideally, we wanted a complete family—father and mother in the home. It was impossible to achieve in every case, but they had a high priority with us.

By then were getting predominantly black applicants, and I wondered, How can we achieve integration? One of the most challenging projects was Dearborn Homes, the first of the high-rises. My goal was to try to get 5 percent white, and I used every manner I could think of that would not cause me a prison sentence.

We did achieve 5 percent in Dearborn Homes, but this was a very tough thing to do in Chicago: trying to find good, solid white families that would be favorable to living in the black community. Also, for the black families we certainly wanted to have the cream of the crop. I still feel the principle in public housing is enabling families to graduate from subsidized housing. I don't believe we can handle the hopelessly unqualified. You can't do it, even with adroit management.

In 1949 or 1950, when I finished the tenant selection stint, I was made Assistant Director of Planning and Development. We had an absolutely superb Planning Department. We were planning for some forty thousand new dwelling units. Martin Meyerson was the head of the department. Dave Wallace, the head of a regional planning group in Philadelphia, came later. Then we had Jack Dykeman, who later succeeded Martin Meyerson at the University of California at Berkley's Planning Department. Reinhardt Lesser was the chief of the Design Department. There was also Herb Gans, the sociologist. These were very stimulating people and stimulating minds.

In the Development Department, you also had Charlie Waldman, who had been the director of engineering for the building of Park Forest.[12] Charlie had taken separate degrees in civil, mechanical, and electrical engineering. To me, he was truly a Renaissance man. Charlie, I thought, was particularly gifted in working with young professionals, bringing out of them more than they had and inspiring them into a very positive direction in their careers.

But in the meanwhile the City Council was vacillating. In almost every case our site selections were canceled because of the opposition of the politicians, whose philosophy obviously was "Oh, we'd like to have the public housing contracts, but not in my ward, not in my ward."

I found this totally frustrating, being vitiated by the bad guys. In principle, I was still committed to the CHA, but spinning my wheels did not suit me. I was very disappointed in its inability to move forward. With all the talent and the excellent leadership, it was criminal that the CHA's plans were not brought to fruition in Chicago.

TED GREENHALGH

During her long tenure as CHA Executive Director, Elizabeth Wood maintained a strong commitment to racial integration. The CHA's Trumbull Park Homes, built in 1937, stood in the center of South Deering, an all-white community on Chicago's far South Side. In 1953, Trumbull Park was integrated when Betty Howard, a light-skinned African-American woman, "passed" for white when applying for an apartment in the project. Ted Greenhalgh was Trumbull's project manager at the time. In 1954, he became manager of the ABLA project, a conglomeration of four public housing developments on Chicago's West Side, where he remained a manager through the early 1960s.

When the Howard family moved in, the community instantly exploded. There was window-breaking and so on. A man walked into my office—I was seated, I didn't even see him. The guy slugged me, knocked me out. I was on the floor before I knew it. Nothing came of it, no court, no nothing. We were surrounded by police for a period of several months, and then the community quieted. It was not a continuing, ongoing, violent riot. Eventually, there was a book written called *Trumbull Park*.[13] I've seen the book. I probably flipped through it. But I never read it from cover to cover. I can't tell you why, except that none of these were pleasant memories, and I didn't want to relive them, I guess. Anyway, after all that, I resumed a fairly normal management process, with programs, regular relationships with tenants, and so on. Actually, I never felt fearful walking out into that project or any other project that I managed. Never did.

I lived in Trumbull, and our relationship with our immediate neighbors was good. As a manager I was out and I knew the people. It was an easy relationship in which we could meet on the sidewalk and speak. We cleaned the stairway, scrubbed it on our hands and knees, and did all the things that tenants were expected to do. Trumbull had three-story apartment buildings and row houses with flowers and shrubbery in the front yard and backyard and so on. As a matter of fact, tenants even planted gardens in the vacant land to the west of the housing project, which was railroad property. Trumbull Park Homes was almost like a garden, beautifully maintained by the tenants as well as by the management.

My wife maintains that I worked every night and every weekend. I don't believe it. I didn't feel driven. I didn't feel like anybody was out there, you know, standing over me. But we did work hard. I felt the Chicago Housing Authority was a good employer. The fellow staff were people I could relate to intellectually. I felt that we shared something important in common. Truly, you went to the Chicago Housing Authority because you wanted to help make things better. We were do-gooders, really, is what we were. And it was nothing to be ashamed of at that time. I guess I was radical, I wanted to do something. When I was doing tenant selection, I would visit families in horrible housing. What a great feeling when I could take them into the clean stairway of a four- or five-story walk-up at Jane Addams and show them a freshly decorated apartment that had hot water and toilets—everything that they didn't have.

When [Wood's successor, General William B.] Kean came in, it was just commonly and generally understood that it was a political appointment forced by the Board and other interests. The man, so far as we knew, had no background, understanding, or expertise in public housing management. Eventually, of course, came the termination of what had been a systematic tenant selection process. We then began receiving virtually all black applications from Central Office. Kean used the rationale that black applicants needed the housing more than white applicants. And that argument doesn't lack merit—except for the fact that it is counter, in my opinion, to the whole philosophy of public housing as an institution that both serves those who are in need and maintains integrated communities.

Several years after Kean came in, I retired and left CHA. I left with a general feeling of disappointment and disillusionment. And I think my disillusionment was probably shared by other people. It isn't that we sat around and talked about it. You just shared the understanding that things were not the way they used to be. We knew that under Elizabeth Wood we were working under a top-notch person with a great deal of integrity and professionalism. We knew that and were proud of it. CHA had a lot of esprit de corps. We were doing something of some social merit.

While I had no particular desire to get into private real estate, that's where I went. It was the only other place I could use my management experience. As a matter of fact, I became the manager of the Mies van der Rohe buildings at 900 and 910 Lake Shore Drive. It was the opposite end of the spectrum. But I enjoyed public housing more.

WINSTON KENNEDY

Win Kennedy worked for the CHA from September 1949 until June 1954, serving as the first manager of the Leclaire Courts project. After leaving the CHA, he became president of Kennedy, Ryan, Monigal & Associates, a real estate sales and management firm. He later went on to become the president of the Chicago Real Estate Board.

On the first of August 1950, and I'll never forget this, my wife and I moved into Leclaire Courts as the very first occupants. The property was still under construction, and they made an effort to get our unit completed first so we could be in residence as the tenants moved in.

At Leclaire, I essentially had a veto over the people who came in. I didn't have a formal veto, but I could express my displeasure at the applications sent from downtown. And I did, on several occasions. And I evicted people.

My very first eviction, I physically got sick! This was a white family. They were just down on their luck, and they couldn't pay the rent. But we had a pretty strong policy. Finally, I just had to initiate the eviction process, which resulted in the sheriff coming out to physically evict them—put them on the street. I think the wife was pregnant. As I recall, the husband was a sometimes alcoholic, and there were two small children in the family. I put them on the street, and I got sick—vomited after that. That was probably in 1951, early on in the game. But primarily we evicted people for not obeying the rules. I was encouraged to do so by the administration, and the other tenants did not discourage that.

Several things can be said about those initial families, and I'm referring to both black and white. They conceived of themselves, for the most part, as upwardly mobile, middle-class families, who expected to be in public housing for the short term. Home ownership was a high priority. While I never tracked the families to any degree, my guess is that many of them went on to do just that, and this applies to the blacks as well as the whites. By the way, most of these families had two parents. The number of residents on public aid was also very small. And when people did receive public aid, it was usually as the result of some crisis in the family, and they would tend to get off of it as their fortunes reversed.

There was a great deal of interaction between the families, including across racial lines. That was not true of everybody. There were people who were withdrawn. But there were some strong friendships that were created there. I don't think we can claim credit for it, but the environment was such that it could happen. We attempted to integrate the project racially, economically, and in family size, and I think that worked out fairly well.

When Leclaire Courts opened, the Authority had a policy of managed integration. We limited the nonwhite residents of the project to between 10 and 25 percent, and it was my job to administer that policy. Oh, in today's terms it could be considered very undemocratic. But, in any case, I think deliberate managed integration worked out well. My recollection is that there were no serious issues of racial tension during the four years that I was there as resident manager.

And outside Leclaire, we didn't have any organized activity from the white residents of the 23rd Ward attempting to drive the blacks off. There were a lot of people in the area that didn't like what happened with Leclaire Courts, but they weren't about to do anything about it. We never had any violence or even strong hints of violence while I was there. I think one of the reasons is that there was a good deal of vacant space that separated the project from the rest of Garfield Ridge.

We really were isolated out there. The closest public transportation was about three quarters of a mile away, and relatively few of the tenants had cars. So there was a staff effort to get the Transit Authority to extend the bus line on Cicero Avenue south of 22nd Street. We also got the bus on 47th Street to come a half a mile further west. The bus lines were important, not only to give people a sense of freedom, but to provide people with transportation, first to find a job and then to be able to get to it. And once those two bus lines were expanded, the opportunities for employment at Leclaire Courts, among its residents, increased considerably.

Land on three sides of the project was vacant, and a number of tenants wanted to grow vegetables. So we parceled out land to the west of the project for private gardens. Although the land was not owned by the Authority, nobody seemed to care. We set up a monitoring system to make sure that we assigned the spaces on a first-come, first-served basis. A lot of people grew a lot of vegetables in those gardens.

In 1952, the Housing Authority asked the Church Federation of Greater Chicago to do something about establishing a religious institution in the community, because the nearest church was some distance away. So the Church Federation asked its membership if any of them were interested in establishing a church and related programs. The only takers were the Unitarians and Universalists. The result was a survey that determined that the community didn't really need a church as much as it needed a social service organization.

And so plans were made, again with the cooperation of other authorities, to establish a social service agency, and space was made available for a settlement house. We also worked with the principal of the new grammar school to become involved in the Lighted Schoolhouse program, which gave the kids in the community a chance to have some additional programs beyond their normal school day.

Another thing we did there, which I thought was positive, was to form a consumer cooperative. Quite a few tenants took part in it because the project was isolated and not convenient to food stores, and also because this gave people an opportunity for some limited control over the quality of groceries that they purchased. So, with the encouragement of the Authority, and permission to lease a building that was intended to be a maintenance warehouse, we established a consumer cooperative and sold memberships.

Only a very small percent of the families were on welfare. They would get on and then in a month or so get off. To my knowledge we had few if any longtime welfare clients. The culture of the Authority was one that said, "This housing is not considered permanent. It is for people with temporary needs." And the original tenants got on their feet and moved out. It was basically a middle-class orientation.

In 1954 I was transferred from Leclaire Courts to Trumbull Park. I came to Trumbull Park shortly after the race riots, when the tension was still very high. And it was during that period that Elizabeth Wood left and General Kean came. Of course, the black families at Trumbull Park during that situation felt very isolated. They literally had to tell the police when they were coming and going from the project by foot or by car. Especially at night, the police wanted to know if they were planning to drive someplace. There was very limited room on my part as manager to implement any kind of policy. Trumbull Park at that point was handled downtown. I was told who would be admitted as a tenant, when they would be arriving, and where I was to meet them under police guard. So I had very little to do with tenant selection, tenant orientation, or community work, because there were other people doing that or trying to.

The frustration of that job was, among other things, that the city had no policy for dealing with race relations except the massive use of force to keep people apart. The classic example of that was a Sunday in August 1954, when the black families at Trumbull decided to test the use of the park, which they had previously avoided. They organized a softball game to be held in the park, and everybody knew about it. So the Sunday afternoon came, and the softball players numbered twenty or thereabouts. There probably were another twenty onlookers, black and white. The entire park was surrounded by about twelve hundred policemen, who were there to keep anybody from interfering with the constitutional right of these people to use the park. They lined the whole park, shoulder to shoulder, because they figured there was going to be a massive white protest. And nothing happened. That's overkill.

DAISY BRUMFIELD

Daisy Brumfield worked at the CHA for about thirty-six years, starting as a clerk in the Planning Department in June 1951 and rising to serve as one of the CHA's most outstanding managers of some of its largest projects. In 1983, she served as the first assistant to Executive Director Andrew Mooney. She was also head of several Central Office departments during her years with the CHA.

By the time I became manager at Stateway [in 1977], we had to lease to all these crooks and criminals without really having the ability to look into their background. HUD was telling us that you've got to be very careful that you don't infringe on a person's civil rights. It got so that you couldn't even ask them if they'd been in jail. Before, depending on what a person had been jailed for, we just automatically didn't house them.

Well, these people would come into my office at Stateway. Many times they were unclean, sometimes they were high, and they had children that you could tell were neglected. I would tell them we didn't have an apartment, and they said, "Well, we were sent out by the Central Office."

I said, "Well, we will call you when we get something."

They would call the Central Office, and Jean Wellborn would call me back and say, "You can't do this. These people qualify, and they can sue CHA. You can't do this."

I said, "I won't lease to them."

Then Harvey Peck [a CHA management supervisor] called and said, "Daisy, you've got to do this."

So what I did was, if I had an apartment on the eighteenth floor in a very bad building, I would say to them, "I have this apartment, and you have children, and I really don't want to put you in that apartment. If you want to wait until I get something"—which was going to be never—"that'll be all right. But if you take this apartment now, I cannot transfer you." Oh, I was terrible. In most instances, they said they would wait. Then about six months later, they'd come back: "You don't have anything yet?" And then they would go back to Central Office, and I would offer them that same apartment. It just went around and around. Here I am fighting the system, but many of the other managers would say, "Hell, if they don't care, I don't."

Yes, the CHA should have fired me a long time ago.

See, they had built in levels and levels and levels of staff down at the Central Office and spent thousands of dollars for retreats and classes and all of this. But none of that money filters down to the developments where the residents are. Now the CHA managers are trying to operate the developments as they do private real estate offices, where you have two or three people. But it's not the same thing. You have people with problems. You've got to have people who work with residents.

I'll use Stateway Gardens as an example. When I went there as manager, I had an assistant manager, a secretary, a rent collector, an income reviewer, three tenant relations aides, a switchboard operator, a stock clerk, and a maintenance clerk. I had twelve employees at Stateway Gardens in 1977. Now, you have five at the most. They don't have enough maintenance personnel to clean the buildings. Take even a good development, the senior buildings at 9177 and 9141 South Chicago. You've only got two men there to clean both buildings, and the buildings are going to the dogs. We've experienced problems in the later years that did not exist in the earlier years. Then, people had respect for their management office, they had respect for their properties, and they were very happy to get in. There's no longer the same attitude. You have people living in buildings tearing out the aluminum around the windows so they can sell it for drugs.

What people forget is that CHA was initially a stepping-stone. People moved in, had safe, sanitary housing, and then went on into their own homes. But people have made it a way of life. Mothers, grandmothers, great-grandmothers, all of them have these apartments here. I believe that our system usurped the incentive for people to get out and do what they could for themselves. With the 30 percent rule, they knew if they made more money, their rent would go up, so they'd feel why get a job?[14] And if they did get a job, they had to falsify the income so their rent didn't go through the ceiling.

I remember once, I went to Goldblatt's, and there was a tenant from Stateway working behind the counter. Now, she had not reported the income from this job, and she became so upset when she saw me. "Oh, Mrs. Brumfield, let me tell you . . ." She just went to pieces. And I said, "I'm sorry, I just want to buy this," and left. Soon after I got back to the office, she came in and said, "I didn't have money to get my kids anything for Christmas. I had to go to work."

I said, "Oh, are you working?"

She said, "Yes. Didn't you see me at Goldblatt's?"

I said, "I didn't know you were working." And then she realized what I was saying to her.

One of the most vivid experiences in my time at Stateway involved this young mother. She was eighteen with four children, and she was waiting outside my office. Her two little girls were sitting on the floor, she was holding the baby, and the other was sitting next to her. One of the little girls acted up, and the mother kicked her, and the child started to cry.

I asked her to come into my office and said, "Why did you do that?"

She said, "I never liked her."

I said, "But isn't that your child?" And I could see she was nervous, tired, she was just ready to do anything. I said, "But you are her mother. You're the one that she looks for. She didn't ask to come into the world."

"But I got no help with them."

I said, "We're going to do something about this. If you promise me that you will work with me."

"Yes ma'am."

Then and there I took her over to the Stateway day care. They could take two of the children for half a day. Then there was the Horizon House. We went over, and they could take one for all day. I said, "Now, if you get them up, they'll even give them breakfast. This leaves you with one child. Now what are you going to do? Would you be able to take care of this one baby and clean house?"

I said, "There is one thing I'll ask you to do. Every day that you have taken them to school, I want you to stop by my office briefly. I want to see you. I want to see that you've cleaned yourself up, and I want see if the baby is clean." This went on for about four months, and then she came in and thanked me. She said, "I don't hit her anymore, Mrs. Brumfield, and I'm a good mother. And my children are having fun because they can play with other kids."

There are so many problems now. They need to do a complete reorganization of the LACs [the Local Advisory Councils, the CHA residents' elected bodies] because the tenants have some of the worst representatives in the world. You've got the mothers of drug dealers and rapists dictating to the managers. You should have guidelines for candidates. If I want to be president, then I've got to have a year's good rent record so that I can encourage others to do the same. I can't be on the eviction list every month and be the president. I mean, why would anyone else feel that they need to do any different?

I'd have a set of guidelines for persons to be eligible to hold office. You've got to have good rent-paying records, good housekeeping standards, and you've got to monitor the behavior of your children. This cancer has been created by permissiveness. It is not only going to wreck and ruin lives in the development, it's going to spread out everywhere.

It's necessary to have the residents have some say in where they live. But I think they've taken it too damn far. It's crazy when you bring in a resident who has had no more than an ADC check to manage, and they come in and cross their legs and tell that manager what to do with the management budget. When they go into various supervisors' offices now and complain about the managers, the managers are called down and threatened. The residents know now that they can get a manager fired. So this manager, if she wants to keep her job, she is not going to call you in and tell you about your children breaking windows. She's not nasty Daisy Brumfield, who's going to call you and say you haven't paid your rent. Because she's concerned the tenants are going to fire her now. It shouldn't be that way. That is demoralizing. Let me give you an example. There is one manager who is incompetent and always has been. He's lazy, limited, but he laughed about keeping his LAC president supplied with her brand of brandy, so she'd speak up for him. It has gotten to that point.

When I started, staff recruitment was definitely on the up-and-up. You had to have the qualifications, otherwise you didn't get hired. You had to present yourself in a positive manner. You couldn't walk in with sneakers and braids. You had to have the appearance of a professional person. But now politics has taken over the hiring of staff. If we're talking about just the family housing—not the senior housing—then not more than 30 to 35 percent of the managers are worth a salt.

MURIEL CHADWICK

After working for the private real estate firm Draper & Kramer, Muriel Chadwick began working for the CHA as a clerk/steno in 1952. Within six months, she was promoted to an administrative position. Chadwick was one of the first black women to work in management at the CHA. She left the Authority in 1985 as Deputy Comptroller.

When I was hired, I didn't have any close personal contact with Elizabeth Wood, but within thirty days after I started at CHA, I was told about the monthly dinner meeting. Dinner meetings were held at the community center at Ida B. Wells, and all CHA came together to this meeting. Central Office, maintenance, administrative employees—everyone came, and I will never forget that. That was the first time I saw Elizabeth Wood. It was a very short meeting, but I remember the spirit of fellowship. Congressman Sid Yates was the guest speaker. I got to chat very briefly with both of them—even though I was a new employee working for a large public agency. At that time in the CHA, it was a family. You didn't have administrative over here and maintenance over there. I can't say when that happened, but it was years later. Under the old regime, I don't think it ever would have happened. The CHA had the sort of employees that you worked with—not for. And there was a feeling among the employees that the idea of public service really meant something.

I began in the Relocation Office, making home visits, and that was tough. You had to sort of sit on the fence. You didn't want to put "bad" families in CHA, but you had a responsibility to these people who had no place to go. That was a very difficult thing. When I started there, my manner was—is there such a thing as too professional?—it was too cold. I learned very quickly after getting an adverse comment on an evaluation by Petrakis, my manager. He said I would be best off going back into private housing. I had worked for Draper & Kramer in their 47th Street office, and they had a very tough site manager. Everything was extremely stringent. Petrakis said I was imposing Draper & Kramer criteria. When I read it, I was very hurt. But his comments made me realize how right he was, and I did an about-face.

In relocation, you are uprooting people, in some instances, from the building where they have lived twenty or twenty-five years. You had a responsibility to put yourself in their shoes and realize why they were hostile. Relocation was a terrible thing, but it was handled with sensitivity and compassion. We did one thing that was not required. If a person was not eligible for public housing, you made all attempts to find them housing in the private market. In going through the neighborhood, you'd see a "for rent" sign, and you would tell the residents about it. You might even go talk to the landlord for them. You're more lenient in a relocation situation than you are in project management. Because in relocation, as I said, you are uprooting these people. You've got to bend quite a bit there, and you may tolerate some things you wouldn't tolerate otherwise. Now, Petrakis was good in relocation. But I cannot see a Petrakis, a do-gooder, in project management. He wasn't strict enough.

After working in relocation, I was sent out to work with Ted Greenhalgh [see interview] at ABLA. I think it was one of the best things that happened to me. He was a very strict manager, a very hardworking manager. But he worked with the staff and you learned a lot. I can remember when the PHA [Public Housing Administration—forerunner of HUD] required us to get all new leases from the residents.[15] We did not believe that employed residents should have to take time off from work to deal with that. How could we ask them to do that? So we set up hours on nights and Saturdays. I can remember on Saturdays, Ted coming down and bringing his daughter—he pulled everybody in and the full staff worked.

We worked ourselves to death for Ted. He was that sort of person. He was willing to train everyone. I told him I wanted to learn to do budgets. He said, "We work on the budgets at nights and on weekends, so if you would like to come in, no compensation, on your own time." I said, "Fine." This is how I got ahead. You came in a little earlier, you stayed a little longer, and you worked. I wanted maintenance experience, so I started working with ABLA's maintenance superintendent, who was supposed to be a monster. But he liked people who worked hard, and he started training me. Then Ted had me out making building inspections. So I became assistant manager in 1959, and then in 1961, I went to Ickes [Homes]. When I was there, we were still inspecting apartments, putting people out for bad housekeeping. When I was at ABLA, people were being terminated for patterns of illegitimacy. It helped if you had a father in the home. There was stricter discipline.

But personally, I am very sensitive on the issue of single-parent families, because I myself am the product of a "broken home." But there was still love, there was discipline, there was self-denial and sacrifice. All of these things were there. A single-parent family is not necessarily a bad family. The minute people talk about a welfare mother, they think of a woman with seven kids by seven men. Which is not true. You have women whose husbands left them, who have no support for their small children.

Anyway, even by the time I started at Ickes, the PHA had relaxed its standards. And then you started getting legal aid and these community groups blocking evictions and complaining about the rules, and that's when CHA started going down. This was in the 1960s. The do-gooders came in saying, "Oh, this poor, poor woman, she came from a rural area in the South, and hasn't had opportunity and so forth." They didn't seem to take into consideration that we'd had people like that in the developments years ago, but we worked with those families. We had people who did not know how to clean house, so we went in and we sat down and we showed them. But if they couldn't learn, they were evicted. And with the courts then, it was cut and dried. You just took the record sheet and ran it on down and ended, "For the good of the Authority, blah, blah, blah," and it was no problem to evict.[16] When you take a soft attitude, you cannot get your hard-core bad family out. Of course you have to have compassion. You're working with human beings, and you've got to recognize that. But you cannot swing all the way the other way and say, "Oh, these poor people." You've got to enforce rules and regulations.

Throughout my career, I was a stickler for CHA policy, and establishing procedures to comply with that. But by the 1960s, the administration said those things are not important. And this I could not tolerate. I had no intention of leaving when I did, but the situation was impossible. I had to leave or lose my mind.

PATRICIA McARTHUR HARRIS

Pat McArthur Harris moved into Altgeld Gardens as a young mother in 1959. She began working for the CHA in 1969, serving in several departments and rising to manager of the CHA's Archer Courts development, located on the Near South Side near Chicago's Chinatown. She passed away in February 2001.

Strong management is needed in public housing, because actually what you're dealing with now are eighteen-year-old young people who don't know what way to go. One thing with young girls, they are very lonely. You've got to be lonely if you have two or three children by the time you're eighteen years old. And to me that comes from a lack of self-esteem. I always used to tell my young people, "I have been like you. I have lived in public housing. I was working poor, but I knew my children had to have shelter."

I was able to have rapport with them because they would say, "You lived in public housing?" They were always intrigued.

I left public housing in 1982 and moved back to Princeton Park [a private development on the South Side], where I had grown up. At that time I was paying a lot of rent in Altgeld Gardens, over five hundred dollars. The neighborhood had deteriorated, and my next-door neighbor had some children, and these children broke into my apartment. After that, I became discouraged with Altgeld. I would say it began to change in the 1970s. I don't think it really started to decline until the drugs became prevalent. When I was living in public housing and was a very young woman, I didn't know of anybody who took drugs. I can remember in Altgeld Gardens, your children could leave a toy out and you would come back and it was right there on your porch. I don't know what happened or what made the decline in society, but I'm sure that it was drugs.

You want to know how I would fix public housing today? If you're not working, I would not put you in public housing. I'd have working families. If you've got a couple of bad apples, then they need to go. CHA fell down on their evictions, and I think that had something to do with the law. The law can be for you or against you. And it has definitely worked against CHA. I know when I was a manager over in Chinatown, at Archer Courts, that was an integrated development. This was how I did it when I was a manager there: if a black moved out, he would be replaced with a black. If a Caucasian moved out, he would be replaced with a Caucasian. If a Chinese moved out, he would be replaced with a Chinese. So I had a racial balance there. Well, maybe it isn't fair, but it worked for me. To my own thinking, it was correct. I did not sin because there are other white people with low income that need housing as much as there are black people who need housing. I don't think it should be predominantly black if whites and Chinese want to come in there. At Archer Courts it worked well because the apartments were mostly one-bedroom apartments and you couldn't have a lot of children there. I don't think there should be a lot of large projects. It's better to have like 116 units. You can keep control of that.

It breaks my heart today when I see people who are political, who are appointed to positions and know nothing about what public housing is about. It's too political now. Just because you know a political person, that doesn't make you a good manager, rent collector, or leasing clerk. You have to have a lot of tolerance and really care about poor people in order to effectively lead public housing.

BEVERLY SHEPHERD

Beverly Shepherd joined the CHA in 1984 and managed individual projects before rising to a supervisory position. Today, she is the head of the Dearborn Homes Resident Management Corporation.

I formerly worked for the City of Chicago, Department of Housing, in an administrative position dealing with relocation. Those jobs were phased out, and Mrs. Daisy Brumfield [see interview] was able to get me a job with the Chicago Housing Authority. I started out as a manager of a single project, and from there I went to the Collections/Eviction Department, where I worked with Mrs. Brumfield.

My former sector was Sector 1, and that was Altgeld Gardens, Trumbull, Lowden Homes, and Madden Park. I really don't think the development has a lot to do with it. I think what has created a lot of problems with the Authority is their tenant selection. Our Occupancy Department needs to be completely revamped. Too often, the resident leaders and staff select the prospective new residents.

They bring in their dope dealers and their dope dealer boyfriends, and they take over the unit. I remember before I came to the Authority, Roberta Coffee was the social service contact, and any problem situations that occurred in the development would be served to her. They used to call these families the "Coffee cases." She had contact with the Department of Children and Family Services about children who were abandoned. There is no social component to the Authority right now. They have a program called resident organization, but there is no component to deal with what we refer to as "problem families," and we presently have a lot. Once the Occupancy Department starts screening tenants, then we can get back on track. And we certainly cannot allow people to move back into the Authority after they have been evicted. That in itself creates a problem. It's not easy to force people out. You've got to go through the legal process. And you know these people know their rights. They've got the [American] Civil Liberties Union.

I don't think that tenant management has been any great shakes. Wentworth is run by resident management. In the past, once a development had resident management, the Authority didn't have anything else to do with it. But with the new administration, after the HUD takeover, they're going to be monitored just like the regular developments to make sure that they are doing the things that they are supposed to. They realize that unsupervised tenant-managed projects was a mistake.

The new administration is recommending putting a number of the developments under private management. They feel that the Authority can no longer carry the burden. When I go to the tenant service meeting, I hear nothing but complaints. I've heard people say, "We didn't realize how well off we were when we were under the jurisdiction of the Chicago Housing Authority."

Some of the maintenance problems that we're facing now are the result of years and years and years of neglect. Years ago CHA was getting a lot more money from HUD than they're getting now for renovating and upkeep. If

CHA had used the money properly, a lot of the good people who moved out would not have moved. The grass wasn't cut. The work orders were not being done. There was a whole series of problems. The neglect is so gross and there's so much money needed.

In terms of moving people to the suburbs, as with the Gautreaux program [which moves public housing residents into white suburbs],[17] I feel that everybody has a right to freedom of choice, but when they go to Woodstock, Matteson, or wherever they go, if they don't keep up the owner's property, they're not going to be there very long. Moreover, it makes it difficult for others who might like to move there when the owners start saying, "No, I don't want any part of that because of what happened."

A lot of our tenants are not interested in moving to the suburbs for various reasons: no automobiles, no relatives, no place to socialize. Some people who received certificates and moved to the suburbs moved back because they could not adjust to the suburban living. Some of the children could not make the school adjustments. Some of the schools that they attended were so far ahead of them. They had difficulty making those adjustments. It's just a matter of the person's choice.

Why did we have people who lived in Stateway Gardens or Ickes, for thirty and thirty-five years, stay when they had the opportunity to move other places? This is home to them, they don't want to go anyplace else. We have a lot of elderly who still live in family housing, and they don't want to move to the elderly buildings, because they heard all these rumors that you have to go to bed at a certain time and you can't socialize.

Most black families like to live in the black neighborhoods, and most whites and elderlies, the same pattern. You can't force integration on anybody. I think that it's nice when people can live together, but if a person does not want to be the crusader, what can you do about it?

PHYLLIS OFFORD

Phyllis Offord was six years old when her family moved to Leclaire Courts in 1951. In the 1980s, Leclaire instituted a resident management program. Offord currently manages the nonprofit social service center that serves the Leclaire development and the rest of the city's Southwest Side. She lives in a high-rise building in Chicago's Kenwood neighborhood.

Racism has always been alive and well on the Southwest Side of the city. We experienced it at its worst when we went to the local public schools. I mean, they [whites] used to chase us home. We had boundaries. Forty-seventh Street was one of them, and if you crossed 47th Street, the teenage guys that I grew up with—my brother and his friends—had to fight to get back home. We couldn't ride our bikes past 47th Street. It was just the law.

It made me very socially conscious, and that is why I do what I do. It made all my brothers and sisters socially conscious. I have a sister who is an assistant principal, and I have a younger brother, he's in banking, and my older brother's an architect. But every one of us is committed to the black community. My dad was not really active in the community, but he was active in his family. He was a Chicago police officer, and he did take part in family activities, but it was my mom who was active in the community.

My mom has always made us aware of who we were. With racism, we talked it out. This may sound far-fetched now, but we would talk about a strategy. She would tell us how to deal with people so we could defend ourselves without being aggressive and angry, so we could talk things out with people when we were faced with racism. When someone called us a name, we were never encouraged to hide it. We were encouraged to talk about it, we were encouraged to tell people how it made us feel, and we still do it to this day.

And it was a good thing for us growing up. It made us much more aware of who we were and how life is. There were some things that we had no control over, but it wasn't a bitter thing.

Leclaire itself was great when we were growing up. Every nationality possible was gathered here. There were Polish, Latinos, Irish, Jews. It was a melting pot. The community had mothers and fathers, and they were a working class of people. There were very few families out here with just a mother as the head of the household. It was like being in a small country town. There wasn't anything in between the development and the airport at that time, so we could sit outside and watch planes come and go.

But the shift took place in the 1960s. People living in public housing were made aware by the media that it was supposed to be only for poor people. And developers moved into this community and began to build these small homes. And that is when the community started breaking up, when people started leaving. There was also a breakdown in other services. That's when this place changed drastically.

I think resident management was set up by the government to fail. When they realized that public housing was too much of a cost, they shifted responsibility to these resident management groups. Look at housing! You know, you create these big systems, these bureaucratic systems, and people steal, shuffle money, and then you expect poor people not to pick up on some of that.

It was set up to fail, and it has failed all over the nation. Resident management of public housing was just part of the whole empowerment package that came down when they were addressing welfare. And now it's over with, and we've moved on politically to another scenario.

What I'm looking at is my experience in Leclaire. I'm watching people put their hopes and dreams into something that they cannot manage. I'm looking at charlatans who have just raped this community for well over ten years on the premise of creating, empowering the residents to be resident managers. I'm looking at this home ownership program that has been shoved down their throat, and they don't know a hill of beans about it, and they can't afford this stuff. But now the Chicago Housing Authority is convincing them that they should have co-ops, which they do not want. It's all just political. HUD does not want this big elephant any more, and they're going to shove it off onto the tenants on the grounds of "empowerment."

When I was growing up out here, Irene Smith, this wonderful lady, was the outreach person at the center. She was a white woman, but she was just a wonderful human being. She had a way with the residents. She took one of the largest apartments out here and brought in social worker students of every ethnic group, and they lived in the community with us during the summer. We could drop in and visit, and they did different things with us. They would take a group of kids all over the city. That's how I began looking at these things, and when I was fourteen, I was nominated for the Volunteer of the Year.

I worked with one of the social workers, and I started working with a group of young boys. They were "real bad little kids," too. But they were wonderful. Now they're all in their forties, and they come and see me. I've been out here like nine hundred years. My first group, some of them are grandparents, and they are doing well, too.

I raised my own kids out here. I lived in the development. My children were participants in every program they had, and I was a volunteer mom who did a lot of things. Today my son is an architect like his uncle, my brother.

I think what people are looking for is a new scapegoat, and the very poor people from public housing are it. They're looked at as people who want to take advantage of public aid. But the system was created to make them dependent on it, and no one has put in a mechanism to get them off of the system so they won't be dependent on it. We still offer the training, but I think people are beat. I think that I'm worn out, too. We're tired. And what you hear is the weariness in my voice, and it's a weariness in even dealing with this stuff. It's just becoming overwhelming. Even President [Clinton] went on TV and said that Chicago has the worst public housing in the nation. And so the children think they're the worst people in the nation, coming out of public housing. It's sad, it really is sad to me. But you know, I'm still fighting. We came up with an idea to do a beautification project in Lawndale. We're planning a garden in the middle of a real violent area.

If I had the chance to remake the CHA, I'd try to create initiatives within this community where people could be trained, so they could support themselves. If I had the money to actually create a training program, I'd start a maintenance company for cleaning offices and buildings. I really think that's the only way for people to survive. Honorable people really want to work. I don't think that they want to manage their housing. They would just as soon that some professional did this.

These people who live there now have lost all sense of hope, and it will take something stronger than you or I to get them to recognize it. Some of them are just waiting to die. And that's real. They do mean and evil things because they're just caught somewhere, and they can't get back to being human again. I spend so much of my time working with folks like this, I don't know who's to judge.

Sometimes if you can capture a person out of a family that's just a wreck, and make that person a transition figure, you can change the entire family. See, you have to offer people hope so they can turn themselves around. But if they don't, people should have to leave public housing. And I'd say right now, about 40 percent of the people in Leclaire would have to go. But before the people were turned out, they would have to be given an opportunity. In order to change these things, there has got to be some kind of hope that we can offer. And if we could offer that, I think that Leclaire would be OK. But it would take a lot of money, and this country doesn't seem likely to spend it.

Chapter 2

Laboratories for Leadership

Public housing provided a nurturing and supportive environment for a group of highly successful individuals who rose from humble, low-income beginnings to positions of prominence in their communities. As seen in the following interviews, these leaders trace much of their success back to the values and experiences acquired when they lived in the CHA's early developments.

The list of high-ranking and successful individuals interviewed here includes a chairman of the Finance Committee of the Chicago City Council, a member of the Cook County Board of Commissioners, a Cook County Juvenile Court judge, a chancellor of Chicago's community colleges, two commissioners of the Board of Tax Appeals, a fire commissioner, an administrative assistant to the mayor, a deputy police commissioner, a bank president, a bank vice president, a senior vice president of the largest public utility in Illinois, and the secretary-treasurer of the Chicago Teachers' Union. No less accomplished are other leaders interviewed elsewhere in this book, including four school principals, two police chiefs, one fire department commander, a double Olympic gold medal winner, and a renowned concert jazz pianist. This list is but a portion of those who entered leadership positions in Chicago after growing up in public housing. Time and space prevented the inclusion of others of similar status.

Those whose stories are told here describe in their own words the strength they derived from their families and neighbors in the CHA's early developments. Public housing created a community that allowed them to thrive. Environment *does* count, and the CHA in its early years fostered a shared sense of purpose and maintained a social discipline that offered many of its residents a chance to achieve their potential. Importantly, those interviewed point to the strong qualities of other community institutions during their childhood. Most praise their 1940s and 1950s schools, churches, and clubs as further positive influences on their lives. Their observations remind us that good public housing by itself is not sufficient. Quality social services and neighborhood-based organizations are essential elements of a healthy community.

CORDELL REED

Cordell Reed spent thirty-seven years with Commonwealth Edison, Illinois's largest electric utility, rising to Senior Vice President. During his career, he helped engineer and manage nuclear power plants and later became ComEd's Chief Diversity Officer. His family moved into the Ida B. Wells Homes in 1941 and left in 1956.

I moved to Ida B. Wells from 45th and Indiana. I was three years old, and we were one of the first families to move into the first building. It was at 37th and what we called South Parkway at the time [now called Martin Luther King Jr. Drive]. It was just me, my brother, and my parents. At the time, my father was working at the stockyards; I can still remember the smell of his clothes. Then he really moved up when we were at Ida B. Wells, and he became a body and fender man at the Yellow Cab Company. He stayed at that job until he retired at age sixty-five. And my dad is eighty-seven now and is still going strong; my mom is eighty-three and also going strong. We moved to Englewood in 1956, and that's where they live today.

In 1941, Ida B. was some of the best housing you could have. We had plenty of heat, and I don't remember any roaches or rats. Our apartment was in a development with three buildings that made a kind of backyard. The floors were concrete, the doors were steel. And I had plenty of kids my age. There were always a couple of baseball games going on. I have a hard time remembering any family where both the mother and the father were not living in the household. And I can't remember any unemployment. The men went off to work, and maybe half the women had jobs.

In my backyard, it wasn't cool to be great in school. The most popular guy in my backyard was the toughest, the craziest guy. I got involved with the church at 41st and King Drive where I'm going tonight. It was kind of a freak of fate for me. I went to daily Bible school because you could get chocolate milk and graham crackers. We kind of had our little gang in the church. And, you know, we weren't perfect, but we had a little teenage choir, and we went places. And that socialization, I think, provided an avenue for us. There were forces in the church saying do good. The church paid my way through college. God, I was kind of working for them. I didn't want to mess up.

I went to Doolittle Elementary School at 35th and Cottage Grove for eight years. We lived only two blocks from Phillips High School, but some of the guys in my backyard wanted to go to Tilden Tech. We were so dumb that we had gone and signed up for Tilden without knowing it was a technical school. The other shock to us was when we found out it was all boys.

But we stayed. We had to stay. That was probably the best dumb luck, because they made us take chemistry and physics and college algebra.

From there I went to the University of Illinois to study mechanical engineering. Three of us from our backyard went through Tilden and then on to the University of Illinois. I graduated in 1960 and was in the upper quarter of the class. I interviewed with fifty-eight companies and got two offers. I remember the man who was last in the class got ten offers. I had letters from people who were just not prepared for a black man at that time. Of the two offers, I had one from Commonwealth Edison and one from Skidmore, Owings, and Merrill, the architectural firm. And somehow I decided to come here. I think I was the third black engineer that Edison had hired. I went into the generating stations—the first black in the generating stations. And I can recall that people were very cordial. If they stepped on my toe, they would apologize. If I stepped on their toe, they would apologize. There was an uneasiness. But since I was no threat, I think people wanted to help me. I don't have one of those sorry stories because people have helped me all the way through.

I was at the generating station for seven years, and then I was selected with three other people to be a nuclear-station start-up engineer. It was thrilling. We were starting up the world's largest reactor. I was at Dresden for three and a half years, and then in 1971, I came down and became a project engineer for a new power plant that we had under construction. So after ten and a half years in the field, I had a big jump on the people who had only been downtown.

And I think being black—being the only black manager or engineer almost everywhere I went—eventually turned out to be a real advantage. If there were a hundred engineers, people would notice me. And being as dark as I am, the effect is kind of magnified. When I just talk normally, people are kind of shocked. They expect me not to use good English. I worked my buns off, but the visibility—being a black guy everyone knew, that the chairman knew—didn't hurt. People have always worked well with me, and I've always had a boss who has shared information, who has been supportive.

So I worked with hardware in the company for thirty-two years, but then I decided I'd like to work with people. The job I really wanted was to become the Chief Diversity Officer for the company. It is an odd title. Basically, I'm in charge of an effort to help people realize their full capabilities. People, because of race and because of gender, have been held back. We know that's the case because 97 percent of the executives at most companies are white males. We don't develop blacks and Hispanics and women enough. We don't put them into those challenging jobs and develop them. It's not necessarily because people are racist or sexist. There are all kinds of unconscious, hidden barriers.

Companies like Motorola and Corning and Xerox, which have become competitive around the world, have discovered that they cannot afford to have 10 or 15 or 20 percent of their staff who are not reaching their full potential because of race and gender. And they're not running diversity programs just to be good people but for good strategic reasons. They have recognized that those barriers exist, and—to be more competitive—they have tried to change the culture. There's a difference between affirmative action and diversity programs. First, affirmative action is something that we've had for thirty years. But affirmative action has dealt more with getting people into entry-level jobs. What it hasn't dealt with is the mobility of people once they get into companies.

There are not the role models for young black males [today]. My father was an automobile mechanic. He just happened to be one of the nicest men, and I really mean that. But my father finished grammar school at age thirty. He was going to Wendell Phillips in the evening to get his grammar school diploma to help him to read the books to become a body and a fender man. But did he want to be an engineer? I had never met an engineer in my whole life. Even through college I had never met an engineer other than the college professors. So the role models aren't there.

Really, the church is the most important institution in the black community. There's a little game I play all of the time when my wife and I are driving around: we count the number of storefront churches in any square block. Every one of those churches has thirty or forty people on a Sunday morning. And at every one of those churches, you'll see ten or twelve young people. The difference between me and those who didn't make it is that there was the church, and there was a loving mother and father. And now, my four boys are doing OK. They have gone through college. I have an accountant, an engineer, a guy in communications who uplinks and downlinks stuff at Intel, and an English major who works at a bookstore.

I've always lived in a black area. I don't believe—I especially don't believe—in taking poor blacks and putting them in a white community. I think that's the wrong thing to do. I think taking poor blacks and putting them with middle-class blacks is how you get the real role models to pull people up. That's what I think the real answer is. There are whites who live in my area and that's fine. But I believe in blacks living in black communities. I'm so proud of my black heritage. I could live in Kenilworth, Naperville [affluent, predominantly white Chicago suburbs], but I've always lived in a ten-mile radius of where I grew up. I could have moved to Morris, Illinois—it's the site of ComEd's Dresden plant—but every day for two and a half years I drove sixty miles each way because I wanted my four boys to grow up in a world that is black.

BENNIE L. CRANE

Bennie Crane moved into the Ida B. Wells Homes in 1943, when he was seven years old. He moved into the South Side complex from a slum tenement at 41st and Martin Luther King Drive (then known as South Parkway). He left Wells in 1954. Crane recently retired from the Chicago Fire Department as commander after working there for thirty-four years. His oldest daughter is an attorney and a professor of law at John Marshall Law School, and a son is a police officer.

I remember very clearly the conditions at 41st and King: roach-infested, vermin-infested. I used to sit up nights and chase the mice away from my younger brothers. There were three of us, and it was a one-room kind of a situation, maybe two. It was a three-story building, which would have been a six-flat, and each of the flats was subdivided at least once. We had twelve families living in a structure that was designed to accommodate six. It was a lot of people and minimal privacy. And I remember moving into Ida B.—the new shiny stoves and refrigerators, and then a living room and a kitchen. It was nice and spacious, clean and well-lit, and it was home!

Ida B. Wells was a step up. We didn't live in what was considered the old housing; we lived in CHA housing. It was a solid sense of community, right from the manager to the newest tenant coming into the buildings. Our administrators took care of the communities. Everybody was accountable. The managers of these projects were out among the people. They were out encouraging tenant organizations. They encouraged the planting of flowers, and our complaints were addressed and answered.

There were gangs when I was in public housing. We've always had these kinds of things. I think that a majority of the kids at least passed through the gang kind of a situation. But it was a phase. I was a member of the Destroyers that were headquartered at 36th and Cottage Grove. We hung around West Point Church. We'd sit around and do *nothing*. We'd just sit around and talk. That's why I got out. It was a bunch of people—and this is my view on gangs today—a bunch of people clustered up out of fear. They're all scared *not* to belong. There were several teams within Ida B. Wells. We had the Sabers, the Small Bears, the Mad Park Bears. We were called the Atomics, the Junior Bears.

My buddy Melvin Wilson [see interview] and I, we got to a place where we said, "Hey, nothing's being accomplished. This is stupid." We got out of the gang. We transferred from Tilden to Dunbar—we played football at Dunbar—and we'd travel over to DuSable, or Wendell Phillips [two other nearby high schools]. We didn't have any problems. We let the gang-bangers do their thing. They didn't bother us.

As a matter of fact, there was a social one night at 49th and King Drive, and the guys from Dunbar and the guys from DuSable were going to get into a fight. So we interceded. We said, "Hey, what's going on here?" Because we had friends on both sides. And then we got a chance to talk it out. We used to do a lot of things like that. We were successful because they were afraid, and we weren't. I don't know that it was smart, but we just decided we weren't going to be afraid.

Overall, I think we had more winners than losers at Wells. But there were losers. There were people who were killed. We started going to funerals in grammar school. It wasn't uncommon for death to take place. It wasn't uncommon for people to go to jail. A lot of the people who went to jail were supposed to have gone down South to visit their relatives. On a civics trip for Dunbar High, we went over to the Cook County Jail, and boy, I saw an awful lot of people that I had heard was down South!

The thing was, it was mostly a good community because the Housing Authority was proactive with the positive people. They supported the concerns of the tenants. They had programs for them. Ida B. was very heavy in sports. The Chicago Bears and the old Chicago Cardinals at that time would sponsor junior football within the park. They provided uniforms and the coaching staff and all of that. And boy, that was a real structured kind of a thing.

Here is the problem with public housing today. It is absolutely insane to put families in twenty-story buildings. That's stupid! How can a mother supervise her kids? She's a world away from them. I have a major problem with that concept. Now, at Ida B. Wells, our tallest building was four stories high and it was a walk-up. We had a good amount of low-rise kinds of things. There was easy access.

The major advantage of Wells over Stateway Gardens [a high-rise development a mile west of Wells along the Dan Ryan Expressway] was that we were a low-rise and we were spread out. This business of taking large families, especially from lower social strata, and putting them in high-rises was a catastrophe.

Now, let's look at the concept. Dawson [a politically powerful black Congressman from the South Side] went to Daley, and they came up with this plan. Each one of those buildings is a precinct. It was for political expediency. The problem is that it is just a rotten situation to the core. Housing has been a dumping ground for political favors. And the management's incompetent. I guess they pay as much for hammers and screws as the Pentagon does. And the tenants are held responsible when things don't work.

The hue and cry today—whether we're talking about public housing or public schools or city government—is about holding things responsible and not people. I just think that people ought to be held more accountable. That is the way I was raised. It's ironic that we're saying that public housing is bad, the public school system is bad, everything is bad except the people that run it.

Thirty years ago Dr. King set the world on its heels. He said that he could see a society that would not judge people by the color of their skin but by the content of their character. And it is ridiculous to me that, over the last thirty years, we have spent more time discussing skin color, affirmative action, and segregation and that kind of a thing than we have about character-building. The name of the game is to build the character, that's what he was talking about. Develop character. Why aren't we?

BERTRAND ELLIS

Bert Ellis is a retired Executive Vice President of the Northern Trust Company in Chicago, where he worked for over thirty years. At one point, he managed its first South Side branch. He moved to Ida B. Wells in 1941, when he was seven years old. His family moved out in 1955, while Ellis was in college. Today he lives in Flossmoor, Illinois, an integrated but mostly white suburb south of Chicago.

There were two boys when my family and I moved into Ida B. Wells. At that time, my father and my aunt had just gone into the grocery business at a store located on 31st and Vernon Avenue. They stayed there until urban renewal cleared that land for what is now Lake Meadows. Then my dad went to work for the CTA. He worked for them until he died at the early age of forty-two. He had blood pressure problems and died suddenly at home. My mother was a domestic for a while and then went to work at the post office.

Life in Ida B. Wells was a wonderful experience for us. We lived at the corner of 37th and South Parkway, now 37th and King Drive. Three buildings formed a triangle, and in the middle of that triangle was a playground. We grew up playing football, baseball, hockey, every sport you could imagine. We had a little yard, it was a pretty good size yard, on the front side of the building that I lived in, and after some time they put up a basketball court there. We had volunteers who taught us how to play baseball. We played softball in our backyard, and we played baseball in Madden Park. And then, of course, Madden Park also had a swimming pool. So we could swim in the summer, and in the winter they would freeze a smaller playground—that's where I learned to ice-skate. We were poor kids in the community, but we didn't know we were poor, really. We had everything kids could ever want.

When I was growing up, one of the things my buddies and I learned to do was play poker. It's kind of funny, but it was a good thing because our parents always knew where we were. We were at somebody's house playing poker, especially on Friday evenings. We didn't do it during the week because we had to go to school the next day. But on Fridays we would play until about eleven o'clock, and then we'd all pile into one car and we'd go out to 63rd Street where there was a White Castle, about 63rd and Vernon somewhere. We'd each buy a dozen White Castle hamburgers, and they sold sweet potato pie there, and we'd all get a slice and a hot chocolate. It was something to do.

Let me tell you what I think about Ida B. Wells when I grew up. To me, and I've thought about this many, many times, and I've had conversations with Cordell [Reed] and other people. I think when I look at my friends, most of them succeeded. I think their success is attributable to a couple of things. One, their families. There was a mother and there was a father in all those homes. And in most cases they were the original parents. The other thing is our homes. We lived in the highest buildings—but ours were only four stories high. Our parents were young people. If we did something wrong, my mom could climb down those four stories faster than you could say "Jack Sprat." Sometimes she didn't have to do that because if somebody else's mom saw you doing something, she just picked up the phone, and when you got home, you had to answer to that. And that was very important. It was a community raising children, and there was care. There was friendship. There was love, and I think that has a lot to do with the way we turned out.

That's not all of it, though. There was some more help. Ida B. Wells, as you know, is named for a renowned social worker. So Ida B. Wells came fully equipped with a community center and social workers who knew that some of these people were recent migrants to the North from the South and there were adjustments they had to make. They had that structure. They had that support system in place for that. I remember as a little kid going there, getting our inoculations for whatever we needed, and dental work. All of those services were in that community. So if you could bring those services to a community, you helped ensure the stability of those people. I think that maybe an inordinate number of people out of Ida B. Wells got out of there in pretty good shape and did OK for themselves.

Ida B. Wells was probably as close as you could get in those days to a middle-class black community. Given that, I think there were influences in our lives that were quite different from the influences today. For instance, the mass media was not as strong as it is today. We were not bombarded with all of the stimuli of immediate gratification that we have in our environment today.

I think of guys we knew who somehow couldn't rise above some of the negative environments around us. It wasn't all peaches and cream. There were gangs. Not like you have now, but there were gangs. I ran many a time to safety from these guys—they made me awful fast. I wasn't too much of the guy to fight, but I could run like hell.

I had grandparents who saw that we went to church. I was always in church. Early on we used to go to Monumental Baptist Church, which is right down the street from the Lincoln Center. It's still there. I sang in the youth choir and in the children's choir. Church was always important to me. In my adolescence I was giving some thought to religion, and I noticed that my poker-playing buddies had started to do the same thing. We all came to thinking about religion about the same time. We all became Catholic, but for different reasons. A couple of my friends said they decided to become Catholic because the services were shorter. I chose to become Catholic because once I got into the instruction process, so many things made sense to me. Mind you, I was eighteen years old, in college. My mind was a sponge, and I was looking for my identity. I was more impressed by cerebral things than emotional things. The Catholic Church really appealed to me because this was a more cerebral approach than evangelical religion. I became a Catholic at the age of eighteen, and my aunt and my grandmother became Catholic at the same time. It was at Holy Angels. I got married at the age of twenty-five. My wife is converted. She is Catholic. The whole family is.

As part of my work early on as a young teacher, I taught in the Couli-Cabrini area. I taught in the Washburne Elementary School, and I saw a community that was not unlike what I had grown up in. The problem was, there was this need to put more people into what they call quality housing. Some of the area that they tore down was pretty blighted. I grant that. But they were putting more people in the space than they actually replaced. And in order to do that, they started going up with the high-rise buildings at Cabrini. And I mean high-rise.

When we were teaching there, I was very active in the community, as was almost the entire staff. We were mostly young guys, and we worked with the Lower North Center, which was a support system like we had in Ida B. Wells. We worked very closely with children and with the parents in the home. When we noticed extreme behavior coming out of the children, we knew where they lived. We could almost pinpoint that those kids were coming out of 500 West Oak Street [one of the Cabrini-Green high-rises]. That was the first high-rise. Then the other buildings went up. And you could see there was a distinct difference in the behavior between our kids that came out of those tall buildings and the ones that came from the older ones, which were the low-rise.

Before Flossmoor, I lived in Homewood [an adjoining suburb] for ten years. And on my block we were the only black family. Some of these young people on my staff have never lived outside of an all-black community. They ask, "Bert, how do you do this?" I say, well, you have to understand. I've had integrated relationships and friends all my life—since high school, because I went to Tilden. One of my dear friends is at my parish in Homewood. He's a white guy. He and I went to Tilden together. We were close friends in school. And I point that out. It's a function of your experience. But I grew up in an all-black community. It wasn't until I went to high school that I got that experience. I've been blessed to have that, and I wanted that experience for my family, my children. My wife grew up in an all-black community in Arkansas and went to an all-black school. She didn't really have an integrated experience until she met me. When we moved to South Shore in 1963, it was an almost completely white community.

As a property owner, I think there's a serious shortsightedness on the part of blacks who want to live in all-black communities. What I saw in integrated communities was that if you're a homeowner, that means you have a universe of buyers available to you. In the case of a minority community—if it's Hispanic or black—you have lost 80 to 90 percent of the market in this country, and that has a negative impact if your home is your major asset. So I think financially, you're very shortsighted to think that you can have a home in an all-black community and expect it to appreciate. I don't mean it will depreciate. It's very common in a black community to look upon investment in a home as a lifetime investment in that location. Many African Americans have not caught up with this concept, and they still think that when they buy a home, it's like they're buying a tomb. So they take the attitude that this will improve my community, and I can live here peacefully and not worry about the rest of the world. That worries me. We're letting the chasm between us and majorities grow wider and deeper in a global economy.

When I lived in Hazel Crest for thirteen years, I was very much a part of many of the programs that took place there. In 1971, when I moved there, I was a pioneer—the 1970 census in Hazel Crest listed one black in the whole community. I was on commissions and the school board. But in Hazel Crest, I think we made a mistake, frankly. We were knee-deep into this bad press over illegal racial steering in the community. The human relations commission decided to go public with a strong statement that Hazel Crest was an integrated community and welcomed all ethnic groups. I said that's a big mistake because we were doing it in isolation. And Hazel Crest now has a large black population. There were people in the South Side of Chicago who had never heard of Hazel Crest. And all of a sudden, everywhere I went, people were talking about that great suburb out there named Hazel Crest. I told the mayor of Hazel Crest—a very fine guy, real good friend of mine—that this was an admirable thing to do, but it had to be done with other middle-class communities at the same time. And maybe even those a little higher on the social-economic ladder such as Homewood and Flossmoor and Olympia Fields. I said that if we could get them to agree to make this kind of statement, we'd have something. Instead, Hazel Crest is hanging out there all by itself with this wonderful humanitarian statement.

I think the CHA's *Gautreaux* program is a bad idea. Now you've isolated them out into a foreign environment without the support systems, because I'm sure they have no support systems out in Woodstock for these people. I've done some studies out there for this bank, in fact. So I know that that's not the right way to do it. I think Vince Lane had an idea that made a lot of sense to me with this Lake Parc Place over here [two recently renovated CHA high-rises that include both working families and very poor residents]. It brought me back to Ida B. Wells. He took those buildings and said what we need in this community are role models. What we need is to show these people who do not have jobs that there are people who have jobs. There are people who work, who believe that work is good and that they profit by that, and that their families profit by that.

My biggest role model was my uncle, my mother's brother. And my uncle was an entrepreneur. Actually, most people think I'm his son—I look so much like him. He was always a very positive guy and very family oriented. He had the first automobile in the family. My brother and I were the only boys in the family, and he would come with his wife to pick up me, my brother, and our parents. He didn't have any children at that time, and we used to go to Michigan all the time, and he would say words of encouragement to me—that I could do things, that I had some abilities. My uncle left Alabama as a young boy to come up here—didn't even finish high school—and he learned the cleaning business. He opened up a cleaners on 55th Street and did very well. He had a bit of a flair for entertainment and opened a supper club on Garfield Boulevard. It was really nice, and he bought a few more. In his later years he got out of the entertainment business and owned a couple of grocery stores until he died. He did very well.

My family left Ida B. Wells in 1955. My mom is still alive, and she lives right down the street from there. My dad died a year after we bought the home. My brother went to Dunbar High School and took a trade; he was a brick mason. He's been on disability retirement for four years, five years now. I have a sister—she's much younger, born in 1945. She was only ten, eleven years old when Dad died in 1956, and I think she might have turned out differently had my dad lived. Her kids are struggling, and she did, too. I certainly was not a father to her. I was in college and she was eleven years my junior, so we didn't have a lot in common. My brother was off working, so she was brought up in a house with a mother who was a recent widow, and I think maybe some of that was the problem. I think the other thing is her early adult life was during the permissive 1970s. My sister, you would hardly think she came from the same family. We get together for family dinners and things like that, but it is a really strange experience. When my kids were growing up, they used to ask me questions. "Why are they so different?"

I have two children, both of them doing very well. My son graduated from the University of Illinois Law School. My daughter is a manager for MCI. Neither have children. I have no grandchildren, as much as I would love to have them. My daughter has a home and lives in Atlanta. When they went out into the world, we had told them that it ain't all like it looks here. You will not have this support system with you forever. They were pretty much ready for it. My daughter and my son were both very active in their undergraduate days in founding and being participants in black organizations on their campuses. Right now, my son is active with what is called BALSA, which is a black law school students organization. He makes speeches down at Champaign all the time to young black law students. One of his protégés is the new representative for the Second District [Rep. Jesse Jackson, Jr.]. He and my son are close. My daughter went to graduate school at Northwestern, and she was involved with the black MBA group there. And she still is.

I think they're schizophrenic. Because while they espouse appreciation for the underclass and want to help the underclass, they really are from a middle-class background, and they don't want to live in those communities. My daughter has a beautiful home in a very white community in North Atlanta. My son has a nice townhome in Flossmoor. They work hard.

My son would tell you—and he is very successful—that he knows he is in his firm because of that firm's need for African-American representation. He knows if it were not for these programs—affirmative action—there would not be a job in some of these firms for him. He knows no matter how strong his talents are, there has to be that kind of a push in order for the doors to swing open for him. And so he is not blind, thinking that he is doing all this on his own, no matter how talented he is.

And my daughter knows the same. When she was recruited from Kellogg, two people from MCI recruited her, and in a minute she's asking, "What is it you want from me? What will I bring you?" And they had to tell her—"We are actively seeking African Americans." If we take away the affirmative action programs, as far as I'm concerned, and my kids are concerned, we start whittling away at the success of a lot of middle-class black people.

LEON HAMILTON

Leon Hamilton developed a thriving business owning and managing apartment buildings, mostly in Chicago's South Shore neighborhood. Now semi-retired, he manages his stock portfolio and remains active in civil rights causes. He lived with his family in Ida B. Wells Homes between 1941 and 1950.

When I look back at Ida B. Wells, I think it must have been a social experiment because it was a world apart from the real world. In that atmosphere we were hardly aware of segregation. We were poor, but we didn't know we were poor, because we lived in this little development.

We had new facilities! Central heat! The apartments were new and clean! Everything! Refrigerators and modern stoves! Here it was, the 1940s, but we had brand-new appliances—the same type that prevailed all the way through the 1960s. So Wells was ultramodern for that time.

Then we had Madden Park. We had a swimming pool. We had a center there that we could go to with activities. So we were like little rich kids. We wanted for practically nothing, and we didn't think of ourselves as poor.

And then we had motivated managers like Oscar Brown. Here was a man who was a lawyer, a graduate of Howard University—a middle-class man with middle-class values. Clearly, the tenant selection process was highly selective, and before you got into Ida B. Wells, your father and mother personally had talked to Oscar Brown or his delegated authorities. At some time or another, you talked to him, and he let you know what the rules were. And your family followed those rules.

I remember the responsibilities for cleaning when we were growing up. My family cleaned the front steps of the building, from the third floor to the second floor. Horace Wilson cleaned the stairs from the first floor to the second floor. In the rear, some other families cleaned. We kids cleaned those halls. And if somebody messed up our hall, we were quick to tell them, "Get that paper off that floor. Don't you do that on my stairs, cause I got to clean it Saturday!" Oscar Brown set those kinds of rules.

For the most part, I would say 90 to 95 percent of the families [in Wells] were intact. Both the mother and father were there. And that was a very important characteristic, because that meant stability. I can't remember, but maybe one or two families that I'm aware of were on public assistance.[18] As a kid, I didn't know what that meant, anyway. We had food, we had clothes. At Christmas time, we got the things that kids expected to get. Even now, I reflect back that when Christmas came to Ida B. Wells, all of us from the first floor would be out in the hall, yelling, "Come see what I got!" We would run to each other's apartments, and that would just be the greatest time!

My father was always one looking for something better. He was an ambitious type of person. For a time he was an automobile mechanic. He had worked in the stockyards, but then he left and opened up a garage and tried that. There never was a suggestion that my family was going to be on relief—my father would just shudder [at the thought] that somebody's going to give him charity. He had such pride about supporting his family. Then he started an automobile "Simonizing" business, and he went around to different car dealers, cleaning and polishing their cars, and within six months to a year's time, he got the down payment and bought an apartment building at 39th and Prairie.

So we were not conscious that we were poor. We did not grow up with any stigma, thinking that we were inferior! We grew up with the idea that if we went to school, if we followed the rules, if we took baths and combed and parted our hair, then we were going to make progress like everybody else in the country.

There was a different attitude when I was growing up. Like, when I was in school, OK, I tried hard. And the other kids that didn't do as well did not criticize me; they were proud of me. I wasn't ashamed. They were proud of me, and they would make comments, you know, "He's the Brain!" A kind of showpiece!

When I was at Ida B. Wells, the whole community wanted the children to do well. Adults would ask you, "How are you doing in school? What do you want to be? You want to become a doctor, a lawyer, a fireman?" There was always encouragement. You'd go across to Johansen's, and he'd ask you, "How are you doing in school? How do you convert from Fahrenheit to Centigrade?" Everybody was testing you.

I attended high school at Dunbar Vocational. It was an excellent choice because the principal of Dunbar was Clifford Campbell, and he was a graduate of MIT. He put together an excellent staff of teachers. Even though they'd graduated from Harvard, MIT, and the University of Chicago, they couldn't get into their fields because of segregation. So Campbell could hire who he wanted. It was tremendous!

There I was, out of Ida B. Wells, at this high school with all of these Ivy League teachers. They saw the potential in guys like me. They took me under their wing and put me into speech class, where I'd get into oratorical contests. And I won one of the contests. The first prize was a week's stay in somewhere like Arkansas! But I couldn't go because it was segregated! [Laughs] So instead, they concocted some consolation prize. I think it was a couple hundred dollars. They gave me a scholarship to go to the University of Illinois. And that wasn't bad at all.

I graduated from high school in the top 10 percent, so I was going to [the University of Illinois at Chicago, then located at] Navy Pier, not under any special programs, because my scores were all in place. Most of the people from Ida B. Wells didn't need affirmative action or any enrichment programs to bring us up to snuff! But when I got to Navy Pier to register, I got the rude awakening of my life, that "Hey! There's something different about you!"

On registration day students lined up single file all along the four walls of the Navy Pier gym. We waited patiently to get up to the booth where you gave your name, and they looked to see if they had the appropriate card for you to begin the registration process.

Well, I got to the front of the line, and it was my turn. A kid in front of me, a white kid, had finished his process and got his card. I got up there, the lady looked up at me, and she said, "Whadda you want?" And I looked back at her, and I didn't say anything because of course she knew what I wanted. And I couldn't figure out what was wrong here. While I was trying to figure it out, there was a Jewish girl behind me who said, "He's next." Well, the lady turned to this Jewish girl, and said, "Can I help you?" And the Jewish girl said, "Yeah, he's next!" And then the lady grudgingly gave me my card so I could begin the process.

So I went on and I started figuring, "My God, you know, that lady doesn't like colored people!" And that was the first instance in my life of discrimination!

When I was in Ida B. Wells, I had contact with white people. The milkman who came to deliver the milk was Caucasian, and he was smiling. The insurance man would come to sell the insurance, and he was smiling, he was jovial. When I went to Johannsen's grocery store across the street, he was smiling. Everybody was smiling! And my teachers at school, the white teachers, they were concerned about my learning and my welfare.

At Dunbar, one of my teachers had been Mr. Samuel Stratton; he taught civics. He was very good at picking out promising students and urging them to go on to college and law school, and do this and that. And he prompted me to get active in the NAACP [National Association for the Advancement of Colored People] Youth Council in the 1950s, just before the 1960s civil rights push. At the time, I'd say it was probably unpopular to do it because even middle-class blacks kind of frowned upon you because they thought you were rocking the boat.

But Samuel Stratton got us all motivated. So I spent time with the NAACP, and we went to Washington a time or two in the 1950s. We didn't get on television with our marches and so forth, but we were carrying on that activity in the 1950s. When I was in the army in 1959 and 1960 at Fort Benning, Georgia, I would go on weekend leave to Columbus, Georgia, and that was segregated. So I felt a duty to try to end segregation, and I tried to organize a group of soldiers. We were going to go into Columbus and integrate the bus station. Integrate some restaurants!

So I contacted some of the civic leaders—black lawyers, some of the other people in the town—but nobody wanted to touch this. And the soldiers were backing off from me. So I went in myself to the bus station and attempted to buy a ticket, and the ticket seller told me, "The colored side is around the other way!" And then he said, "I don't care whatcha are, but go around the other side there." So after doing what I thought I must do to satisfy my conscience—I did not just passively fall into line with the traditions of segregation—I went ahead and followed the route.

I applied to go to the Officer Candidate School, and my application was turned down. So I appealed it. I went to see my company commander, and he said I had to go see the battalion commander. So I went to see the battalion commander, and we proceeded to talk. He asked me some questions, and I answered him. Then he'd cut in with another question before I'd finish, and I'd attempt to answer that question. Finally, he was about to cut in again, but I kept talking to answer his previous question.

He said, "Don't you know to shut up when an officer's talking?"

So I said, "Well, Sir, I attended the University of Illinois, and I have worked with the NAACP. I talked to Representatives, I talked to Senators, and I talked to college professors. I guess I can talk to an army officer."

So he said, "Your application is denied!" I suppose they were just testing me, to see if I could follow the discipline. But, you know, I'd always thought, somehow or another, that maybe something else was wrong. So after they passed the Freedom of Information Act, I went back and I looked at my old army records, to see what had happened.

I found out that my activities with the NAACP had been monitored by the Red Squad. [Until the early 1970s, the Chicago Police Department maintained a division, known as the "Red Squad," that tracked suspected left-wing activity in the city.] There was this write-up on me in the army records that said, "This enlisted man would make a fine army officer, but see the incoming communication." And the incoming communication was from the Red Squad. That kept me out of Officer Candidate School.

I had gotten my degree in business management from Roosevelt University before being drafted into the army, so I started looking for jobs in a junior management training program. I went to places like First National Bank, and they would all tell me, "You're well qualified, but our program's not open to coloreds yet." They would say that. I went to an employment agency, and the fellow told me, "I should be able to get you a job, but to be frank with you, I don't want to waste your money."

This was about 1962 or 1963 when I was being told that. I decided that I couldn't get a job in an executive program, so I applied to the CTA to get a bus driver job. Well, when I got there, they told me, "You got too much education!"

So I said, "My God, what do I do now? I've got too much education." I ended up going to work for GMAC [a subsidiary of General Motors] as a field representative, collecting delinquent car payments. I audited car dealers and repossessed automobiles. This was the closest that I got to an executive job at that time!

I decided to go into real estate. I started selling real estate, and things went really well for me. I sold with Dempsey Travis for a couple of years, then I opened up my own real estate office. I bought buildings in distress, with problem tenants in them, and I put the buildings back together. I kicked out the tenants who were dealing drugs, and then I selected the right families and put them in. That way, they became stable and sound investments. That is the principle of making a project work: it's selectivity of the tenants.

For instance, I bought a building with twenty-four apartments a few years ago, and I was going to rehab it. To help with the rehab, I selected a fellow who had been with me about seven or eight years—he was the janitor at a large building with seventy apartments and he had been to college. For some reason, though, his life got all jumbled up, and he was drinking and so forth. But he related to me, and he kept the building clean. And I liked that. When I bought the [twenty-four-apartment] building, I told him, "I will give you 20 percent interest in this building if you oversee the repair." I allowed him to put the building back together, which he did excellently. I also allowed him to manage the building. He selected the tenants, and they moved in. For a month or two the rents came in and it was a very profitable building. But after about three or four months, the building practically exploded, because there were people that had bad habits, alcohol habits, dope habits, and a lot of social problems! I say it happened because he didn't know how to select. He selected people that he could relate to. And yet, he was a good janitor—he's still the janitor of that building. But I [bought out] his 20 percent interest and I took it back over. In order for me to regain control of that building, I had to get with the local police department and go to council meetings so I could clear out all the problems.

In my experience in managing properties, I admitted many female heads of families, but again, I've been selective among those female heads. Because there are some female heads that want their children to do well, and they're going to keep watch on what the children are doing, and you can talk to those parents about what their children are doing. So you've got to have that selective process, and you've got to monitor it and be able to identify where the problem's coming from and go where the problem is originating and get to the root of it.

There's one thing that Ida B. Wells never prepared us for. It prepared us to do well, but that background did not prepare us to face a world that was not willing to give us a chance. There were fellows who had far more potential than I did, who had nervous breakdowns, who committed suicide when they hit this world. My younger brother went to the University of Illinois and then to Howard University. He was in pharmacy school, but at twenty-two, he committed suicide. And I've seen a number of other suicides in the group.

We had our hair combed and parted right. We were cleanly scrubbed and we had done well in school. But when we got out there and we hit the real world, it was not allowing us to do the jobs that we were capable of doing.

In a way, Ida B. Wells was just like the experimental biosphere that they had going for a time. We were reared in this biosphere. Then they opened the door and said, "Well, go ahead out!" And they didn't tell us there was no oxygen out there.

ANDREW GREENLEE

Andrew Greenlee is a retired Deputy Superintendent of the Chicago Police Department. He moved to Chicago from Mississippi in late 1943, and moved into Altgeld Gardens in the fall of 1944. He lived there with his parents and eight brothers and sisters. Since 1974, he and his family have lived in Kenwood, a racially and economically mixed neighborhood on Chicago's South Side.

Back in 1943, there was a lot of migration to the city of Chicago, especially from the South. My father had been a builder in Mississippi, but during the war he left Mississippi and went to Tuskegee, Alabama, and helped build an airfield down there. After that, he moved to Chicago in early 1943 in search of work. We still lived on a farm in central Mississippi, Mom and the bunch of us. At that time, my folks had eight kids, or was it nine? There were so many, I can't hardly remember. About November 1943 the rest of us moved from Mississippi to Chicago. We lived in a rooming house at 3242 Vernon.

For a family of our size, of course, it was very crowded. We stayed there until the summer of 1944. When school was out, my folks sent my younger brother and me back to Mississippi, which was the custom in a lot of families, and I spent the summer with my grandmother. By the time I had come back, my folks had moved to Altgeld Gardens, 922 East 131st Street, known as "Block 1." That was the first block that opened up out there. It had just opened up, and it was a lot better living than where we were in the rooming house, but there were still ten of us living in three bedrooms with one bathroom. And they were not large bedrooms. Two of them were fairly good sized, but the third bedroom could not even accommodate a full-size bed. So, it was not the Ritz by any means. We stayed in that unit from the summer of 1944 up until we moved in 1953.

Dad worked initially at the Pullman Shipyards. During the war they used to build ships over there. And that's where he worked up until after the war. Most of the tenants were working-class people, pretty much the same as my father. Most of them were mother-and-father families. I recall only a few female-headed families at that time.

Out there at that time it was a very cohesive neighborhood. Believe me. I mean, people took what they had and fixed it up nicely. I recall my dad building a little white picket fence around our unit, and Mom had beautiful flowers in the yard. It was just really a wholesome place to live.

We were very happy at Altgeld. I mean relatively speaking, relative to living at 3242 Vernon, which was a crowded ghetto neighborhood. Just imagine, here's a youngster coming in from the country where he's used to horses and dogs and wide open spaces and plenty of room to run around in, and outside all the time with plenty of fresh air to breathe, moving into a rooming house at 3242 Vernon. I remember it so well because things were so filthy around there. Most of the furnaces were burning coal at that time, and coal dust settles everywhere. Every time you touched anything, it was dirty. To me, that brief period of living there was devastating.

Well, at Altgeld, we had a mixture of good and bad teachers. Some were very dedicated. Most of the teachers that we had out there, almost all the teachers I had in grammar school, as I recall, were white. And they didn't want to go all the way to Altgeld to teach school, so they didn't exactly get the best ones. They were teaching there because they obviously didn't have no place else that they could go.

After the war was over, new income restrictions were applied to Altgeld, sometime during the Truman administration. My father was not in a position to buy a house. With nine kids, you need a pretty good-sized house. Or a heck of a large apartment. We were subjected to some pressure to move, and I recall this very well because my mother sat down and wrote a letter to President Truman explaining her plight, and consequently we were given a reprieve. Later on, my father was able to buy a two-flat building, and we moved away from Altgeld. This was in 1953. By that time things had gotten better.

I remember certain blocks were getting awards for best-kept blocks and most beautiful flowers. Going out there and seeing the way things are today—there's no comparison between the two. But then, almost all of the necessities of life were there. I mean, we had a doctor's office right around the corner. I'm convinced that the key to the whole thing is the integration of socioeconomic [groups]. We're going to continue to have devastation when we lump socioeconomically depressed people together and confine them to an area and isolate them.

One of the problems was Lyndon Johnson. We have been a depressed people for a long period of time. When you take a depressed individual or a depressed group of people, they don't need handouts, they need handups. When you start giving people aid and relief and requiring nothing in return, you neuter that individual. You destroy his will to do for himself. I think therein lies the problem. People need assistance, but they don't need total subsistence. We have youngsters who come up in the welfare system and that's all they know. They know "I'm going to get to be fifteen or sixteen years old and I'm going to have me a couple of babies," and this is just natural to them to think that way. This is the way the welfare system has operated. I think it's wrong, and it's degenerating to just continue to give people the necessities of life without insisting that they do something for themselves. Everybody loses in a situation like that.

We didn't get in this position overnight and we're not going to get out of it overnight. The alternative is education. Now you cannot wait till the child gets to first grade to start with their education. He's too far behind. You've got to start his education from the time he's in preschool. And you not only have to educate that child, you have to educate his parents, or whoever's responsible.

Today, almost everybody that's black that lives in Chicago lives in segregated areas. I don't, but I made a special effort not to. Someplace along the line I realized the importance, not so much for myself but for my children, to bring them up in an area that was not segregated. I'm comfortable with white people. I want my children to be comfortable with white people. I want them to go to school with white children so they will know from the beginning that they can compete with anybody and be successful. It's an attitude that has to be implanted in the youngster's mind. Of course, I didn't get it till later in life. I had to get these things for myself. I can't rely on my children being lucky enough to get these things.

This is why I chose to live in Kenwood. I've been in Kenwood since 1974. I don't regret it one bit. It's a nice place to live, it really is. But the main reason I moved here is because I want my children to feel free and to know that they are just as important as anybody else, and not to feel as though they have to look at somebody else in awe because of their different race or different culture. And the only way you can do that, I think, is by having people live together. I'm all in favor of it. To me it's vitally important.

JERRY BUTLER

A legendary rhythm and blues singer, Jerry Butler grew up in a cold-water flat near the Frances Cabrini Homes (now part of the Cabrini-Green complex). He moved with his mother and two brothers to a high-rise within the development when he was fifteen. Butler still sings on occasion and is active in the entertainment world, but since 1985 he has been a member of the Cook County Board of Commissioners.

The neighborhood around Cabrini was integrated when I lived there. That was the real melting pot of this city, right in the middle of Cabrini Homes. Everybody was there, almost any nationality that you could think of. Patrick Reilly was one of my friends in school. There was Dominick DiMaggio, who was an Italian fellow. There was a Jewish family that I recall. There was a Polish family that I knew. I can't remember their names now, but that was pretty much the mix.

I used to attend St. Phillip's. They used to have these festivals with the Italian sausage and red wine and old cigars and all this stuff. I just thought it was marvelous. I never really gave much thought to racism in the city until, I guess, the neighborhood started to become predominantly black. And then it was like, where did all these other races go, and why did they leave? By the time I got to Washburne Trade School, there were only nine white students in my freshman class.

I studied culinary arts at Washburne because I wanted to own a restaurant like my Uncle Johnny Bennett. He owned Pearl's Kitchen, which was near Cabrini. He came back from the Navy in 1942 and opened up the restaurant. To our family, he was the best of the best. Many people who came up from Mississippi first had a job in his restaurant before they found other work to do.

He was a little guy. I doubt if he was over five-one or five-two. Muscular build, hard-set jaw. "Good morning, and how are you?" was a long conversation to him. I mean, he didn't talk a lot, but he was just the pillar of society. All of the ministers, all of the policemen, all of the number runners, all the pimps, all the prostitutes—you name it—they all came into Mr. Bennett's place to eat. And they all referred to him as Mr. Bennett.

When the neighborhood changed, when it became single-parent families and people on welfare, his clientele disappeared. From 1942 until about 1955, he had working people—the policemen, the bus drivers. The restaurant was always packed: big breakfast, big lunch, big dinner. After the neighborhood started to change, you'd have a big breakfast, no lunch, a little dinner. Then little breakfast, no lunch, and no dinner. So he moved his place to 71st and South Chicago, to a much smaller restaurant.

When we moved into Cabrini-Green, we moved from what I considered being poor to being middle-class. Most people don't think of the projects as that, but that was my reading of it in those days. I had come out of a three-room basement flat with cold water. Now I go into a five-room apartment on the seventh or eighth floor with a shower, a tub, hot and cold water, a refrigerator and stove, and a good view—the whole nine yards. But it was not a community.

It wasn't the low-rises. It wasn't the Mother Cabrini Homes where you walk out in the street, and the guy next door is sitting in the front yard and says, "Hey, how ya doin'"? It wasn't that. No, you can't develop a feeling of community in a tall building. I just don't believe that. 1117 [N. Sedgwick] was a very large building, very tall—maybe twenty-two, twenty-three stories. I didn't know anybody that even lived on my floor. I might know the kids—you know, what they looked like—but I didn't know their names. There were lots of kids, and kids have a habit of wanting to play with elevator buttons. So I thought that was a problem. And everybody was on welfare—that had a definite impact.

You know, going back to the [low-rise] Mother Cabrini Homes, I would say right off the top of my head, maybe 15 percent were on welfare. I would think less than 30 percent of the families were headed by single mothers.

My mom lived at Cabrini until about 1959 or 1960. I made my first recording in 1958. In those days income had a lot to do with your ability to stay. Because people heard my voice on the radio, I was considered rich and famous, and it was assumed that my mother no longer needed that apartment, so they asked her to leave. I bought a building out on the South Side of the city on 65th Place, and my mother moved in there.

I don't really know how I got into music. I mean, I never planned a music career. I sang in choirs, I sang around the house, I sang on street corners. I just sang for the love of singing. I sang what is popularly known as doo-wop, street-corner singing. My first recollection of singing was gospel songs on my mother's knee. When I was a kid, I went to the Catholic church, to the Baptist church—I went to any church that I wanted to because my mother believed that there was one God called by many names, served by many different kinds of people in many different fashions.

My friends and I sang on the street corners of Chicago—in Franklin Park, all around Cabrini. And then in 1958 there was a little recording company on South Michigan Avenue, VJ Records, which was owned by a black couple from Gary, Indiana. Vivian Carter was the wife. She had a radio show in Gary called *Living with Vivian*. And we went to her recording studio, sang a song that I had written while I was a student at Washburne called "For Your Precious Love," and she recorded it. It became a big hit.

Since then, it's been peaks and valleys. Peaks and valleys. But I was fortunate in the sense that my first recording contract was a three-year agreement; it was assumed in the industry in those years that that was about the life of an entertainer. The second contract I had was with Mercury Records, which was up here at Wacker Drive and Wabash. It was for seven years, because that was assumed to be the extent of a singer's career. I have gone far past what normally would have been considered a successful career for someone who just started singing on street corners.

If you're a black man, they take you to jail—directly to jail. Do not pass go. My own sons were driving down Cottage Grove in a new four-by-four. They'd been out to a joint on the South Side, The Godfather at 87th Street. A newspaper truck makes a U-turn in the street, they put on the brakes, can't stop, hit the truck. The police come—two white policemen. They say to the guy driving the newspaper truck, "Go ahead and finish your route, Joe. All right, you guys, up against the car."

My son said, "Wait a minute. What the hell you mean, up against the car? He's part of an accident. Don't you have to make a report?"

"Yeah, we know who caused the accident, kid. Get on the ground."

He argues some more, and they kick him, handcuff him, and throw him on the car. They take him to 51st Street. And they call me at three o'clock in the morning. See, that's why we start to have this breakdown among black males.

Though Butler has never been associated with the Nation of Islam, he did travel to Washington in 1995 for the Million Man March.

People say black men don't care about anything, you can't get a bunch of them together without having a fight. They will steal you blind. And I purposely went on a bus that left from 47th Street. I rode with Howard Saffold. He was the chief of security for [former Chicago Mayor] Harold Washington. Then we had a deacon from some church. We had a guy from Independence Bank. And then we had some people who were not even employed. The whole spectrum was on this bus.

It was awesome. I came back and I looked up "awe." It said awe is a mixture of feeling and reverence. And I said, "Ooh!" That's what that was. Reverent in the sense that you could pull all of these different people together. I will say to you that there is probably no people in America as diverse as the black race. And the reason it's diverse is because we've been caught up in everybody else's culture. You've got Catholics, you've got Protestants, you've got Lutherans, you've got Muslims, you've got Buddhists, you've even got Jews. You name it, we got it. Well, to have a million—or six hundred thousand or four hundred thousand or whatever number you like—come together in spite of their differences, based on the commonality of being black man in America and having this stigma—it was awesome.

We got to Washington, D.C., at 7:30 in the morning, and people were coming in droves. I felt like I was standing in a room full of gunpowder, expecting somebody to light a match—because I felt it could be that easy to start something that would be uncontrollable. And if it had started, it would have been uncontrollable. I don't care how much National Guard, how many police—there was no way you would have been able to stop that.

In Washington, there was a request that you would come and be peaceful, and that if you see somebody getting out of line, you put them in check. And so I saw all these black men with a spirit of camaraderie coming together for one common purpose. I didn't see anybody drinking. I didn't see any brown bags. I didn't see any beer bottles. The only guy I saw smoking was me, and I was smoking a pipe. I did not hear any angry words. As a matter of fact, I didn't hear anything vulgar. It was just a bunch of men. It was a mind-blowing experience.

I don't think people came because of Farrakhan. It was his idea, but I think some people came in spite of him. There was some who said, "Yeah! I'm with Farrakhan, blah, blah, blah." There were some who were silent on the question. And there was this deacon that I told you about. He was Christian, probably as far away from Farrakhan as anybody could be. He said, "I am going because I want to show unity."

As a matter of fact, I think that Farrakhan and Jesse Jackson learned from Martin and Malcolm. Martin and Malcolm could not come together because of their religious differences. We put aside our differences. We put aside Muslim and Christian. We put aside rich and poor. We put aside everything except that we are all black men in America, and we all suffer because we are black men.

MELVIN WILSON

Melvin Wilson moved into Ida B. Wells in 1940, when he was six years old. His parents had five children at the time and would soon add three more to the Wilson family. After years of labor activism and a career in education, Wilson served from 1984 to 2001 as the Treasurer of the Chicago Teachers' Union. His wife passed away in 1998.

We were one of the earliest families in Ida B. Wells. We had three bedrooms, a living room, kitchen, and bath. Oh, we were just fascinated with it. It was four boys, so two in each bedroom, and our parents had their private room, and we had just a wonderful kind of arrangement, considering what we were living in prior to moving into Ida B. Wells.

It was a step up, no doubt about it. I lived there up until I was married. My parents were there up until the late 1970s. My parents put a tremendous amount of work into raising us. And we pretty much had to toe the line. Ida B. Wells was very strict with their tenants in those early days. You had to maintain the house, the hallways had to be clean, and they would rotate that kind of duty between the two families that were living across from one another. And the same thing would apply to the landscaping and groundskeeping. So children didn't play on the grass.

If the janitorial staff told you to do something, there was no question as to whether or not you were going to do it, because it was understood that they were in a position of authority. Your parents said, "If the janitor or a responsible adult tells you to do something, you better do it, as long as it's reasonable."

The church was very important. My parents were Christian people, and it was understood on Sunday, you go to church. I attended the Catholic church with my wife on a frequent basis. I made that commitment and I followed through on it. But I'm a firm believer that the church is within the individual, you are the temple. I try to treat people right and try to live by the word.

I graduated from Doolittle Elementary School and attended Dunbar Trade School [now Dunbar Vocational School]. At Dunbar it was more or less like a family arrangement with about six hundred students at that time. First, I enrolled in the print shop and I enjoyed it. I took a series of other shops—welding, sheet metal, and machine drafting. In my junior year I had to make a decision which one I was going to major in. So the instructor in the print shop said, "Well, once you graduate, I'm almost sure I could get you a job at the *Defender*. You seem to be a good student. You pay attention to what's going on." My instructor in the sheet metal shop sort of did the same thing. This was Dixie Davis, a Jewish fellow. He said, "Well, listen, you're a good mechanic, I can probably get you into a program within the sheet metal trade." Dixie Davis talked to my parents and told them that he thought I would make a good sheet metal mechanic. After that, I said, "Well, maybe I will try it," since he was so persistent. So I majored in sheet metal.

In my senior year, 1952, I went to interview at two plants and I had a choice to go to either Shop A or Shop B. So I picked the one that was a little closer to home. Phil Lazarra and his brothers owned that place. I would go to school for maybe two hours and then I would go to work. They expanded and wanted me to stay.

I was oriented in support of unions at that time because my dad was in the union. He worked for Revere Copper & Brass during the war. But the Lazarras didn't want the union. They led me to believe I was supposed to tell the others not to vote for the union. There was a total of maybe about twenty-five workers. I remember one of them, his name was Albright. He asked me, "Melvin, what should we do? Should we go for the union?" I told them "Yes." But let me tell you, the boss was so angry. He came out of that office and unplugged the Coke machine and said, "No more breaks."

Well, the workers wanted me to be the union shop steward. And so I said [to management], "That's not right, you can't deny them a break." That went on for a few days. Lazarra put so much pressure that employees started quitting! He said, "We're not going to have no union around here, I don't care what happens. If I have to shut it down, I'll get rid of everybody." Eventually he got rid of enough people so he achieved what he wanted—the next time the union wasn't voted back in. He fell out of favor with me, and several months later I quit.

Some of my classmates were employed in other shops in the inner city, giving me easy access to finding employment within a short time. A good friend and classmate Bennie Crane informed me about a shop that was hiring—Ledal Stainless Steel. I worked there for fourteen years, and during that time several students from Dunbar Trade School were employed by the company.

I was the union's shop steward and then the shop foreman. It didn't take too much to organize a union there because it was the Teamsters Union, Local 714. The way they organized in those days, they would go in and scare the hell out of the owner, and the owner would come out and ask the employees to sign the card! [Laughs] I served as a shop steward there for about eight years.

Then the boss said, "Melvin, how about coming into management? When I open the plant next door, that's gonna be your shop over there." Sure enough, he bought the building next door, and I took over that program, and I gave up the union. I became a manager—that was about 1964—and I stayed at that another six years. I got decent money.

Then in 1967 I started vocational teaching at night in the public schools. Martin Luther King and the Southern Christian Movement had a strong impact on me. So my contribution was made when I was in the classroom. It gave me a sense of sharing and reaching out and trying to pass something on to somebody else. I keep up with a lot of the kids; I have a number that call me all the time. They're doing quite well, and that makes me feel good.

In school I was immediately a member of the union. I got elected to be in the union's House of Representatives. And I joined a few of the committees. The treasurer of the union at that time—Mr. Hambrick—was one of my teachers at Dunbar. So I joined his PAVE [Practical Arts and Vocational Education] Committee. After I worked with him for a few years, he said, "I think you should become chairman of this committee." So I took over the chairmanship of the PAVE Committee and became more and more involved with the teachers' union.

Mr. Hambrick was my mentor, and he shared a lot of information with me. He said he was going to be retiring, and so I said, "What the heck?" I submitted a letter and said I'd like to apply for the job of treasurer. I had to go before the Executive Committee. I knew a lot of the people there—we had worked together—and so the president said, "Okay, Melvin, you're going to be a part of the union slate." So I began to do my little campaigning, got myself a leave from school for a while and started visiting schools, talking to teachers. And they voted for me.

During my tenure, we were faced with many serious issues dealing with benefits relating to health care, class size, recertification, and major changes in vocational programs. I am proud to say that there were significant changes that we were able to get into our contract, such as reducing class size by giving additional support staff.

Many times I think having integrated schools is beneficial to minorities. But black students still need something extra. You see, blacks are coming from behind. When you start talking about four hundred years of slavery and all of that stuff, it's a situation where you have to be conditioned to come back into the mainstream because there are so many times where we have heard black kids being told—even by their parents—"You can't do this, you don't have the intellect to do so and so." And it takes time to get over that.

JOSEPH BERRIOS

One of the first Hispanic politicians elected to citywide office, Joseph Berrios was the Commissioner of the Board of Tax Appeals. His family moved into Cabrini-Green in 1958, when he was six years old, and left in 1968, "the weekend after Martin Luther King got killed."

When the riots started [after Martin Luther King's death in April 1968]—the shootings and everything else—the people in the building [most of whom were black] all wanted to make sure that my parents and my brothers and sisters were safe. They were there for us. They were saying, "Don't worry about this family, they're part of us. They've been here forever and nothing's gonna happen to them." In Cabrini we all treated each other like family. As long as you knew someone in the neighborhood, you were safe.

I lived in one of the seven-story buildings. Our building was unique because we had approximately sixty-five apartments, and everybody knew each other. It was a good experience for me. I'm one of seven kids, and we had lived in a small two-bedroom apartment on Elm Street before we had the opportunity to move into Cabrini-Green. My parents didn't make a lot of money, and they were both working, so moving into Cabrini-Green was a step up for us.

I had a lot of friends in grammar school over at St. Joseph's, and I had friends that went to Jenner. So within our group we were very close. We played baseball together, we played basketball, we did everything together. You know, I had more black friends than I did Hispanic and ethnic ones. But we treated each other well. Everybody took care of each other back then.

There was gang activity, but it was not as prevalent as it became in later years. When I lived in Cabrini, there were a lot of two-parent households. That started to change when the laws started changing. Under public aid rules, a family would not get as much if the husband was there, so the husband moved out. You're always trying to make it better for the family, but I think some of those programs hurt. When you had fathers leaving, kids felt that they had to bring money in, and, all of a sudden, gangs out there gained more and more power.

I started working when I was about thirteen years old. I started out as a dishwasher at a place downtown called the Tower Club. My aunt got me the job by telling them I was sixteen. I was sixteen for three years at that place. They kept asking me, "When are you gonna be seventeen?" I kept saying, "Not yet, not yet." Then I became a kitchen helper and then a busboy and then a waiter. I went through the whole scheme of the restaurant business. I worked there for seven years.

My parents were always trying to make sure that we got a little further than they did. It was mandatory for us to go to school. All my brothers and sisters ended up finishing high school. I got accepted at Lane Tech. I was lucky. Five of my friends took the test to get in, and I was the only one that got accepted. And it was a big deal back then. It was a good school. Then I went to the University of Illinois and got an accounting degree.

I not only had my parents, I had people in politics beating the heck out of me, saying, "You got to do this [get an education]." We moved up to the Northwest Side during my junior year of high school, and I got involved with a political organization through my precinct captain. And the funny part is that I never intended to go to college. But the powers-that-be said, "You have to go to college." I was graduating from high school and State Senator Ed Nedza came up and said, "You've got to go to school." I knew him pretty well, and then we kept a relationship throughout the years. My parents were also saying, "Yeah, you're going to school." So I had a double whammy. I got myself into college and made it through.

My first job out of college was over at the Bureau of Parking for the city, in charge of the parking meter collection. Later I came here to the Board of Tax Appeals as a chief clerk. In 1982 I had the opportunity to run for state Representative. I was elected three times to the legislature. When [former Commissioner] Harry Sungro passed away, I decided to take a chance and run for Commissioner [of the Board of Tax Appeals, now called the Board of Review]. I've been Commissioner since 1988.

I feel comfortable anywhere in the city. It doesn't make any difference to me. When we go out campaigning, I've had people ride in the car with me, and we go into different neighborhoods and sometimes people might feel uncomfortable. "We're going where? That's all black," or "That's all white," and "Are we gonna be alright over there?"

I say, "Yeah, we're fine, don't worry about it."

I've had a unique opportunity to be able to grow up within the black community and then to move to a Hispanic community, where I live now. But I've always been able to relate back and forth because I grew up within Cabrini. And the black community has got the same problems we have. They've got the same dreams that we have. We all have the same beliefs. That's what I truly believe.

NELVIA BRADY

Nelvia Brady was both the first woman and the first African American to serve as Chancellor of the City Colleges of Chicago. She served during Mayor Harold Washington's administration in the 1980s. Until 1960 Brady lived in the high-rise at Henry Horner Homes that would later house the two brothers profiled by Alex Kotlowitz in his 1992 book There Are No Children Here. *She then moved with her family to Rockwell Gardens, a nearby West Side development.*

I had an immediate reaction to Kotlowitz's book when I read it: there was something missing for me with that book. I realized that these things were true, but it wasn't my experience in public housing.

Our playgrounds were nice. There wasn't grass, but there wasn't glass either. The swings worked, the sliding boards worked, the children could come out and play in relative safety. The parents cared not only about their own children but about the children of other families. If you did something wrong and the neighbor saw it, your parents were going to know. There was unity within the community. The laundry rooms were clean and neat, and garbage areas were cared for. We knew the janitor. I guess they called him the "Engineer." If there were problems, the janitor could come up and take care of them for you.

When we were there, drugs were starting, but it was certainly not the problem that it is today. When I was in Rockwell, I was old enough to know that drugs were there, but I couldn't tell you where they were being sold. Of the families on my floor in Rockwell, I would say 80 percent of them were healthy, normal families. My mother is still in touch with many of them.

My father was a postal employee. My mother was a housewife. There were four children when we were in Horner, and then there were three additional children born while we were in Rockwell. All but two have gotten college degrees, and those two are in excellent positions in the telecommunications industry.

I was in the projects all the way through high school. I even spent one year in the project when I came back to Chicago in 1970 to teach. At the time my husband was in the military, so I taught on the West Side and lived at home. My parents didn't leave public housing until the early seventies.

When I grew up, public housing was not housing of last resort. It was housing that was valued and respected by both the tenants and the management. But over the years, like everything else in the cities, I could see the decline. I think there was probably a decline in the financial support to public housing. If there was not a decline in funding, there was certainly a *change* in the way people were admitted to public housing.

We were interviewed as a family. Screened. Fully screened. And later I know that stopped. I know that the family structure of the residents changed substantially. I recall that early on, the families that moved into public housing were *working people*. So something happened in terms of policy that allowed it to become available to a broader population.

From a child's perspective, the standards were fairly rigorous and rigid—in terms of the laundry facilities, in terms of the use of elevators, in terms of where children played. We were very familiar with what we could do and should do, and what we should *not* do. When you have large numbers of people living in fairly concentrated and dense quarters, that ought to be in place. It's no different from rules that are in place at a high-rise building on North Lake Shore Drive.

At Rockwell we were in a thirteen-story structure, and we lived on the thirteenth floor. At Henry Horner we had a seven-story structure, and we lived on the fifth floor. The high-rises were OK when we lived there, but I think there were some serious design issues. I mean, it's just not right when you've got thirteen stories and only two elevators—*two elevators*—for that many families and that number of children. The problem is the density. And those elevators were not enclosed—they were exposed to cold, to snow. Looking back now and knowing what I know about public purchasing habits, I doubt if they got the best structures in the first place. The work went to the lowest bidder.

I feel it's important for African Americans, or anyone, for that matter, to never forget from whence they came, to always find ways to give back to the community that nurtured and developed them. When I became Chancellor, one of the issues that I wanted to address was how the City Colleges of Chicago could help the residents of CHA. I embarked upon a three-year initiative that took us to the nineteen largest public housing developments. We did a door-to-door campaign, bringing the City Colleges' resources directly to the residents of public housing. We had on-site registration for classes; we had financial-aid support. We worked with all the welfare agencies in order to expose public housing residents to the adult education programs, the GED programs—all of the programs that we had available.

I know that we touched the lives of many through that effort. I remember meeting a woman. We knocked on her door and said, "Hey, this is City Colleges of Chicago, can we help you?" This was a young woman who had five kids, and she was in her late twenties. She had never thought about going to school. But she decided she was going to go because we knocked on her door. And she ended up getting a nursing degree and another associate's degree. We not only impacted her, but we impacted the five kids in her family. Once she started school, she wrote to us and talked about how she had begun to be more helpful to her kids with their homework, and how they studied together.

My point is that there are families in public housing today that want the very same things for their children that you want for yours, and I want for mine. And in many instances it's only a matter of them knowing what's available, or someone coming out and grabbing their hand and helping them get to where they need to go. We can't save everybody. But I don't think there's anything that's beyond our ability to address.

JAMES FLETCHER

Jim Fletcher was the president of South Shore National Bank, now Shorebank. His was one of the first families to move into Ida B. Wells. He moved out in 1953, and he passed away in 1998.

I moved into Ida B. Wells around 1941 with my mother and father and younger sister. I was five at the time. We had been living in a converted garage at my uncle's six-flat. There was a long waiting list to get into Ida B. Wells, but we had a fire, so they moved us up the list on an emergency basis. At Wells we lived at 509 East 38th Place, and we had two bedrooms. Next door were one-bedroom apartments, which were elderly housing. Growing up, one of the responsibilities we had was to knock our neighbor's door when we got home from school. My parents said to see if she needed anything done. That was part of my job, to see if Miss Shepard needed anything from the store or what have you. I never thought about it when I was a kid, but what they really did was to surround these elderly people with families so that they had somebody there to sort of take care of them.

But I wasn't actually an angel growing up. I remember having one heck of a couple days because I swung on a tree and broke a limb. A janitor saw me, and of course he came over that night and told my mother. Then my father came home from work, and I didn't swing again in the trees for a long time. As I think about the kids that I grew up with, I don't recall anybody who was from a single-parent family. Oh, there was one family divorced or separated. But I knew the father as well as I knew the mother. The large bulk of the people there were married. The mother and father were there.

Looking at my circle of friends—everybody's parents worked. I think the population was different than today's, where a great many of the families are on welfare. There was a notion at that time that—as good as that housing was—at some point you were going to save enough to maybe go buy a home. There was a different way that people thought about public housing.

I had a great childhood, I really did. You know, my grade schools weren't some of these prep schools up on the North Shore, and they probably could have been better and prepared me so that I could have gone to Harvard or Yale. But all in all I enjoyed grade school. Most of the teachers in those schools were truly interested in the students they had. Even as traumatic as high school was, I enjoyed it. I went to Tilden Tech in 1948. Prior to my class, you had to go two years at your local high school before you could go to technical school. But in 1948 they allowed freshmen in, and they got the largest influx of blacks they'd ever had. There were a few white teachers at Tilden who I felt would have loved it if blacks had never come to campus. But for the most part that was not the case.

Tilden was a very interesting place then because it was in the Back of the Yards [a white ethnic neighborhood located near the stockyards]. It had a lot of kids whose second language was English—Polish, Irish, German. Up until 1948, there were probably twenty-five or thirty blacks at Tilden. Now a hundred came into the neighborhood each day. You had to fight to get in and fight to get out.

Talking as a bank official who deals with affordable housing, it is a little difficult to predict what public housing of the future should look like. We at South Shore Bank think that sound public policy means congregate mixed-income housing. We think that approach provides the best kind of social environment for moderate-income people as well as for poor and working poor to thrive in. If you've got an environment where everybody is at the lowest end of the economic scale, you tend not to have any real market for goods and services in that neighborhood.

Public housing, as it came on in the 1930s and 1940s, was good public policy. It served its purpose. Since then public housing, for who knows what reasons, has gone awry. We need to go back and take a look at the whole issue, but I think we did well with Section 236 housing [a federal program providing tax subsidies to private builders to construct low-income housing]. And we seem to have been moderately successful with Section 8 [the federal program that gives low-income residents vouchers to use in the private housing market] because developers can make money. That's one way to approach it now.

Now, what should that public housing look like, and where should it be, and how should it be structured? I think public housing ought not to be built just in the inner city and not just in poor neighborhoods. We ought to look at a lot of additional places. In certain communities it makes a lot of sense to put a three-flat here and a four-flat there. In other communities you can build 150 units, and it works because the environment is different. Part of what you've got to do in some of these communities is figure out how you make the housing attractive enough so working people want to move back into it. And the dream in America is still a single, detached home.

When my family moved into Ida B. Wells, there was a very limited market that we could afford. You didn't have a lot of choices. Today, similar families have more choices. Now the black middle class is moving out of the older neighborhoods, leaving those neighborhoods a lot poorer. In many of the neighborhoods you don't have the diversity of income you once had.

Friends of mine have moved into "white situations" and just did not like it. They will tell you that they moved for better education and wound up with damaged kids because the kids weren't accepted or one thing or the other. Others say the education choices in all-black neighborhoods can get them all the things they want. You see, the big driving force for housing for families is still school—we must provide good schools for all black neighborhoods.

WILSON FROST

Wilson Frost is a Commissioner on the Cook County Board of Appeals. He served as an Alderman from the 21st Ward and then the 34th Ward between 1967 and 1986. During his political career, he rose to Chairman of the City Council Finance Committee and served as floor leader and president pro tempore of the City Council. After Mayor Richard J. Daley died in 1976, he was interim Mayor of Chicago for eight days.

I moved into Dearborn Homes with my mother and sister in 1950. I was twenty-three at the time and had just finished college. I remained until 1953. My sister remained until 1957, and my mother remained until 1963. It was a great improvement over where we had been living, which was in an area that was scheduled for demolition. We were among the first families to move in.

At that time there was no stigma about moving into public housing. In fact, my mother had made an application to Ida B. Wells, and she was discouraged because we were receiving public assistance at that time, and she had heard that was a bar to admission. But we had no problem being admitted to Dearborn Homes.

Dearborn Homes was a brand-new building on State Street with modern facilities and great transportation. It had a real community feeling with a mixture of old and young families. Many of the older people had ailments, so the neighborhood children would run errands and these older people in turn would baby-sit for them.

They were not primarily people on welfare. Rather, they were wage earners who did not enjoy high salaries. In fact, knowing about housing as I do, there are many instances where the only difference between public and private housing is the amenities provided. In the particular building we lived in, most of the families who lived there when we arrived were still there when we left.

Attitude, pride, and tenant makeup have changed since we were there. There is, of course, nothing wrong with an eight-hundred-unit project, as long as the screening process is substantially different from what it has been in the past twenty years.

I got into Fisk on a sports scholarship for basketball and track, both of which I commenced at Madden Park, the Ida B. Wells park. I would say, quite candidly, that in reviewing what makes Wilson Frost run, sports had a greater influence on me than anything else because it had rules and you had to prepare and train for it.

One thing I enjoyed about Fisk was that it was a black school. It had high academic standards, but from the day I walked on campus, any social activities they had, I was a part of. The school had five hundred students. I knew virtually all the student body, and they knew me. We had close relationships, and many of them are still my friends today.

Chapter 3

Gateway to the American Dream

The people who come to life in this chapter tell a similar yet surprising story: the move to public housing in the 1940s and 1950s represented a gateway to a better life. For the fortunate few, public housing was a privilege, a step up, and a way out. It offered a healthy environment, a shared community, and a new hope for struggling but upwardly striving, low-income families.

The former residents interviewed here speak happily—often lovingly—about their experiences. They remember a wonderful ambiance that promoted a common purpose and self-respect. While other family members were often role models, many found inspiration from the neighboring families in the projects. For others, a set of lasting friendships developed in public housing that continue to this day. Annual reunions of former residents allow these positive memories to survive—a window to public housing's past rarely viewed by the public.

The stories in this chapter are not "rags to riches" anecdotes, though a few of those interviewed have achieved substantial financial success. Rather, these are individuals from solid families, often with a strong mother, who moved to the projects to better their lives. The resulting move put them on the path to the American Dream, including accomplishments in career and family life that make them solidly middle class. The "salt of the earth" characters in this chapter are not exceptions; they more closely resemble the "rule" because their favorable experiences and later successes are not untypical of many early residents of public housing.

The CHA selected its families in the 1940s and 1950s from among thousands on its waiting lists, but it did not "cream" the most desirable families off the top of its pool. Instead they were "screened" by a conscientious CHA management team. Over eighteen thousand African-American families applied for the 1,660 apartments in the Ida B. Wells Homes when it opened in 1941. The Housing Authority gave priority to those living in the worst of the slums and those with the lowest incomes, but also to those who demonstrated good housekeeping. A check of police records and a personal "home visit" by a social worker provided an important safeguard for keeping out potentially destructive residents and those who could not adapt to community living.

The voices in this chapter destroy the typical stereotypes surrounding what public housing was and reveal what it still can be. They are not idealized types, but rather form a spectrum of the American middle class. Their voices are clear and cogent, as well as humbling, and they deserve to be heard.

ERMAN AND DOROTHY SING

The Sings met and married in Altgeld Gardens. Both moved to Altgeld as children when it first opened. They began raising their three children in Altgeld but moved in 1960. "Conditions changed. The people changed." Erman worked for thirty-seven years at the Sherwin Williams plant just north of Altgeld, and Dorothy worked for thirty-four years at Children's Memorial Hospital in the Lincoln Park neighborhood.

Erman: With some of the old-timers at these different Altgeld alumni parties, the subject is always brought up: If the same people could move back, everybody would move back. We had a lot of successful people from Altgeld Gardens. Charlie Hayes, he became a Congressman. A big group of guys went on the police department and the fire department.

Dorothy: Altgeld was like one big family, believe me, it was. Everybody in Altgeld Gardens knew everybody. Vandalism was zero out there. If you broke a swing in the playground, your family paid for it. So you know what happened? We didn't break the swing. We played with the swing and we went home.

If my mother's friends would come by, they opened the door and hollered, "Mrs. Mitchell, Mrs. Mitchell?" If nobody answered, they'd close the door and go on. And then they'd say, "Oh, I was by your house earlier today, you weren't there. I yelled in the door." This is how we were. There wasn't a lot of crime. I don't think I remember having a key to our apartment as a teenager. You just went out and closed the door!

Erman: The neighbors were beautiful. They were urbanized people. They had been in Chicago for years. Most of the teenagers and the youngsters, I'd say 95 percent of them, were born here in the city.

Dorothy: I know you were screened to get in. People came there and asked questions. They wanted to know if the kids get into trouble, do they go to school every day, was there fighting around the neighborhood. They asked a lot of questions.

Erman: I was sitting on the front porch and this guy drove up in a staff car, a government car, and asked for the Sing family. At the time my parents weren't in, and I explained to him that I was a Sing.

He said, "I would like to see the apartment your family is staying in."

I said, "Well, I tell you what I have to do. I have to get the landlord." So I went and talked to the landlord, and he says, "Okay."

And this guy came in and he looked. He said, "How many of you are staying in this apartment?"

I says, "There's four of us."

He says, "Tell you mother it's been OK'ed. I'm from the Federal Housing Authority."

Dorothy: They had rules when we moved in Altgeld Gardens. If the grass needed cutting and you didn't cut it, they cut it and they charged you. If they saw a paper on the ground with your name on it, the family had to pay five dollars. If something went wrong—if the knob came off your door and needed to be replaced—you were charged for that. So everybody took care of their apartments; all of the apartments looked very good.

Erman: Now you go out there and you ride around and say, "I used to stay in that apartment," and you can't believe the place! The storm door's missing, windows broken out. I just can't believe it! And the people's attitude! I don't understand it.

Now they've got private owners trying to run public housing, but they're just in it for the bucks. When the government runs it right, you're going to set up rules like we had in Altgeld Gardens. If they saw garbage by the incinerator by your house, they found out who put it there. Everybody took care of their apartments, and all of the apartments looked very good.

Dorothy: You know, my sisters and I were very poor growing up. My mother used to order little scraps from Sears Roebuck; we used to call them remnants—different kinds of material. We learned to sew skirts for ourselves. My mother learned to do hair; she worked very hard. Now, when I think about it, we were very poor, but my mother never once, I don't *ever* remember her telling us we were poor. And your morals had to be very high. She demanded that. Now, these twelve-year-olds that are out in the street killing—the family has no idea what's going on with the kid. Some of these mothers will say, "Oh, where is my son? He's thirteen years old, but I never see him." That was unheard-of when we grew up. If your mother put three meals a day on the table, you better be there, or you better have a good reason for not being there. So you've got to get back to the morals in the family. Just got to pull it back together.

None of the five of us had children before we were married. A small percentage of the families had single mothers when we were at Altgeld. I'll say

10 percent. My dad was not in our home, but we were disciplined. My mom was a very strong person.

I worked from the time I was a sophomore in high school until I graduated from high school. I worked as a page girl in the Altgeld Library, and one night a week I had to work until they closed, which was nine o'clock. I almost missed that job because my mom said, "You won't be here when we eat."

And I thought, "Gee, how important can that be?" But that was important in the family—that the whole family sat down together to have dinner and to talk. You might have a problem, and we could all come together and help you—we would talk about it. We had each other in Altgeld Gardens.

Erman and I left when our third child was just a year old. We decided we didn't want to raise our children there because we could see the writing on the wall. Some people were being forced out because they were over the income to live in Altgeld Gardens. We thought, "Well, we better get out of here, too."

Erman: See, basically they were letting people in the housing that weren't responsible for paying rent. You had a different type of people coming north to these cities—people that were coming because of the welfare benefits. They were putting these people in the housing projects, and they would have to *hire* people to show them how to turn the stove on.

I was born in 1931, when things were hard for my family. But we had never known anyone sending you a check in the mail. We couldn't go anywhere and live for nothing. You had to have a *job* in order to pay your rent and your overhead. And in fact, that's how Altgeld and most of the public housing was.

When we moved here to the Southwest Side, it was all white. Now, it's just another way of life with me. It's OK. It's better, the neighborhood is better. We've been here thirty-five years. And all of my neighbors made improvements over the years.

Dorothy: We built Saint Thaddeus Catholic Church from the ground up; it's always been all black. That's one of the few Catholic churches that we built from the ground up. The priest is Irish—John Collins. He's been there now about twelve years. Very nice, very good. We have had a black associate priest there. But the people, we just love our priest. When he's standing there doing the Gospel, you don't think, well, there's a white man. We don't think a thing of it. That's your priest. That's your church leader. That's John Collins, you know.

Some people have more money than others, some people live a little better. But whatever a little better is, we've had a good life. We've raised our children, and we were very fortunate. Neither one of us got laid off during the time the children were growing up, and they were in private schools, which cost us quite a bit. And two of our children went to college. I mean, my life was good for me. Our life was very good.

EDGAR JOHNSON

Edgar Johnson moved into Ida B. Wells in late 1941 with his mother and three sisters. He was ten at the time. He moved out after graduating from high school in 1949. He taught in the Chicago public schools and retired after thirty-two years of teaching.

There was a sense of community in Ida B. Wells, and believe me, there was a lot of pride among the people there. Because the housing they were enjoying was, in most cases, a step up from where they had been. The guys I grew up with were involved in athletics. We played basketball, we played softball, we ran track. Madden Park [a nearby public park] had a track facility, a field house, a swimming pool, and several softball diamonds. That park was a magnet to enhancing socialization among the children.

There was a strong sense of respect for adults in Ida B. Wells. Generally, the parents had a lot to say about the children's social acquaintances and activities. The parents at Ida B. Wells were not "too busy," let me put it that way, to raise their children. When I was there, the family units were family units.

We had a female-headed family. My mother was the spiritual fountain as well as the authoritarian law in our family. In many of the families where there were men, the women were equal in terms of breadwinning, and many times the woman brought in more than the man did. Of the six families in my building, there was only one man head of the household who was working, and he worked on a part-time basis.

Delinquency, while always prevalent, was on a minor scale. I'll give you an example. We used to go to the lakefront many times to swim and enjoy ourselves. We passed merchants along Cottage Grove as we proceeded to the lakefront. They always put their fruit and stuff out, and we'd always grab some potatoes as we ran by.

We played hooky. I failed sixth grade because I played hooky too much. But the shame of having to repeat a grade, knowing that I had the mental capability to pass, was a motivation in itself. As far as serious trouble, we'd have, maybe, a brush with the law every two or three years, but I can't think of anybody in my social group who ever went to juvenile detention or anything. Now, as adults they got involved in things that got them incarcerated. I remember one of the leaders of our little group ended up going to prison, and I think out of the ten or twelve guys, only two of them ended up actually serving some jail time. But this was after they had left Ida B. Wells. Delinquency, as you see it now, was unheard of.

I'll tell you something else. Probably the most shocking thing would be to take a brick and break a window, and that didn't happen very often. Destruction wasn't done. You had a janitor who was charged with the responsibility of maintaining the place, you had a whole bunch of adults and children who assisted him. We took pride in where we lived and as a result, we picked up things. I remember we planted victory gardens during the war. There was a sense of community that doesn't prevail nowadays.

When I was a resident, Ida B. Wells was comprised of a great number of people who I would have to describe as working but poor. I think that if the sociological circumstances were the same today as when I lived in the project, many more people would be willing to move in. Public housing has become a sort of dumping ground for—well, I can't say the truly down and out, but for non-wage-producing people. What I see in many of the housing projects today are people who are unemployed, and the prospects of employment for them seem very limited. And it may not be all their fault, because of the technological changes and things like that. But it just seems that, for whatever reason, they are probably less employable than many other people.

Today we are bombarded by media. We see things that we will never have. For instance, a young kid sees guys driving big cars with beautiful women on television all the time. And he looks at his very squalid surroundings and wonders why it's not so for him. It becomes incumbent upon the head of the household, the parent, to put that in the proper perspective and channel that frustration into aspiration.

Our credo was that if you get education, they can take the clothes off your back, they can beat you, but they cannot take what you have in your head. So education was the passport to the things that you wanted to enjoy. Now, even though that wasn't true, that was a good motivation to keep us going. The country as a whole, I think, has become so immorally enmeshed in getting things. As long as you get something, how you get it is not important. They're more concerned with image than they are with integrity. Believe me, as a teacher, I had kids tell me that they made more money than I did. "I don't need to go to school because I can make more money by being lookouts for dope houses," and things like that. The things that we held as legitimate goals to strive for no longer have validity. You know, fatherhood, nine-to-five job, things like that. The idea is to get it any way you can.

The girls and boys in my day seemed to have differences in terms of—I won't say "ability"— achievement. The boys did well in school, and the girls just sort of went along with the program. I did not see them achieving at any greater rate than the boys. Matter of fact, I felt the boys were better adapted to handling schoolwork than the girls; boys took more hard subjects than the girls did. There has been a sort of reversal in academic achievement in terms of the black society. When I came up, the guys seemed to have the edge over the girls, and it kind of mirrored the dominance in white society.

But historically, the black female could always get a job. The white male has allowed her to work when he wouldn't give her husband a job. I don't know whether that was done purposely. But many times, the black male would have to stand around the neighborhood, you know, and just generally socialize. The black male now is dropping out of school, getting incarcerated, and things like that. It seems to have a snowball effect. They stay unemployed for a while and then they begin to think that they're unemployable. They're not preparing themselves for the work-a-day world. As a result, they will refuse to take a job that has low social status. As a result, the black male seems to be more or less digging himself into a pit.

In the meantime, and thank goodness about that, the black woman is saying, "Hey, I will continue to strive to achieve, and if you come along with me, fine. If you don't, I will socialize with you, but in the meantime I am going to be able to take care of myself."

There was a strong belief in God then, and that kind of kept the black community together. I do not believe that the black folks could have existed without a strong belief in a supreme being. One day we would go over to Grace Presbyterian down on 37th and Bowen; the other one we would go to was Mount Calvary Baptist Church. The church wasn't important, but the religion was. My mother became a Catholic. And of course, her main missionary fervor was to convert us to Catholicism. So through her urging, I went to instructions, and in 1948, I converted to Catholicism, over at Holy Angels Church. I'm a practicing Catholic, as contrasted to, you know, a passive one. I attend church regularly. Color loses its importance in religion, I think. When you love somebody in a Christian way, it doesn't make any difference whether he's white or black. Truly it doesn't.

If this were a color-free society, I could accept the argument against affirmative action. But for years, the dominant white society has taken the advantage of, well, everything the society has to offer. Whites would not enjoy their dominant position if they had not brought the black over here in chains and kept him enslaved while they used his shoulders to step up on to become what they are. Many of them came over from Europe, escaping the very same thing that I'm complaining about, mainly lack of opportunity. And if you're going to limit my opportunity by giving me poor books and no books at all—I'm old enough to remember seeing ads in the "world's greatest newspaper," the *Tribune*, that said, "Only white need apply."

When I was eighteen and went in the post office, there were guys who went in there with lesser test scores than I did, but they got five points veteran's preference. Is it fair? I would say it was fair. They served the country. There's always some sort of compensatory aspect. It wasn't a very big shift to take. I submit to you that by affirmative action you're not going to change the composition of society in general. You're just going to extend the opportunity to other people who may not have had an opportunity to benefit.

I prefer living in an all-black neighborhood. There is a constant quality that exists among black folk, in spite of all the negativity that modern-day life brings. And by that, I'm saying the cars getting stolen, houses broken into, things like that. I don't care whether you're in the suburbs or in Ida B. Wells. It's gotten to the point now where people are going to steal from their neighbors. But I feel a warmness in spite of that in the black community. I get up in the morning, go to get my newspaper—I see black faces, and we exchange greetings. There's just a sense of, I guess you have to call it, "community."

This is why I'm somewhat distressed about places I used to have an emotional feeling for. I don't want to use the term "love," but I have appreciation. Like Ida B. Wells—I pass by there and see the graffiti and the damn windows boarded up, I hear about crimes being perpetrated in that area, or someone being arrested, and I say, "Gee, it wasn't like that when I was there."

If anything, I have lovely memories of my childhood in Ida B. Wells. I not only enjoyed the physical surroundings, I enjoyed the people with whom I interacted. And basically it could have been two hundred people, it could have been two thousand. I contend that it's not the edifice, the physical structure, it's the quality of the people who reside in the structure. Take Lake Meadows [a private, mostly black apartment complex on the near South Side], or Presidential Towers [a federally subsidized but upscale development near downtown]. If they took some of those people out of Henry Horner Homes and put them down in Presidential Towers, they would still have the same problems.

If I were running the CHA today, first of all, the selection process would be one in which you mixed different types of family compositions together in harmony. You cannot take a family of eight children and put them next door to just a husband and wife and expect things to be fine. So, in the selection process, not only would I be concerned with the size of the family, I would also be concerned with their income and educational background. In the lease, you've got to tell people, "Hey, this is what we observe. And if you make trouble and cannot remedy it, we'll give you a certain amount of time, but then it might be better for you to find some other place to go."

You should give the population in the building an opportunity to have some say-so over the behavior and conduct of the building. I would like to think that people would be involved and concerned enough to take an active interest. I saw this among the people in Ida B. Wells. We had what we called "Wells Town." We had a mayor of Wells Town; we had people involved in electing representatives to participate in residential government. And I don't see why, in this enlightened age, where people make more money, you couldn't do the same.

JOHN WILSON

John Wilson is a certified public accountant who owns an independent accounting firm in Chicago. His uncle's CPA certificate from 1923 hangs on the wall behind his desk. "Arthur Jewel Wilson was the second black CPA in the United States. I'm the ninety-fourth black CPA in the United States. And now my daughter, she's the star accountant. In this century, my family has had three CPAs. That, to me, is an accomplishment." In 1941, at age eight, he moved into the Ida B. Wells Homes.

Before I moved to Ida B. Wells, my mother and I lived with my aunt on 54th and Calumet in sort of a rooming house situation. There were a lot of us in one apartment. I had a sister in the South when we moved to Wells, and my father wasn't in the home. So it was just my mother and me at first.

My father and I had a relationship, but it was a little stormy. He couldn't help it, and I was too young to understand. My mother lived to be about eighty-seven, and in her whole life, she probably never had a paycheck of three hundred dollars. When we moved into the projects, she made approximately thirty dollars a week working in the laundry in Evanston. She was a seamstress repairing old clothes, overalls and pants—work clothes, primarily.

We were never on public assistance. My mother was too independent. She was a God-lovin', God-fearin' person. She always told us that Jesus was in the house. She was from Mississippi and had just a second-grade education. But she believed in the Lord, so we went to church.

When I went away to Northwestern University, I had a period where I walked away from the church. Like many college kids, quite frequently you think you have the answers to things and that you don't need anyone but you. But I'm now back—as John F. Kennedy would say—"with vigor." It's so important at this stage of my life. Like Solomon, I'm praying for wisdom now.

I went to Northwestern when there weren't many blacks on campus—probably less than thirty in my sophomore year. I had always been in a black world, so to speak. I got to Northwestern the second year that they allowed black men to live on campus. All the campus groups were organized around white people. I did join a black fraternity, but there weren't enough of us to sustain a chapter at Northwestern.

I don't think there's anything wrong with a black person wanting to live in a black community because they feel more secure. I don't see the Irish boys running away from each other, or the Italians, or the Jews. But you also must understand that this country is based on diversity, and for it to work, we've all got to work together. That's the American way, right or wrong. So I don't believe that it's necessary to break up these good neighborhoods. And secondly, I don't know how you would do it.

We all tend to fall into the racial discussion, but class is also important. I see the CHA's high-rise buildings at Robert Taylor, and people say they're congested with black folks having trouble living together. I go to the North Side and I see private buildings just as congested, but it's high-priced congestion.

Obviously, the living conditions in public housing now aren't ideal. But there are differences between 1940 and what I see now. We had gangs then, but there was one pistol for fifteen guys. Now there are four pistols for each guy. There was dope then, but there was no one around in the cocaine trade. And the guys that used heroin—they were so few and far between that it really wasn't a problem at all.

It's also an important factor that back then we had migrants from the South. They brought with them some of the traditions and mores and spirit of country folk. Everybody did believe in God, and everybody did go to church, to an extent. And everybody cared for each other. If I did something wrong and somebody saw it, they would slap the hell out of me and tell my mama, and she slapped the hell out of me again. That doesn't fly anymore.

Even though people were able to get aid, I think people were less dependent on help from the government. Then we started taking these handouts. And once you start taking handouts from someone, black or white, you're losing something in your life.

We were poor, but, you know, life wasn't so bad that we even knew we were poor. I never thought of myself as being poor. In high school, I needed money, and I knew I couldn't get it from my mother. I wanted to play basketball, which prevented me from having a regular job, so I developed a *Defender* route. I would go down to the El [elevated train] on South Park and sell fifty *Defenders*. My hands would be so cold I couldn't even make the change. I'd just pour the money out and people would take the change.

I developed another route where I would sell anywhere from fifteen to twenty-five pairs of stockings a week. I sold Susan Gale hosiery to my teachers. And I would make about a buck off of each box. That was a lot of money as a kid. But I don't know if the environment encourages that now. I don't know if a kid in a project could develop something like that today. The opportunities aren't there.

I don't know how far we have progressed in the last fifty years. It's true, there's been some progress. I can go now to Jackson, Mississippi, and stay in one of their fine hotels—if I've got the money to do it. And sure, there are people like me out of the projects that have been successful, with the grace of God and with luck and their hard work. But you haven't met those guys that died along the way. You haven't met those guys that went to the penitentiary. You haven't met those guys who didn't get through school like me and those who, for whatever reason, didn't have mamas and papas to discipline them enough for them to make it through.

Sure, black people have made some progress. But if you look at us in total now, we don't control our communities. Frankly, in America, money is a very big thing. Until we can control our own community, we can never get in the mainstream. Sometimes I think I see things going backward. Folks still hate me because my hair is kinky and my nose is wide and my lips are thick. You can't hide from that, and I don't want to, to tell you the truth. At this stage of my life I'm proud of what I have because God made me. And you know what? I believe that many of us, if we were to leave this planet and had the chance to come back, I think we'd come back as we are, because we're proud of being black folks. But, you see, they never taught us our history. They don't teach us our heritage.

I hear some people saying that we don't need affirmative action, and I'm not knocking that point of view. Maybe they just made it on their ability. Clarence Thomas, up on the Supreme Court, maybe he just made it because he was the smartest darn lawyer that ever walked the aisles. However, guys like me, I wouldn't have even had a chance to go into a corporation if it hadn't been for affirmative action.

Before I set up my own firm, I worked for a major corporation in Chicago. I worked my way up from general accountant to treasurer. Yet there was still a glass ceiling on my head—there was still a difference in treatment. If we went over right now and talked to my former boss, he would never admit there was any difference in treatment. And maybe in his heart he didn't think there was. But there were certain decisions—treasurer's decisions—that I was never involved in. The board of directors, they didn't care whether I was there or not. I worked for over nineteen years, and I saw white boys with less skill than me coming in and running the company.

My oldest girl went to Wellesley. No scholarship, all of this was on daddy. She was president of the Black Student Union and almost got run over by a truck when they had a sit-down strike against school investments in South Africa. She went to law school at the University of Michigan and just passed the bar. Last month she passed the CPA exam. Now she's working for Coopers and Lybrand, the big accounting firm.

My second daughter went to Spelman. She joined her sister at Michigan and got a master's degree in human resources. She got a very good job with Sara Lee in North Carolina, but after about five months she came home and said, "God has blessed me. I've had good parents, a good upbringing, and I want to give something back to my community. I want to teach, especially young black males, because we're losing them to dope and gangs." So she moved to Philadelphia and started substitute teaching. While she was teaching, she earned a master's of science in education from the University of Pennsylvania. So she has two master's degrees and she's twenty-six years old. She took a 50 percent cut in salary, but she says this is something she's got to do because she just believes that God is directing her to do something for these kids. And she's so happy about it. You know, I'm an accountant who's always looking at the bottom line, but I just say, "Alleluia, Alleluia."

I have been real blessed with my children. We offered them an education and they took it. In this day and age I have plenty of friends who can buy and sell me. But to say that your children have done what mine have done—all of this before they're thirty years old—all I can say to my Maker is thank you, thank you, thank you.

ACEY HARRIS

"Yeah, that's my real name. It's Acey." Harris has worked for the Chicago Streets and Sanitation Department since 1973. He moved to Ida B. Wells with his parents and three siblings in 1941. "It was a very beautiful place to live. The neighbors were wonderful. The neighbors looked out for you and kept you in, you know, kept you together so you wouldn't be running around, acting up and doing the wrong things." His brother Dillard Harris became deputy principal of Wendell Phillips High School. Acey is an amateur photographer and has captured many Ida B. Wells residents on film.

I was proud of Ida B. Wells, but I would say my brother Dillard, he wasn't too proud of it. No. Like he told my father, he said he was going to do better things in his life. When we were living in Ida B. Wells, we were on relief. He always went out and got himself a paper route and things like that. He got his own clothes. He was such a good paperboy that people used to give him good presents, nice presents, like shirts and pants and different things, you know. He was very diligent to do whatever he had to do to move into a better status.

My father told me I was sort of the one going wrong. He told me once, I'll never forget, "Your brother Dillard here, he's gonna be something one day. But you, if you don't get yourself together, you ain't gonna be worth a damn." He said, "You have to take care of you, because one day if you live, you gonna have some kids."

I said, "Dad, what you mean I'm going the wrong way?"

He said, "With that damn hat on your head like that. That hat don't go on your head like that." See, I used to wear my cap to the side like the kids wear them today. He said, "The damn bill is supposed to be on the front of your head to block the damn sunlight." That's what he would say. My father was a janitor. He did a little work around. He wasn't employed. He worked at little companies here and there, you know. He worked.

When I was growing up at Ida B. Wells, there was a police officer, Officer Frazier, he was on 35th and Vernon. We honored him in 1977, and after that he died. He was always on my mind because when we were kids, he always used to see us on the corner. He used to just holler down the block.

"All right, clear that corner down there. All right, Thomas Polmlind, Acey Harris, Don Holmes." Called our names out. "Clear that corner, I don't want to see you on that corner no more."

My father took me to the police station one day and told Officer Frazier to lock me up. Officer Frazier said, "Oh, Mr. Harris, I'll come down, and I'll check him." My father said, "No, no, no, Officer Frazier. You're not gonna come by my house to check him because he's not doing right in my house and he's not gonna be there. He's not gonna be under my roof any more."

He said, "Mr. Harris, I will honestly come by."

My father said, "No, no, no. I want him locked up." So he took me downstairs in the police station and locked me up, put me in a cell. I was fourteen. I was just sitting up in this small cell by myself. I sat there for about an hour and a half, and then Officer Frazier came down and drove me over to the Audy Home [a juvenile detention center]. When I got over to the Audy Home, I was looking out the window at young kids my age while he was talking about me to the people at the desk. I'm looking out the window, and it's like a big prison. Well, in my mind, I'm saying, "Dang, I'm locked up over here. I can't go to the Peps, Tank Town, Bird Land." Those were all the places we used to go dance. I'm saying, "I can't go there if I'm locked up." Then Officer Frazier drove me home.

When I was a kid, a guy named Mr. Frank McBride lived in the project. He came over to the park where we played softball and threw his arms up in front of me. He looked down at me and said, "You like to fight, don't you?"

I looked up at him and said, "Yeah, I like to fight, Mr. McBride." And I always loved to.

He said, "No, no, no. I'm not talking about out here in the street. I'm talking about in the ring."

Mr. McBride said, "Okay, tomorrow we'll get together and I'll show you a few pointers."

So he took me over to the gym. That was the Capital AC Gym on 35th and State. That was before the Stateway Projects were built.

So Mr. McBride said, "How do you hold your guards?" I just threw my hands out like this here, and he tested me on the shoulder. I had both legs together straight, and I stumbled back. He said, "What are you, left-handed or right-handed?"

I said, "I'm right-handed." So he took my left leg and he brought it up. Then he touched me on the shoulder again and I leaned back like this and I was able to keep my stance. Yeah, he took me over there and taught me.

Another friend of mine really helped me, Lewis Trula. He didn't live in Ida B. Wells, but he lived close to it. He's a drug user. He was shooting drugs. So I asked him one day when they were shooting drugs to let me shoot some, because they looked like they was feeling good. He said, "No, little Ace." He said, "You is my little partner. I don't want you to mess your life up. You're a hell of a little athlete." That's what he told me.

I said, "Oh, Lewis, man." I'm trying to talk hip, you know.

He said, "Oh, little Ace, oh, man, let me talk to you." So he took me out of the kitchen where he was shooting the drugs at, and he took me into the front room and sat on the couch and told me to sit down.

So I said, "Oh, Lewis, if I don't dig it"—trying to talk that hip talk— "if I don't dig it, I'll cut it loose."

He said, "No, Ace, it ain't that easy. You're not gonna cut it loose like that." He said, "You're gonna love it because you're gonna be feeling good. The first thing you're gonna do is clean your house out. Clean your house out and your mother and father. You told me you love your mother and father. But you gonna take everything they got to sell to get you drugs."

He said, "Now, Ace, I don't want you to go that way, because you my little buddy." He said, "Let me show you one thing." It was a real hot summer day, and he had a long-sleeve shirt on. He pulled his shirt all the way up and showed me the lines on both arms that he had been shooting these drugs in. Then he pulled his pants leg up and showed me the tracks on his leg, on his ankle.

He said, "Now, little Ace, I'd rather see you go ahead and drink you some wine than to be shooting." He gave me a dollar. He said, "I'd rather see you go that way than do this." Oh, yes, he really had me devastated, because he was a dealer. He was selling it. I don't know if he is still living or not.

I didn't finish high school. And that's why I tell a lot of kids, try and finish it. Go to school and take a trade. Learn how to do something that needs to be done, like pipefitting. Yeah, I've been pretty persuasive. Friends of my kids come by my house. They come by. They say, "Ace, I know you used to keep us from doing different things. I'll never forget it."

I ride the bus a lot. I talk to kids and take a lot of pictures of different kids on the block. I can get a better conversation with them once I take their picture. I used to have a Polaroid, but I like the 35-millimeter much better. Yeah, I got a lot of pictures. Like when we go to the picnics. Ida B. Wells has a [reunion] picnic every year. I go every year and take pictures of a lot of people. There are some that have achieved from Ida B. Wells. Oh, many people—good friends of mine. Cordell Reed. He's the Senior Vice President of Commonwealth Edison Nuclear program today. He was telling me, "Acey, I'll never forget the day me and my brother was standing out front"—they lived on 37th Street—"and these other guys was going to jump on us, and then they saw you coming. They said, 'Oh, man, here comes that damn Acey.'" Because during that time they would respect you if you knew a tough guy, and I was sort of known as the tough guy in the neighborhood.

I knew Barbara Jones [the Olympic gold medallist from Ida B. Wells]. We ran track together. She ran for the Olympics, but I was, like I said, with my cap to the side. Like I tell a lot of young people today, you guys got problems with these caps, because if you wear your cap this way or that way, they kill you. I said everybody wants to live. I tell them, "I'm almost sixty years old, and I'm telling you all what my father told me years ago. I want you all to get yourself together and cut out all this gang fighting stuff. You got all these here guns and all these drugs up here."

I talk to kids today, when I see them, while I'm working or while I'm on the bus. I work for the city. Rodent control. I worked for the rodent control since 1975. I was on the garbage truck for two years before that. I do my job, but I keep a little camera in my pocket, and I see something interesting, I take a picture. A lot of people say, "Man, you spend all that money on them pictures." I say, "I love my job, and I can explain to people better with a picture." See, I don't know all these big words, but I think that a picture is more interesting than a big word.

When I first started, I'd be out there in the alley dumping this garbage. I said, "Man, I'm gonna bring my camera to work and take some pictures with all this garbage out here." These people be piling this stuff up, you know. Maybe if they see the picture, they'll do something about it. So a little guy that worked with me—bless his soul, Harold Lee, he died—he said, "Yeah Ace, man," he said, "Confucius say one picture is worth more than a thousand words." And when he said that, I started bringing my little camera with me.

MARGARET AUSTIN

In 1954, at the age of eleven, Margaret Austin moved to the Harold Ickes Homes, a mid-rise development on Chicago's near South Side. She briefly explained her life before Ickes: "The apartment that we lived in, it only had one bedroom. There was my mom, my dad, and I think there were two sisters at that time. And it was a small place." Today, she lives with her husband, Gene, in a single-family home in Park Manor, a largely black middle-class neighborhood on the South Side.

You would not believe how the Ickes Homes looked when we first moved in there. Gorgeous! They had green grass, they had flowers. Beautiful flowers, like a bouquet out there in the grass. There were swings for the kids, there was a playground, a small playground, where the moms would come out and sit with the babies. And there were no—as far as I know—there were no drugs at that time, and there was no fighting. You could walk up and down at night, nobody would bother you. But of course, my mother made us come up at nine o'clock. Oh, but go down there now and look, ooooh!

When I was there, there were a lot of fathers there with the mom, with the kids—a lot of just ordinary people. And none of the kids down there were bad. It wasn't like it is now, where it's mostly moms with their children. We didn't fight, you know. Maybe a little argument or something, but no fight-fight-fight. We didn't have problems with gangs. We didn't have those problems! Because everyone there knew everybody. We could leave our doors open. I mean, everybody knew each other.

My mother would have us out there on our floor cleaning those bricks. She and the other neighbors on our floor, we kept our floor clean. We had janitors at that time. There was no problem. We would get out there and mop the floors. There's no dirt here! Our places were nice.

We had the Henry Booth House. That's where all of the activities were for the kids in the Ickes. They had skating, they had dancing, they had arts and crafts. You could go on a field trip. It was really nice. On Friday night we'd go to dancing, then during the day they had skating, you know. As a matter of fact, I met my husband there. He didn't live there, but he was visiting some friends of his in the building. He was hollering out the window at me—that's how I met him.

My mom was a maid at the Country Club Hotel on Lake Shore Drive. And my father was a mechanic at North Pier Terminal, downtown. My mother was there for many, many years. And so was my father. On Sundays, or Saturdays, my father would take us riding. We would go to the airport, go up on the deck, and watch the airplanes take off. I don't know if they still do that now.

My father would also take us riding out north, in the white area, to let us see homes out there. We would stop and get hamburgers and ice cream and stuff like that. But every Sunday, my mother took us to church. We sang in the choir, we'd come home from church, we'd have dinner, and then we could go outside or something like that. But we went to church.

Well, I stayed in Ickes until I was nineteen, and I got married. After I had moved out and my parents were still there with my sisters, then they started getting in people that didn't care. That's when my father decided that it was time to move out. People were moving out really to better themselves.

My precinct captain from Ickes, Charles Bowen, got me my first job. I worked at the Chicago Board of Health. From there, I went to the Mental Health Department in the Ida B. Wells project. Then I had my son [Mario], and when I came back to work, I worked at the Chicago Traffic Court for two and a half years. Then I decided I wanted to get out of politics, so I went to Sinclair Oil. I was a keypunch operator at that time, and I worked there for—oh, God, I don't know how long. And then the company merged with Atlantic Richfield. The big shots, they kept their jobs. Out of all of the other people, there were two people that kept their jobs, and Margaret Austin was one of them. They sent me to the Atlantic Richfield research lab out in

Harvey, Illinois. So, all in all, I worked for Atlantic Richfield for eighteen years.

When we moved into this house [in Park Manor] twenty-five years ago, there were maybe two blacks on this block. My neighbors were all white. Most of my friends and myself, when we moved into these areas, there were black and white. So, naturally, a lot of the whites started moving out. When they start seeing blacks moving in, then they start moving out. My son was four years old when we moved here. And we had no problems, none whatsoever. But I guess, you know, as they say, "As blacks move in, whites move out." I don't know.

My son lives in Wisconsin. As a matter of fact, where he lives, he's the only black. He's the state manager for Seagrams, up in Menominee Falls, Wisconsin. He moved into his house last October. When my husband and I were up in Wisconsin, all of the other neighbors came over, and they introduced themselves to my son and said if there was anything that he needed help with, feel free to let 'em know. My son is thirty years old. He got his B.A. from Drake, and he got his master's here from Roosevelt. I'm proud of my son. He's a very good boy. I have never had any problem out of my child. And people would say, "You only had one child, he's spoiled."

You know, with our son, whatever he participated in, we were there. My son won the national championship in his division in karate. And my son's got trophies this tall [gestures], upstairs in the attic. Every tournament he participated in, we were there. My son also played Little League ball. I kept a chair in the back of my car. When I got off from work, I would go and watch him play Little League. We would go to his karate classes. We took my son out for dinner, so he would know what silverware to use with what. When we went on vacation, we took our son with us, so he would know how to act. And that's what it takes.

Every time I got a raise, I put it into my credit union. Because my husband and I had to foot the whole bill for my son's college education when he went to Drake. They said we were making too much money to get aid, and all of that type of stuff, so we had to pay all of the money for my son for his four years in college. He did not disappoint us.

My husband did not want my son to go to an all-black college. He wanted him to go to a mixed college because he felt that when my son got out of college, he would be better at getting a job. And sure enough, he was. My son is doing very well in the field that he went into. He took up marketing, business administration, for his B.A. And for his master's he went for international marketing. So my son can work all over the world.

See, we pushed our child, we pushed him to go to school. I don't have any college education. My husband does not have any college education. But at the time we were coming up, you could get a job with just a high school diploma. Nowadays, you need a degree to sweep somebody's floor! So we pushed him. We wanted our child to do better than we did. The same as my parents wanted us to do better than they did. And it's just a repetition thing. You know? And naturally, maybe my son, since he's got two degrees, when he gets married, maybe he wants his kid to get three.

CHARLOTTE YOUNG MOORE

Charlotte Moore moved into Altgeld Gardens with her parents and younger sister in 1944. Her family was one of the first to move in, and since then Moore has been a leader in the community. A dynamic woman, she has worked as a travel agent, a car salesperson, and a real estate agent. Moore was a past president of the Altgeld-Carver Alumni Association. "If someone came from Altgeld, I wouldn't care if they were the janitor, I'd want to meet them."

I go out to Altgeld, believe it or not, every Thursday. I'm with this program called the Altgeld-Carver Alumni Society. Most of the people in our group moved out to Altgeld in 1944 and 1945 as the project was first built. So our organization has the old-timers in it. We've decided to reach back and try to work with the students that are in Carver High School. We give scholarships, and we also go out to Altgeld every Thursday and deliver fresh bakery goods. So we still love where we came from.

But when I started going out again, three or four years ago, I could not believe the way the people lived. When I listened to the young people's stories of the conditions that they live in—seeing people getting shot and killed—I said, "Charlotte, maybe you could go out there, and if you could just save one child's life, that would mean a lot." Since then, I've met many families. I go into people's homes. But my children won't go with me.

I feel so sorry for kids now, because Altgeld was the place to be. It was like a heaven. I cannot forget how the mayor would come out to Altgeld, and we'd have this picnic and this parade every year, and they'd go out and select the prettiest lawns and give awards for the prettiest flower gardens. They'd give you money to buy the flower seeds, they'd give you lawn mowers to cut your grass with. Then we had our baseball teams. And we'd have our Friday night dances.

I had a free life, a lot of freedom. My mother had a lot of trust in me and my sister, and I got to go where I wanted to go and do what I wanted to do. My mother worked, so from the time that I was in fourth grade, I did all the shopping. I went to Household Finance, which was right on 111th, and paid the bills. I went up to the office at Altgeld and paid my mother's rent. I did the cooking and had my mother's dinner on the table for her.

We had only two children in our family, but it seemed somehow that the larger families lived better. My father worked for the Santa Fe Railroad and my mother worked for R. R. Donnelley, but I went to bed many days on nothing. Waiting on my dad to come home because he was out there with his girlfriends, and his family did not come first. Plenty of times, with two children in the family, he took my mother's money. We had a poor life, we lived poor, but we shouldn't have ever lived poor.

You know, working for the Santa Fe, all these big shots rode the train. Dad would come home with Rita Hayworth's picture, telling about how much she loved him. He'd have clothes from Jerry Lewis and Dean Martin. Daddy wore a Stetson hat and Florsheim shoes when we were kids, and I was walking around with holes in the soles of my shoes. Sometimes we would be sitting there for days, a week at a time, waiting for him, but when he got home, he didn't have nothing. And there wasn't any reason to live like this. Maybe because of this, I decided that my children would never go hungry. They would never go without.

When we were at Altgeld, everybody worked. I did not know anybody that lived where we lived [raps the table for emphasis] that did not work! Nobody! Everybody's mother and father worked, and they lived well. And that was because Altgeld was built for people that were working during World War II. So everybody had a job.

We moved out of the Gardens in 1956. The only reason that we moved is because they were bringing in what you'd call bad elements. That's when everybody that we knew was told that their income was too high and they had to move out! So we moved out in 1956, and this was the beginning of my travels.

For one year, right after I got married to my first husband, we moved into Stateway Gardens [a high-rise development on the near South Side]. But I didn't want to raise my kids up in a project. I grew up in a project, but Altgeld was a different atmosphere. Stateway was low-income, and I did not want to live that way, so we got some money together and bought a house in the Englewood area.

In 1963, by the time my son was a year old, I had left my first husband. I wanted more out of life, and he didn't understand that. I had dreams and goals, and I just wasn't going to let nobody stand in my way. I worked in the post office until 1973, and then I became a real estate salesperson. I got my broker's license, and then I got my management license. I was at home one day and a guy came to my house selling me this carpet. And I says, "Shoot, if you can sell me this carpet, I can sell it to somebody else." So I started working with him, and I've been selling carpet ever since. And I work for a travel agency on the side. I was also a foster parent, even though I had three children and was single. I had four different foster children within a three- or four-year period.

I live a full life every day. I stayed up till four o'clock this morning, trying to get out flyers for our dance at Altgeld. Things that I want to do, the average person does not want to do. And it's still that way. My children don't understand me. My husband now to this day does not understand me. I just went to Korea to do my Christmas shopping. Everybody looks at me: "Going to Korea to do your Christmas shopping?" I like doing that. I do it every year: Korea, Hong Kong, somewhere. I work at a travel agency, so I can get reduced fares, reduced hotel. You do what's necessary to do the things that you want to do! I live the American Dream! I do something constantly. My mind is one of these that just cannot sit down.

I have three kids. Trina just got her degree in industrial engineering a little over a year ago. She's still looking for a position. Pamela works for Apple Computer. She's doing well on her job. And my son does social service work for the Department of Children and Family Services. I'm very proud of my son because he started out in elementary school with a learning disability, and he had to have a lot of special help. I took him to the University of Chicago, the University of Illinois, Michael Reese. And he's the only one of my kids that went straight through a four-year college and graduated. I've never had any problems out of all three of my children. Thank God, I can knock on wood [knocks], no drugs, no nothing.

The only thing—there is one thing that I want to go back to—is that we lived in a very hazardous environmental community. So many of the people from Altgeld are dying from lung cancer.[19] My mother died of lung cancer in 1959. My father died of lung cancer in 1976. My sister died of lung cancer in 1993. My best friend, Patricia Sullivan, her father just died of lung cancer in 1992. Everybody in my family has died of cancer! Everybody I know has some type of cancer.

This is something that I don't understand. Even though we lived out there, everything seemed clean, the air was clean and fresh, everybody loved to come out to Altgeld. I don't know whether it's coming from the ground, whether it's coming from air, but the toxic chemicals are out there.

You know what it all boils back down to? It boils down to people having this idea that they can do better. They do not have to stay in that situation. Of all the friends that I went to school with at Altgeld—and I can count 'em!—I don't know any that are not doing well. I am very serious. I mean, I can give you name after name after name. We did a thirty-year reunion, and, I mean, the people came out. And all of those people are doing well!

TROY L. YATES, JR.

Troy Yates was a thirty-year veteran of the Chicago police force before retiring in 1994. At his retirement event, he received a standing ovation from an audience of nearly five hundred admirers, both black and white. In 1941, when he was six years old, Yates moved from a crowded two-flat at 48th and Michigan Avenues into Ida B. Wells with his parents and sister. He left Wells in 1953, when he got married.

The difference, I think, in what's happening with the family of my day and the family of today is we came up with more love. It was a different time. I don't care if it was your teacher, your neighbors, you always said, "Good morning," "Good evening." If you didn't say something to them, or you looked at them the wrong way, they called your parents right there. If you were on a streetcar and a lady was in your presence, you automatically got up and gave her a seat. That was just the training that you had in those days.

Within our group, if anybody had gotten pregnant, they'd say that "something happened," and they would probably take her down South somewhere till she had that baby. There weren't too many babies having babies. In those days we knew that when we grew up, we had to leave our mother's house, and we had to work and get a job. Whether you went to finish your education in college or whatever degree it was—you had to work.

I was like my father. He worked everywhere. He worked at International Harvester, and before he died, he had retired from United Airlines. He always worked. One time he had a job working as a custodian for a car place that sold Kaiser-Frazers. He was working at the auto show one year, and he would talk about the cars. One of the salesmen came up and looked at him and said, "What are you doing here?"

He said, "I'm a custodian, I'm working."

The salesman said, "You know quite a bit about these cars."

"Yeah, I work around 'em."

So the salesman said, "Come back down here tomorrow to see me." My dad's down there the next day selling cars. No education. I don't think he even finished grammar school. But what he had was common sense. He was like the Godfather to his side of the family and my mother's side of the family. Everybody came to stay with us. When they came from the South, they came to see him. One time we had two or three families staying with us.

Every day I give love. Every day I say "Good morning" to somebody. I don't care if they don't respond back. I say, "Good morning, have a good day." Because we're not used to saying good morning to each other. Now people down South used to do that. "Good morning! Good morning!" Here we scarcely say good morning. I teach all of my sons to hug, and we kiss. There is no shaking hands. You hug, you give that love to the man the same as you would give to a woman. 'Cause they need to do it, and whenever they have kids, they can teach their kids love.

We belong to the church. I'm at Third Baptist Church at 95th and Ashland. The pastor used to be Elmer Fowler. He's a pastor emeritus now. He is like a father to me. I love him. Some people, they go to church all their lives, their mother put them into church, and as they get older, they say, "Well, shoot! I ain't going to church no more." I got away a little bit, but it wasn't that far. I always loved church music, I always loved a lot of different things, so I couldn't stray that far. I had been out of the church for a while and I came back. My second wife and her mother were going to this particular church that Fowler had started. I went and listened to the pastor. I think that's what really got me there. I've been going to that church ever since 1967. Now I'm a deacon, on the board of trustees for the church, and I've been in the choir twenty-eight years. My kids have gotten away from church. So I went and got my grandkids and took them to church. Now the grandkids are bringing my kids. Sometimes, you have to go another way and use reverse psychology.

When I came on the police department, some of the white guys wanted to work with me because they said I was different. They said I could take jokes and could get on with anybody. There was an incident at the station. One of the black policemen was saying, "You know, the white guys are prejudiced."

I says, "Oh, they are?"

"Yeah."

"So why?"

"Because they don't speak to me."

I said, "Well, do you speak to them? Well, just watch." Now, there were these two white boys. One boy was coming up the steps, one was going down the steps. They didn't speak.

I said, "Oh, are they prejudiced?"

He said, "No."

I said, "Well, they didn't speak."

I said, "Now watch this." I went down and spoke to one of them and said, "Tell me, what's happening, baby?" We hugged, and I came on back up and asked, "Was he prejudiced against me?"

"No, he hugged you."

I said, "Because I spoke to him, he spoke to me. If you speak, they'll speak to you."

But I know things aren't perfect. We still need affirmative action. I cannot see a black man that reaches a certain point and tells you that we shouldn't have affirmative action. When a black patrolman makes rank, most of them think they're better than someone else and they think they got that way by themselves. But nobody in this world got to be nowhere unless somebody helped them. I don't care if it be mamma, daddy, the man next door [raps on table], nobody in this world has made it nowhere till somebody's helped them. In fact, Jesus Christ himself had to be helped by God above.

A lot of my friends that came on the job, when they started working with me, they said, "Troy, I watched you." They said, "When I came on this job, I was ready to get out there and beat me some heads, you know." I'm talking about both black and white. They just want to get out there and show "I'm the police." But when I would do things, if I caught a guy drinking, coming down the street, I would call him to the side and say, "Do me a favor. Take that beer, put a little bag under it. When you're finished, throw it in a garbage can." Now if I see you selling reefer, you're not only hurting yourself, you trying to hurt somebody else. If I see you selling, you're going to jail. See, it's all right if you're going to hurt yourself. Hurt yourself, don't hurt anybody else. And this was my attitude.

I was a security guard at South Shore High School from 1965 to 1973. All the kids—black, white—they all thought I was crazy. But I saved a lot of them from going to jail. If the kids did something in the morning while I was at the school, and I couldn't catch them, in the evening when I went to the police department, I got in my squad car and went right to their house and got 'em. They'd say, "You can't . . ." and I'd say, "Yes, I can. I'm in the Chicago Police, all day." I would go to people's houses, knock on the door, and say, "I want your son." The parents wouldn't ask me nothing. They knew I wouldn't hurt them.

I got three kids in college. But I stay around. If some stray, then I'm there to pinch them. You know, you can lead a horse to water but you can't make 'em drink. But they are going to remember the pinch, even if it heals. They are going to remember this little sore. So that's what I'm there to do. Pinch them. See, I can't stop you from walking through that wall. But if I tell you things about that wall, provide a padding, it won't be as hard as you walking into it if I didn't tell you nothing. And then you learn.

HENRY AND ELOUISE MESSIAH

The Messiahs lived in Dearborn Homes from 1950 until 1954, while Henry worked and attended the college at the Art Institute of Chicago. A few years later, he began teaching visual and graphic arts at Chicago Vocational High School, where he remained for eighteen years, until his retirement.

Elouise: When we were first married, we lived with family members for almost three years. I felt that we needed a place of our own with more space for our two children. It was then that I applied for public housing.

Henry: I was not too happy with the idea of moving my family into public housing. However, when I went to visit the site, much to my surprise, the apartment was nice. There were two large bedrooms, a living room, a bath, and a kitchen. It was significant because everything was all new, which impressed me very much.

Elouise: The owner's manuals were there for the stove and the refrigerator, in clear view, on the sparkling countertop. The fixtures in the kitchen and bathroom had never had any use. After we lived in the apartment for a few months, the manager would show it to other prospective tenants. We were one of the first families to move into the nine-story building. I think this was the first building to be occupied. All the families seemed proud of their apartments. We were given designated days to make sure the halls and stairs were clean. No one seemed to mind.

Henry: On the day that we were moving into the complex, I remember that everyone was happy and jubilant. There was laughter, talking, and a sense of bonding with people who were to become our neighbors. Dearborn Homes was the newest and sharpest housing at that time. There were really some wonderful families living in public housing. Some families used it as a stepping-stone to seek something better in the way of housing. For some, it was a place to live and raise a family for several generations.

Elouise: Our daughter was thrilled as she watched the building of D. H. Williams Elementary School. She called it "my school" and looked forward to attending it. She had just entered kindergarten when we moved away from Dearborn Homes. We might have stayed longer, but our income increased and we had to move on. The income limits caused a lot of tenants to be reluctant to report an income increase because they did not want to move.

Henry: Mr. Payne, the manager, and the office staff were open to new ideas and did not put limitations on the tenants and their input. You could walk into the office at any time to discuss a problem. We asked for and got permission to start a newspaper, which we called *The Tenants Voice*. We had freedom about what kinds of things we printed in the newspaper. I was editor, and I remember running into some controversial subjects. There was an article about birth control, which caused me to be called into the office by the manager. He said, "I cannot tell you not to run the article, but I don't think you should, because it will put St. James [the local Catholic church] in an uproar." It was my feeling that the information was essential and relevant. It was not telling anyone what to do, or what not to do, nor was it offering any advice. So, the newspaper staff and I decided to print the article. Then I received a letter from Elizabeth Wood praising me for the good work that the newspaper was doing. I will always remember that letter.

Elouise: I think Elizabeth Wood was responsible for starting the "flower show" in public housing. She would hold meetings downtown with delegates from all of the public housing sites. My husband made some of the posters promoting the show. Groups of delegates were assigned to visit flower gardens at other housing sites. At a special meeting, the flower gardens were judged. The flower shows brought tenants from various housing sites around the city together. I still remember dear friends from the Ida B. Wells Homes.

Henry: My wife was attending college when we married, but when we started our family, she devoted all her time and love and caring to our children and me. I was always a "women's libber," so I wanted her to have other interests. When the Dearborn Homes Women's Organization was established, my wife was elected president. I was so proud. I said to her, "See, I knew you had what it takes."

Elouise: We were a very productive organization. We discussed and solved many of the problems the tenants were experiencing. Mr. Payne and the office staff were very cooperative. We organized many activities. There were classes in sewing, dance, and crafts, as well as card games. There were also after-school activities for the children. Sometimes on Saturday, there were trips to the zoo and parks. Some of the parents would alternate supervising the children on the playground.

Henry: The Christian Family Movement, formed by a group of Catholic men and women, came to Dearborn Homes. This group was led by Pat Crowley and his wife, Patti, who held meetings with several families. One week, the group went on a retreat to Notre Dame. That was quite an experience. One day at Dearborn Homes, Pat Crowley observed me talking to a group of kids of different ages. He said to me, "You are a natural-born teacher." He planted the seed of teaching in my mind. Pat and Patti were great role models and were an asset to the families in Dearborn Homes.

Chapter 4

Reflections on Integration, Segregation, and Choice

American society has struggled with racism throughout its history, and in Chicago the effects of the city's often ugly racial politics on the perception and mission of public housing have been particularly pernicious.

As a preface to the reflections on integration and race in these interviews, it is essential to recall the extreme residential segregation and poor housing conditions faced by Chicago's African Americans through much of the twentieth century. After a major migration of African Americans to Chicago during World War I, white real estate interests established a well-defined boundary around the city's "Black Belt" on the South Side (and later a smaller belt on the West Side). Restrictive covenants blocked nonwhites from access to "white" neighborhoods, and periodic violence by whites also enforced the city's color lines. During a second and much larger migration after 1940, new arrivals had few choices but to crowd into the existing Black Belt, straining the housing stock. Apartments were cut up into ever-smaller "kitchenette" units, and families also doubled up to weather the deep housing shortage. Overcrowding caused rapid deterioration of buildings, and substandard conditions became endemic in black areas of the city. After the Supreme Court declared restrictive covenants illegal in 1947, the borders of the Black Belt slowly began to crumble. African Americans moved into neighborhoods vacated by fleeing whites, and a massive transition of housing took place on the South and West sides of the city between 1950 and 1970. Nevertheless, integrated areas of the city are few today.

Under Elizabeth Wood, the Chicago Housing Authority was the only public institution in the city that acknowledged and addressed the housing plight of African Americans. Before and during World War II, the CHA developed several first-rate projects in black neighborhoods and one racially integrated project on the near North Side, Cabrini Homes, opened in 1942. Besides Cabrini, the temporary veterans' projects (1946–1954), Leclaire

Courts (1950), and Archer Courts (1951), each contained a successful mix of black and white tenants. Wood put tremendous energy into integrating these developments, often over the objection of less liberal CHA commissioners. She achieved integration by carefully placing black and white families up to a desired racial balance, usually around 20 percent black. In practice, this balance operated as a flexible "quota," but one unopposed by the city's African-American institutions, including the Chicago *Defender*. The former tenants, black and white, who lived in these integrated projects virtually unanimously praise the CHA for its integration policies during the Wood years. Nevertheless, in August 1954, she was fired for her efforts.

Her successors did not share her commitment to integration, and they no longer worked to maintain racial balances in projects. With black applicants far outnumbering white applicants, and with white turnover far greater than black turnover, the tenancy in the integrated projects slowly changed, until by the end of the 1960s little balance remained. By that time, the Chicago City Council had taken firm control of public housing's site selection and made it impossible to build in white neighborhoods where integration might be sustained.

With all projects after 1954 built in black neighborhoods, white interest in public housing dropped off. Few if any whites were willing to be pioneers and move into the Black Belt projects like Stateway Gardens or the Robert Taylor Homes. More important, negative publicity and attacks by real estate interests tarred public housing with a stigma. For many white families, moving into public housing was perceived as a step down in status, even when the housing was located in white areas. For black families, however, the move out of overcrowded slums into public housing had an opposite effect—it raised their status during the 1940s and 1950s. As a result, blacks admitted to public housing in that period had, on average, higher incomes than their white counterparts.[20] In fact, in its early years, public housing offered considerable prestige for black families.

The former residents interviewed here had a range of experience with segregation and integration. Many who lived in the integrated developments reflected positively on the experience and chose to live in integrated neighborhoods after leaving public housing. But one of the significant themes of these interviews is the low priority placed by many African Americans on residential integration for themselves. Those who lived in all-black projects took great pride in the communities they developed as a refuge from the dominant white culture. They valued public housing's good conditions, treasured the strong sense of camaraderie that developed in the early projects, and felt no inherent need for racial integration. When these families left public housing, they tended to move into primarily black neighborhoods and suburbs by choice, expressing satisfaction at being surrounded by, in their words, "our own."

The overwhelming desire expressed loud and clear in the following interviews is for the freedom to choose where to live. Some have selected all-black communities, others desire integration in varying degrees. However, all want the right to choice in the matter. Divergence occurs only in the degree of integration.

Significantly, the interviews here express some opposition to policies that move poor black families to outlying suburban areas in order to achieve a degree of token integration and social engineering. This approach has been a basic element of several current programs originating from the landmark *Gautreaux* case of 1969, which found the CHA's site selection policies to be discriminatory.

In the course of discussing integration and choice with former residents, the conversation often turned to affirmative action. While ambivalent on integration, almost all interviewees believed affirmative action to be essential. Often, they referred to their own frustrating experiences with discrimination. They keenly recognized the continuing underrepresentation of blacks in the upper reaches of corporate America and the professions. Consequently, they argued that despite educational gains, affirmative action is still necessary to open doors and break down barriers for their children. Wherever they lived and worked, the African Americans interviewed here want a most basic freedom already assumed by whites—freedom of choice in where to live—as well as equality of opportunity.

SIDNEY AND BERNICE BILD

The Bilds live in the South Side's Kenwood neighborhood, a racially integrated community noted for its gracious old homes. Sidney is a retired physician. Bernice, a force of nature, works with the Coalition for New Priorities, a Chicago-based group that promotes a progressive political agenda for the nation. In 1950, early in their marriage, they moved to the sixth floor of a Dearborn Homes mid-rise, when Sidney was in medical school and Bernice was pregnant with their first child.

Sidney: Dearborn Homes helped us get started—it really gave me an opportunity without which I wouldn't have made it. It helped us while I was going to medical school and during my internship. My income as an intern was minimal. I started out with nothing, and then they raised it to twelve dollars a month. Financially, living in public housing was very helpful.

[Former CHA staff member] Ed Holmgren encouraged us to move to Dearborn. He thought it would be a fine idea to have a few white families there, and he thought good things would happen. This was prior to the civil rights movement taking off, but civil rights [activity] existed before the civil rights movement. We believed in civil rights then. Still, it was the first chance we really had to meet and be friends with black people on a social basis. We were next door, in the same building, baby-sitting for each other. They were our neighbors, and we were their neighbors. All the white people that we knew seemed to get enormous amounts out of it. Their social life was enriched during that time by the people they met. In fact, Dearborn *was* our social life.

Bernice: Right. There were rent parties where everyone would come and bring a little booze, bring a little food, and pay to get in. And there were "bid-whist" parties. We did all sorts of things in there.

Sidney: We were never lonesome. We were, I guess you'd say, comfortable.

Bernice: There was really total acceptance, as far as I remember, by everybody.

Sidney: We were the only white family in our building, but we never ran into any animosity.

Bernice: I was elected chair of the tenant council, and I remember thinking it's inappropriate for a white person to be chair of this totally black organization, so we had co-chairs. There was a grocery store on State Street, and there were various stories that came to our attention where tenants were being treated poorly. At one point, I guess, the owner pulled a gun on a kid. And their cat was sleeping in the greens, too. So we protested to the Board of Health and picketed the store. The Board of Health closed it down. We eventually formed a citywide tenants' council. We tried to get all of the tenants all over the city to work things out together.

Sidney: The high-rise didn't bother us. It was no big deal. It was different than Robert Taylor, where you come out of the elevator, and there you are on an exposed area with a fence. In Dearborn, the elevator opened indoors.

Bernice: Our gripes with management were not with the fact that Dearborn was a high-rise project. The elevators worked, and there were stairways. You'd have six or eight apartments, and all of them were on a central space. I remember we used to put Gene's playpen out there so he could watch all the kids playing.

Sidney: We sort of turned the elevator area into a playroom. The doors [to apartments] would be open. It was very close, and we would go in and out and the kids would crawl around.

Bernice: But we moved out of Dearborn after three years. We had to sign a loyalty oath [to stay] in public housing.[21] We refused to sign a loyalty oath. So we moved to Midway Gardens.[22]

Sidney: Midway Gardens was fine. They had nice facilities, there was a playground in the back, and the building itself was well appointed. The majority of the people there were black, also. But there was much more companionship at Dearborn. These were our friends. This was our neighborhood.

Dearborn was much more of a village. I'd come home to Dearborn, and it was like coming to the village square. You come down the street, and there we were in this little compound. Midway Gardens was a typical apartment-building dwelling. You didn't necessarily know who lived next door to you. Midway Gardens was more middle class, and people thought of themselves as middle class. There was less interdependence, and we didn't have rent parties, for instance. But at Dearborn Homes there was sharing, there was caring for each other.

Bernice: Who had a rent party at Midway Gardens? Are you kidding?

GWENDOLYN DUNCAN ALEXANDER

Gwendolyn Alexander is an administrative assistant to John Stroger, president of the Cook County Board of Commissioners. When asked about growing up in Cabrini-Green, she very pointedly says, "It wasn't Cabrini-Green, stop using Cabrini-Green! It was Mother Cabrini Homes." Her family was one of the first to move into the 586-unit, low-rise complex completed in 1943. Later additions, including the Cabrini Extension (1958) and William Green Homes (1960), created the larger Cabrini-Green community.

Cabrini was ideal because I was free to go anywhere I wanted. There was a sand lot between the row houses where kids could play, and there were jungle gyms. I used to sleep on the back porch. I would bring my pillows and sleep out on the back porch all night! You wouldn't even think about it now. You can't even sleep with the windows open today.

Cabrini was really ideal. We had Mexicans, we had Irish, we had Italians. My best girlfriend was German. It was very homogeneous.

Do you mean heterogeneous?

We were closer than heterogeneous. We were truly a homogeneous neighborhood. Everyone looked out for each other. There was a mixture of racial and national groups, and it was great.

At Cabrini, there was always something for the youngsters to do, and it was always centered around the administration building. I was a [Girl Scout] Brownie, and we used to have our Brownie sessions at the administration building at 900 North Hudson. It had an activity room, a pool room, and a kitchen. I believe they rented it out, so if you lived there and made a reservation, you could have parties and functions. You could utilize the activity center.

But when Elizabeth Wood left, it started going down. The really dramatic change was when they removed the grass from close to the houses. We used to have victory gardens and a lawn, but they put tar in where there used to be grass. And then they took away the trees—all those things that make for decent living within the city. Once they took that away, people didn't have a lawn or garden to keep up, so they would just throw trash out there. People became callous, and the callousness became fighting, because you had to clean up behind someone else. The Housing Authority became more relaxed and less careful in their screening. They didn't care what the person did. The vigilance wasn't there. They only wanted the dollar.

My principle on integration is that you should be able to live where you want, nobody needs to tell you where to live. Now, I don't want to live around all black folks, and I hope I'm not in an area where I'm living around all white folks. In the condo where we live now [in Hyde Park], the people on the third floor are of German and Welsh extract, the people on the second floor are Haitians, and we're African Americans. You need to live where you want to live.

STEPHEN PUGH

In 1943, the Pugh family moved to the Frances Cabrini Homes, when Stephen was one year old. In 1958, he left Cabrini to begin instruction as a Catholic seminarian, though he soon switched to studying law. Today, Pugh is a partner in Pugh, Jones and Johnson, a Loop law firm.

Cabrini had a wonderful persona. It was separated from all the other projects and had its own little identity. It was set right on the back of Montgomery Ward and right close to downtown. So we had access to downtown and the lake. We'd walk down Oak Street, and we'd pass the Gold Coast and be at Oak Street Beach. It was just a wonderful place.

Cabrini was racially integrated, but the concept was a little bit different then. It meant there were approximately 25 percent African Americans, but there were really no Hispanics around at that time that I can recall. We had Italians, Germans, some Asians—we had everything there.

One of my best friends back then happened to be a white guy. He lived across the street, and we ran around together. But you know, even then, whites presumed that they were better. It wasn't as though I couldn't go to some white house and play with the kids and vice versa. The kids got along—that wasn't an issue. It was more an adult issue. Even though whites lived next door, it didn't matter. They were still perceived as having more access to society, to capital. They felt they were able to do things that we couldn't do. I understand that now.

Still, I've gotten to a point where I feel comfortable doing certain things with people of any race. I really think that started when I lived in Cabrini-Green. I knew a slew of different kinds of people. I wasn't afraid. We had black teachers and white teachers—primarily white teachers. And it was that way throughout the neighborhood.

When I was in eighth grade, I had Father Rainer as a teacher. He was a good model. I can remember him. He was quite a decent guy, a white guy. He was not like any of the other priests at that time. A lot of people have given me help along the way in one way or the other.

In the family we had my aunt, my mother, myself, my two sisters, and two cousins. With my mother and aunt, one was on welfare and one worked. One went to work at Montgomery Ward, and the other one stayed home and watched me. So from time to time they went back and forth between being on welfare and off.

When I was growing up, one of the things that helped us at an early age was that we got jobs right away. We were all paperboys and worked in grocery stores and things like that. And that helped focus us. We had parents who were very strict, for the most part. And I think that that helped a lot. There was a moral environment that is not there today.

My black male role model was my uncle, the husband of the aunt who lived with us. They were separated, but he lived close by and came by often. He got shot up in the legs a little during the Second World War, but because he was a great veteran, they allowed him to be on the police force. I can remember him in his police uniform with these black boots and his gun. He was a humongous man! And he used to play with me—not like my mother and aunt played with me, but like a man played with a kid. He'd punch me, throw me around. And my mother couldn't understand it. But to some extent he is my personal model when I think of a strong black man.

When I was in the military in the 1960s and I'd tell people that I was from the North Side of Chicago, all the blacks thought I had to be rich because there were no blacks on the North Side. Cabrini was like an oasis. We had very good people, very close relationships.

You could see Cabrini changing while we were still there in 1958. We lived in the original row houses. But then the mid-rises and the high-rises started to open up. When they built those buildings, things began to change a little bit. By then, the neighborhood was predominantly black—I'd say about 80 percent black. But there was still St. Joseph's School, St. Philip's School, and St. Philip's parish. And the Catholics still stayed around. In 1961, more high-rises—the gray buildings [the William Green Homes]—were built. That's when I remember that the neighborhood was no longer my neighborhood, it was somebody else's.

My father-in-law often says—and I kind of believe him—that the worst thing that can happen to the black businessman is civil rights. He said, "Before, when we had our own communities, they [African Americans] had to come and spend their money with us. They had to come to our cleaners, they had to come to our movie houses, they had to come to our churches, they had to come to our stores. Once civil rights came, then they no longer had to use the resources of the community, and went out and spent their money in the white areas."

I think that people should live where they want to live. But I think it's also important to be open and not to exclude themselves. If integration happens on a natural basis and it's not forced, then it's OK. Not after some regentrification effort, but when people really feel free enough to move in and out of each other's neighborhoods, particularly when white people move into black communities. Now I live on the near West Side, in University Village, right near the University of Illinois campus, an almost completely integrated area.

My son, he's in his second year of NYU law school. He went to Cornell. My daughter is at St. Albert's High School. My wife is going for her second master's, in library science at Chicago State. So you got a mixture of things happening in the family.

White people don't mind if there's one or two black families in a building of five hundred families. That's fine. It's just like the big law firms down here. They want one or two black lawyers, but they don't want 30 percent. Universities have been doing it for years and years. They've always let a couple of people in because of family relationships or whatever it is. They say there's value in that. And that diversity brings something different to the table, a different point of view, and that has value. You know, if we're going to be competitive as a nation, we need to utilize all of our resources. We have to find a way to do that.

ANDREW THOMPSON

Andrew Thompson moved into Harold Ickes Homes in April 1955, when he was eleven years old. He lived with his mother, two sisters, and two brothers on the third floor of a nine-story building. "My dad was not with my mom at that time. My mom was on ADC. We lived there through about 1961 or 1962." Since 1988, he has worked as a salesman of heavy truck parts for a small, white-owned firm. At the time of this interview, he lived in a predominantly African-American neighborhood on Chicago's South Side.

When we moved in, there were a couple of buildings that hadn't yet opened. In terms of the housing that I had been in, I'd say that Ickes was an improvement. We all had uniform rooms, we had good storage space, and it was a brand new structure. Oh, I was pleased. Each floor would have one person responsible for keeping the hallways and windows clean every week. Our apartment was right next to the incinerator—which in some cases is negative. But at that particular time it was fine, because we all made a point of making sure that our garbage was dropped properly. It was well kept. I was proud to live in it.

The antisocial behavior in Ickes was limited to people outside of the projects, coming down trying to do something that we didn't want them to do. Now, we didn't have a gang. I could walk from my end over to the south end, and anywhere inside the project, and I was never threatened. In the project there were no problems. The only problems you had were those that arose between people with opinion differences. That's in any neighborhood. Ickes was integrated, but the families that were not black lived on the south end and in 44 West [Cermak]. This was one of the first buildings that they opened. It wasn't all-white, it was mixed. But not all of them were mixed.

I felt the integration when I attended grammar school at John C. Haines. This was a multiethnic school. We had Chinese, Italian, white, black, Hispanic—everything. When we left school, sometimes we had to fight our way across the viaduct that separated Wentworth and LaSalle. We had kids out throwing rocks and bottles, you know. But we didn't have those kinds of problems in Ickes itself.

After Haines, I went to high school at Tilden Tech. Tilden was like 80 percent white and 20 percent black when I attended. Miss Kline's store—right there on the corner of Union and 47th Place—that's where the black students went. We would go in and play the jukebox and buy something to eat and stand around and talk and dance and maybe do homework. We would do it in our own particular store.

My feeling about integration is this: I think we should have, if we want, a place that we can frequent, but by the same token, we should have access to the other areas, too. We've got white friends that want to hang out with us sometimes, and they should feel welcome at our place. By the same token, we should feel welcome in any place around the school that's rendering services to the students. We don't make a person that's not black feel as uncomfortable as some whites make us feel when we come to their place.

My wife was reared in Mississippi. She says that one thing about Mississippi, there is no segregation when it comes to housing. You live here, white family lives there. She said the public segregation comes into play when that school bus rolls up. What I'm saying is that an institution should not be separate and equal. When it comes down to church, school, movies, the whole nine yards, there should be no separation. That's my opinion. Integration ain't got nothing to do with it. I'm not all fired up about living next door to a person of another ethnic group. I mean, it doesn't bother me, but it ain't my aim.

I'll never forget the first time I went south to college, in 1961. I walked in the front door of the bus station in Tyler, Texas. One of the clerks said, "Hey, boy, what's your problem?"

I looked at him and said, "I ain't got no problem. Do you have one?"

"Well, you're not supposed to use that front door."

I said, "Right, right. I know that"—just like I'm going to go back out the door and come back around the side. Well, I walked right into the bus station, picked up my bag.

"You can't come in here and do that."

I said, "I tell you what. You're not going to stop me." It was just that simple. You know, I got an attitude. Once, we were riding the bus going down [to college], and when the bus stopped, we were in Kentucky. Well, they had two waiting rooms, still, at that particular time—1961.

So me and the guy that I rode down with, Ron Higgins, who came out of Stateway, we got off the bus and walked into this black waiting room. And it's so tight, and it's hot and greasy, they're cooking food. So I said, "Man, I ain't waiting here." We walked right around the little partition to the big, air-conditioned white waiting room. You're damn right we did. We walked right around, we got to buy those newspapers and comic books. Most of the other people had peered over there, looking at us like we had done something wrong, like something was going to happen to us.

Racism won't stop here. It's not going to stop here in America. This whole country was built on racism. When kids are in primary grades—maybe as far as fourth grade—they're fine, they don't see color, it ain't a factor. Because they haven't learned anything to associate with that color. But when they get to sixth grade, seventh grade, eighth grade and high school [slaps his hands], that's when the separation starts. And I think that happens from either home experiences, home conversations, and/or the damn media.

I don't have a problem with tall buildings. But if I got a choice, I don't want to live above the fifth floor. In our building [Ickes Homes] we had only one elevator. So if that one was out, everyone above me had their problems. My opinion, in terms of high-rise buildings for low-income families, is this: make sure to have an adequate number of elevators. One for service and two or three for regular transportation. That's my opinion.

I don't agree with the people who want to tear down the high-rises. I think they should be rehabilitated, and low- and moderate-income people should be able to live in them. Matter of fact, the example that kind of works real good is Lake Parc Place [two CHA high-rises on the South Side near Lake Michigan]. Those buildings have been rehabbed, and you have multilevel people inside it, and I think this is good. Matter of fact, I think it's perfect, because you have the same thing in a building that you do in a neighborhood.

PHILLIP AND JEFFERY ROBERTS

Phillip and Jeffery Roberts grew up in Ida B. Wells during the 1950s. Phil was an Assistant Dean of the dental school at the University of Illinois at Chicago. During his tenure, he instituted significant improvements in the school's affirmative action policies. However, a conflict over these policies developed between Phil and the university, and on the afternoon of our interview, a maintenance worker changed the locks on his office door, effectively barring him from his office.

Jeff worked as an affirmative action representative for Allstate Insurance for several years, then took over his own independent Allstate agency in Chicago.

Phil: Everybody worked at Ida B. Wells. We had a church. We had the YMCA. We had all those institutions that make a community. As in any community, you've got people whose lives took wrong turns. But it was no different or out of proportion from any other community. There are a number of guys who are dead, who are drug addicts. But I can't think of more than four guys, maybe, and a couple of girls. Most of them, the families are doing fine. We are representative of the types of men and women who have moved out from Ida B. Wells, and they are all over the place. I'm a dean, and Jeffery is doing his thing. My sister is a teacher, one of my brothers is a small-business man, another brother works for the CTA. All of us are college graduates, several have master's degrees. When we were growing up [at Wells], there was a very supportive environment, but all of the factions that we encountered—social workers, the health workers, the policemen, the church, the school—were key in terms of the affection that we received as kids. And the demands that were made on us as kids—we were expected to excel.

Jeff: I won a writing contest that was sponsored by the *Daily News* and *Sun Times.* I was one of six boys picked in the city of Chicago to be a batboy for the White Sox. The principal at Doolittle [Elementary] was Mr. Beavers. I was the "school pet" type of kid. I was always the president of my class, you know. Mr. Beavers would call me down to the office, and all the kids would go, "Ohhh, you're in trouble." Well, Mr. Beavers and I would sit and talk about all kinds of things. There was another teacher—Mrs. Skoronsky, a Polish lady—who was like everybody's mother. If I got in trouble doing anything going up to school, it was like, "Mrs. Skoronsky wants to see you, Jeff." And I'd go to her office, and she'd say, "Now what happened on 36th Street when you were . . .?" We had many white teachers, but there was never a thing where a teacher was the least unfair to me. What they said was, "You're going to be the greatest thing in the world, you're wonderful, and you're going to do every teacher we have proud." So, it wasn't until I got to Tilden that racial differences were being made.

Phil: My two oldest brothers were voted the top students when they graduated. They won the America Legion award when they graduated from elementary school. I was the valedictorian when I graduated. There are six of us in our family, and we were all big achievers in school.

Jeff: I have a bachelor's degree from the University of Illinois–Champaign in journalism, and a master's in public administration from the University of Illinois here in Chicago.

Phil: Let me give you a little history. In 1968, I, along with five hundred other black students, went down to the University of Illinois in Champaign under something called the "Private Five Hundred." Dr. King had been killed, and the University of Illinois was under a lot of pressure to admit black students. And so they hurried and recruited five hundred black students to attend the University of Illinois at Champaign-Urbana. We were the experimental group. We had been on campus less than a week when, on September 9, 1968, we all got arrested in a student sit-in over housing arrangements and financial aid packages. Everything was just really screwed up. The [Chicago] *Tribune*, by the way, ran a headline, "Negro Students Tear Up Illini Union." Now if you're familiar with the Illini Union, you know there's no way you can tear that building up.

The point is that we enriched the university. In 1968, the university in Champaign had more foreign students than they had black students. It was a culture shock to everybody. Nobody had been exposed to one another before at the University of Illinois. But after that, the place was never the same. They went back and traced our class, and four hundred or so had either graduated from the university or gone on to other universities. And in Chicago, now, in the leadership of corporations, I run into so many of these people.

In 1969, there were two black kids in the University of Illinois's dental school, and I think there was one in the medical school. Among public universities, the University of Illinois is now the leading producer in the country of black and Hispanic health professionals. I'm one of the guys who developed a lot of the affirmative action programs on campus. But now the leadership of the University of Illinois has said, "We can't let this continue."

You know, the University of Illinois and I have a very different way of seeing. I felt if we brought in more minority students, it might improve the whole operation. Now, after we brought in black kids, white females started flooding in. We began to markedly improve the total product because we brought such rich experiences and new ways of seeing things. We have grown so far beyond just dealing with affirmative action.

See, I never would allow myself to fall into this thing of "You're the affirmative action guy." I said, "No, I'm the guy that's going to come here and make some things happen that need to happen, and then we're all going to grow together." But about five or six years ago a tremendous resentment began to develop at this university, because the culture is beginning to change. And fear has set in. Tremendous fear. I've had many whites tell me, "We don't fear your color, we fear your culture. We fear the dynamism that you bring to what you're doing. We fear the way that you say, 'Hey, there may be a different way.'"

As the dean here, it's a daily struggle to continue to maintain and to expand opportunities. I was invited to come here to develop all kinds of programs, but I catch it coming and going every day.

Jeff: I ran for a state Representative position in the area that we grew up in. We had one principle: that being born and raised in that particular community, we could best represent that community and plan for its future. But what we found people saying was, "You're too successful, so you must have some other agenda. Even though you came up in this community, and even though we've known you your entire life, we don't trust you."

Phil: Something very interesting happened during the course of one of Jeff's campaigns that drives the point home. One of the precinct captains was losing his precinct to us, and he was going crazy. So this guy, he came up to me, he pulled out a knife and started cutting his fingernails. He had his henchmen with him, a couple of big dudes. He said some things that were not too nice, you know. But then he said, "I checked you out"—he's pointing his finger at me—"I've checked you out! I can't believe that anybody who grew up at Ida B. Wells doesn't have a police record!"

We were too clean. It got so bad that people would say, "Hey, come and take some money." And we'd go, "Take some money? What do you mean? You going to contribute to the campaign?"

"No, we want to give you some money!"

Now, I'm the guy who's taking care of the money in the campaign, right? And I'm saying, "We don't play that way. Now, if you want to contribute to the campaign . . ."

"No, no, no, no, no! You want some dope?"

"We don't smoke dope."

"You want some cocaine?"

"No, we don't do that either."

And then it became "We can't trust you, man. You all look different."

We said, "No, we're not different, we're just about trying to . . ."

"No, man, you don't smoke, you don't drink. . . . Well, let's go and do some women."

"What the hell you mean, 'do some women'?" That's when I realized there was a tremendous gap in terms of where we were in our development and what we were trying to represent. And that was a heck of a decision that we had to come to in terms of dealing with it.

Now, we were running against Larry Bullock, and Larry didn't mind getting underneath that table. Larry would see Jeff on the street and would want to start fighting him! We said to Larry, "No, brother, this is a campaign, we can discuss things."

Jeff: Now I live on the Northwest Side of Chicago, in the 36th Ward. I made a decision that for the sake of my family, it was best to buy a home on the Northwest Side. I just had to walk away from that particular area [near Wells]. We live out on Harlem Avenue, near Oak Park. One of the status symbols in the neighborhood is to have the Tru-Green lawn service. [Laughs] Everybody spends a tremendous amount of time fixing up their properties and keeping their properties up, and race has absolutely nothing to do with it. Up and down our block at Christmastime, everybody's got their little lights up. My dad, when he first moved in with us and saw us putting up all the lights, said, "Somebody's going to steal that stuff." But everybody puts up Christmas lights and nobody steals them.

I used to wonder why my dad sits in his bedroom window every night. Because he wants to check everything out. See, he's like a one-man security system, check it out every day, you know, the movements. He spent forty-five years in Ida B. Wells. Then he spent seven years up north in the West Rogers Park area, lived there in the building that my sister owns. But the hardest transition that he's had is moving in with us, because it's a totally integrated block. My son sits outside the house talking to all these little white kids. Hispanic kids ring the bell, Filipinos live next door to us. Dad will always talk about Harlem Avenue as Western Avenue. I never could figure out why he did that. But then I realized, it's because in his mind Western is the furthest point that black folks can go in the city of Chicago. He was a cab driver, and living way out on Harlem—that is just mind-boggling.

WILLIAM SHAW

William Shaw retired as the Deputy Chief of the Chicago Police Department. In 1945, at the age of six, he moved to Chicago from Georgia with his parents and four brothers and sisters. At first, the family lived with his maternal grandparents at 5544 South Parkway. "We lived in one little room that the residents of the building used as a storage bin." After seven months in the basement, Shaw and his family moved to Altgeld Gardens. During his career, he served as Police Commander in the Altgeld area.

When we moved to Altgeld, it's almost like I died and went to heaven. For so many years, as long as I had been living, we were always bundled up, we never had rooms of our own. Altgeld Gardens afforded us the opportunity to spread out, to have some form of privacy, and to live as a family, truly as a family.

If you lived in Altgeld Gardens during this period of time, there was a feeling of family throughout the entire development. I lived in what we called a "block"—block 5. Block 13 was on the opposite side of the housing development. We knew kids there, we knew families there, we knew their parents, we knew their fathers. And it was a safe situation. If we were on the opposite side of this development and there was a problem, we were able to go to someone's home and seek some type of assistance.

If I was on the other side of the development in block 13, most of the people in that area knew me and knew my parents. Listen, if you did something wrong, they would take the belt to you right there. And I'd be so afraid to tell my parents, I'd beg them not to tell. "I'll take the whipping, just don't tell my parents!" Frankly speaking, those ten years that I spent in Altgeld Gardens I still consider the best of my fifty-five years.

You had pride in your home, because that's what it was, your home. We took care of it. South of 134th Street, there was vacant land and we all had vegetable gardens. No one violated the other person's garden—not even to take a tomato. That was a no-no. After school, after I did my homework or some chores around the house, I'd go to the garden and cut weeds. Saturday morning, no doubt about it, regardless of the temperature, that was the job.

We also had a flower garden, and we took pride in those flowers. No one would step on those flowers. And you never stepped on the grass. There was a guy by the name of Mr. Rothings, he was a security guard. If he caught you on that grass, you got a whipping. And the whipping that you'd take was no problem. You didn't go home and talk about it.

I used to get in so much trouble. Altgeld had a big flagpole, and I just loved to sneak out of the house at night and get that rope and run and swing in the air! The janitor knew someone had been messing with that, so one night he was waiting at one o'clock in the morning, and he caught me in the air! I couldn't get away! But he was nice. Mr. Wilkes was his name. He took me back in the building, and I expected he was going to fan me. But he just sat there and talked to me for about ten minutes. I never bothered with that again.

The administration, during the period of time that I lived there, gave out a feeling of caring for what happened to each apartment and the family that lived in it. I recall, every once in a while, someone from the development came by and talked to the family and inspected the apartment. We didn't consider this any invasion of our privacy. No, not at all! The administration during that period of time wasn't the enemy. They were concerned about the residents.

In 1955, my family decided to move to the West Side of Chicago. I continued to go to Carver High School [near Altgeld, on the far South Side]. Naturally, during this period of time, being a young male, I became attracted to girls. I felt no need for continuing high school. Eventually I dropped out and started to work. Then I joined the military, which was quite an experience for me, lacking discipline. The military put me back on the right track. I spent three and a half years in the Army, stationed in Hawaii. I returned to Chicago in 1962, and a couple months later I married my childhood sweetheart, who was also a product of Altgeld Gardens. I've been married to the same woman for thirty-three years.

I drove a CTA bus for approximately four years before becoming a police officer in 1966. At that time I realized the need for education. I went back to school and obtained my bachelor's degree and master's degree in criminal justice. Strangely enough, in 1988, I became a District Commander of the Kensington Police District, which encompassed Altgeld Gardens. I had an opportunity to go back there and do some things for that community that I thought would be positive. As District Commander, I was able to get a satellite police department located within Altgeld Gardens. Not so much because of the crime rate, but because of the geographical location of Altgeld Gardens. It's located on the border of Indiana, on the south end of Chicago. When I was a kid, when we left Altgeld, we would always say that we were going to the "city." We felt so isolated and away from the mainstream of what was occurring in Chicago. We were isolated. We were cut off from a lot of opportunities. Altgeld became a third world.

When I was in Altgeld, there were very few troubled families. I would say less than 5 percent. When I returned, I saw that the 5 percent was still residing in that development, but so were their children, and grandchildren, it was just a procession. That 5 percent had expanded to 85 percent.

Yet from the original group, most families succeeded because there was an understanding of community during that period of time. The families whose kids had respect for their parents moved on to better things. The void they left was filled by families that didn't have those values. The key to it all—there has got to be a screening mechanism.

I know Altgeld was exclusively black, but there are a lot of positives in living in a mixed neighborhood like where I live now—in Beverly [a racially integrated South Side neighborhood]. Sometimes—I hate to say it, but I've got to be honest—the number one issue is crime, OK? People who have an investment in property will take care of that property. There are, of course, many black communities in Chicago that are stable, where people have the same concerns. But many all-black neighborhoods, they are subject to change, like so! [Snaps fingers] Just like so! I mean, just a matter of two families moving.

I have no intention of ever moving into an all-black neighborhood. I would love to stay where I'm at forever. I've got good neighbors. They believe in being neighborly. We do some of the things that you hear about in storybooks, such as on Christmas Eve. Truthfully, in my community, we all get together. Like, if there's a lot of snow, we'll pull a sleigh. And we sing the Christmas carols, we drink the wine—all over the neighborhood.

ADOLPH SLAUGHTER

Adolph Slaughter moved into his grandfather's home in Ida B. Wells as a little boy. An outstanding student, Slaughter was voted "Junior Mayor" of Wellstown. He went into journalism and became one of the first black members of the National Press Club. He ended his professional career as a public relations officer for HUD in Washington, D.C.

My father was killed in Chicago back in the 1930s, and at that time, he was a small-business man and a precinct captain on the North Side. By 1930, he and my mother had five children. To make things easier for my mother, his parents, who lived at Wells, decided to take care of me and my [fraternal] twin brother. Rudolph and I used to go home to the West Side to spend every summer with my mother and the rest of the family. We would return to Ida B. Wells after the summer.

One year Rudolph said he would prefer to be with my mother on the West Side. My grandfather asked me what I would like to do. I said, "Remain here with you." My grandfather said to my mother, "Ruth, you may take Rudolph with you. Adolph will remain here." And that was it. He was the kind of person that you couldn't get too close to. He was authoritarian, he just ruled the roost. What he said went. My grandfather worked all of his life, until he got ill, and was a very strong member of his church. He was one of the deacons who ran the church.

I graduated from Morgan Park High School in 1947 and got a scholarship to University of Dubuque in Iowa. High grades were part of it, but also I was an active member of the Grace Presbyterian Church. I became the moderator of the Presbyterian of Young People here in the city of Chicago while I was still in high school, and vice-moderator of the Presbyterian Young People in the United States. I was also "Junior Mayor" of Ida B. Wells. I guess as a result of these activities, a number of colleges offered me scholarships. I stayed at the University of Dubuque for one year. I found it a rather disappointing and disconcerting experience. The university had a somewhat fundamentalist approach to religion, which did not satisfy me. I completed the year, but did not return.

I volunteered for the Army and was shipped first to Fort Sheridan. After basic training, I became a classification and assignment officer at Camp Cook, California. I wanted to go back to school, and enrolled in the Army's Foreign Language School. I stayed there forty-two weeks. You had to pick three languages, and I chose French, Spanish, and Japanese. Japanese is the one I got. And that's how I ended up being sent to Japan. I was stationed at Camp Drake outside of Tokyo. I was released in 1955.

Aterward, I came to the University of Illinois, where I stayed until 1958. I studied journalism. When you go on the break, senior year, you are asked to visit publications in your community to seek employment. You let them know that you would soon be a graduate of the university in journalism. Unfortunately the Chicago *Sun-Times*, the *Herald*, the *Tribune*, and the City News Bureau were not hiring minorities, certainly not blacks. I had done some writing on the Chicago *Defender* while I was at the University of Illinois. Enid Withers, who was the editor in chief there, offered me a position, but I had to leave school and begin working right away. So I said, "I'll take it now." Which I did.

That was the beginning of my journalistic career. I worked for the Chicago *Defender* until 1962. I got married in 1961. My wife was born here in Chicago, and she was the daughter of Dr. and Mrs. William Glover; her father was a dentist here. Although she and I are divorced, we are both close to our daughters. She is now the principal of a high school in New York City.

I went to Washington to become Claude Barnett's Washington Bureau chief for the Associated Negro Press. We opened the office, and I stayed in that capacity until he died, I figure 1965 or 1966. I joined the National Press Club in Washington, D.C. I was about the fourth black to become a member. During that time, I became associate editor of the Associated Negro Heritage Library, a company out of Yonkers, New York, that put together the first encyclopedic history of black people in this country. We produced about ten volumes.

My youngest daughter graduated from Troy State, a racially integrated university in Troy, Alabama. Troy State solicits black alumnae from the school and assists them in attaining doctorate degrees so that they can come back and teach at Troy State. They want to further enhance minority representation at the faculty level. She was solicited, and after she receives her doctorate from Howard, she will give Troy State three years as a professor.

My other daughter got her master's and law degrees at Rutgers University. She became the clerk of the Chief Justice of the Supreme Court of the state of New Jersey. The largest and most prestigious law firm in the state of New Jersey selected my daughter to work for them during the summer for two years prior to her graduation, and then decided to bring her into the firm after she completes her internship with the Supreme Court Chief Justice. This law firm had only one black member, and of all the law students who graduated with her, black and white, she was the only one chosen. While I do not believe that that was done because she's a woman, or because she's black, I think that the firm was not unmindful of either of these facts.

I believe that while my daughters are both most competent, they achieved what they did in part because they are black females. I certainly think that minorities in this country should receive consideration because of past injustices, and that it should reach youngsters like mine. That was what affirmative action was all about—and I think that should continue on.

Public housing was not designed to be permanent for any one family. It was anticipated, and expected, that those who lived in public housing, once those families got on their feet and moved up the ladder, would be able to move out and make room for other people to come in. There's one thing that has not been mentioned yet, which affected the building and the institutionalization of public housing, and that's the political ramifications. At the time Dawson was Congressman. I think that political machinations affected the decisions for public housing, causing deteriorated, segregated public housing. I believe there was an agreement with Dawson and Mayor Daley. While on one hand I laud Daley for pushing for more public housing in the city of Chicago, I also decry him for the collusion, which forced so many underprivileged and poor people into what I call "concentrated ghettos." Those political decisions have, in my mind, done a lot of damage. The white politicians and the black politicians colluded in the destruction of public housing.

I think those families with poorer prognosis ought to have the same opportunity to live in decent housing as we had. But those persons are going to require a greater public assistance, more educational opportunity, more health services, and far better job training. Many of these families require social services in order to help them move up the ladder in terms of what we perceive to be acceptable ways of living and conduct. If that had been the case for the last forty years, public housing would not have come to the pass it has today.

ANGELA WILLUWEIT

Angela Willuweit, who is white, moved to the Frances Cabrini Homes (now part of the Cabrini-Green complex) in 1943.

The war came along. I had gone to California to be with my husband, and when I came back, there was absolutely no housing. At that time they reserved Cabrini for service people. We were mostly service wives and children—very few men. We gave each other encouragement and strength. It was a very close community, closely knit.

I remember when Cabrini was built. It was a model. People came from all over—even Europe—to see it, because this was something new. The designer had done something that was really remarkable. The townhouses were built so the housewife could look out the kitchen window into the front. We had our own little yard in front, and that's where everyone had a jungle gym or a sandbox. It was small, but we had everything: a bathroom, hot and cold running water. If anything went wrong with the plumbing, the repairmen were right there. It was very well run. It was one of the best apartments I'd ever lived in. Altogether, it was darling.

Cabrini was like a little village. We did things for each other—baby-sat the children and stuff like that. In fact, one of the other service wives and I, we convinced a small manufacturer, just two blocks away, to split a shift between the two of us. It took about three or four months to convince him that it would be fine. She took mornings and I took afternoons, and we met at lunchtime. We punched one card.

We were very politically active, also. We tried to vote in our own alderman. We had a woman run. Of course, she didn't get in, but we put up a good fight. We worked very hard for our candidate. We were poll watchers in the 42nd Ward. It was very dangerous. The people that were entrenched in politics there, they stood around with guns in their pockets and nobody said anything. The polls were crooked: they stole the votes, they brought in bums to vote. So we tried to challenge them, you know. We were women. We were brave.

Then, what happened was, as the men got out of the service, the women stayed home and had babies because you had waited all through the war. So everybody was having babies. The fellows, most of them, went to school; they took advantage of the G.I. Bill. We were all struggling to get that degree. I think those were some of the happiest years, even if we were so poverty-stricken. We were all in the same boat. We used to swap clothes for the children. You'd get hand-me-downs through somebody that had older children. If you had more babies and you needed a larger apartment in Cabrini, the CHA shifted you gladly. You didn't have to wait too long, maybe a couple of months, that's all. Every building had one or two four-bedroom apartments and they allotted you the unit according to the family size so that you didn't feel crowded.

In 1946, Cabrini was practically all young people, most of them going to school. If the wife could find a part-time job, she did. But you really couldn't, because if you made too much money, you went above the scale and couldn't live in Cabrini. And you couldn't find housing anywhere else, which was sort of a Catch-22. It still is. I mean, it's a ridiculous thing. Well, you tried to hold a part-time job without going above the scale.

We were all one big family: black and white, Mexican and Japanese, German, Irish, Polish, Italian—you name it. We lived upstairs in a two-flat, and there was a black family that lived downstairs. Nobody thought anything of it. Then two doors down, it was a Mexican family. Across the street, it was an Irish policeman. We had a Japanese family right across from us. He and my husband were underneath our car one whole summer trying to get the thing to run. We were quite an intermixed neighborhood. There were intermarriages. We had Jewish people living near us, but I never heard the word "Jew." Everybody got along.

I don't remember how or when it started, but there was a controversy. Somebody threw up their hands and said that Cabrini had a racial quota. Elizabeth Wood did not deny it. So when the tenants discussed it in the tenants council, we split as to whether it should be opened to first come, first served, or whether we should try and maintain the quota so that it would be a sort of international village. You know, integrated. Elizabeth Wood came to some of the tenants council meetings. Well, she was dead set against lifting the quota; her theory was that the quota would maintain a balance, and that Cabrini couldn't survive without a balance. I was on her side; I believed in a quota, too. Because Cabrini was in the middle of an area that was becoming more black, and logically it would just turn black, too. The surrounding area was poverty-stricken. We were just a little cleared-off space surrounded by this horrible poverty and decay. There were a few tenants that believed there shouldn't be a quota, ever. But you have to be practical, according to the situation.

Well, I saw the atmosphere change from sort of an ideal little community into a place that you wanted to get out of. It changed from highly motivated college students and working families to just poor people. Oh, and a lot of broken families. When we first moved there, the blacks there were complete family units, with a father and a mother. But then there came just women with children. They were on ADC [Aid to Dependent Children, welfare]. Well, we got more and more of those in. Some tried to raise themselves by the bootstraps, doing filing and stuff like that at night. Quite a few of us women worked at Montgomery Ward. We started at six in the evening and worked until eleven o'clock. We were escorted by this security guard right to our door. They didn't pay much, but you were escorted.

My husband worked nights, and he came home around two in the morning. He was attacked a couple of times. It started getting rougher and rougher in the surrounding area. Every year I felt worse and worse, you know. I wanted to move out, but we had three boys and the housing was scarce. Finally, we came out to Lombard in 1953 and built our own home from a shell house. You know what a shell house is? The contractor builds the shell, and you put up the plasterboard and the flooring. You finish the house yourself. Sweat equity. There was quite a few of them around this area. You finish it and save around five or six thousand dollars. A lot of us did that.

I am very concerned about people in the slums today. They're trapped. We know, because we were in that position ourselves. We couldn't go on to anything else. We didn't have enough money. You couldn't save a dollar. You're really trapped, you know. I can relate to that very well. It's a horrible feeling.

DEBORAH GILLIAM MAYES

Deborah Gilliam Mayes is a Vice President and Branch Manager of LaSalle Home Mortgage/LaSalle Bank. She grew up in Leclaire Courts (near Midway Airport) in the 1960s and 1970s. Beginning in the 1980s, Leclaire was run by a resident corporation. The corporation was dissolved in 1996, however, after its leaders were charged with misusing development funds.

After I married my husband, who is from Leclaire as well, we moved into a house virtually adjacent to Leclaire. Originally this area was predominantly white, but as Leclaire progressively became more black, everything seemed to change. I personally have no problem living in an all-black neighborhood. However, if I had my choice with no other family considerations, I would prefer to live in either Oak Park or Beverly, both of which are perfect examples of well-integrated areas.

In terms of where people want to live, income plays a far more important part than people realize. Living in a clean and safe environment is of great importance to me. I'm not going to say that habits correlate with income, but people's habits have a lot to do with whom you want to live next to. There are a lot of blacks and whites that I would not like to live next door to. It has nothing to do with color or ethnic background.

I don't live at Leclaire anymore, but I see certain things that go on, and I've noticed that there has been feuding. There is no place for this type of thing if you're trying to run a successful business. Housing should be run like a business, and you have to have someone who has the know-how to run a business. It's fine to get residents involved like they did. We should always have tenants involved, but only to a certain extent. The basic management decisions should be made by professionals who know the housing business.

Personally, I think that a row house is far better than any type of public housing. You have the illusion of home ownership. I really don't approve of scattered site housing because you are sending people out to a place they are not familiar with, far from their families and friends, and their economic and social similarities.

I have worked for LaSalle Bank for eighteen years now. When I am asked to approve loans, I try to be 100 percent fair to everybody. When we have to reject an application because the family does not have enough funds or is receiving public assistance, I try my best to explain it to them so that they don't feel that they have been treated unfairly. There is certainly no "redlining." There are situations that some underwriters don't understand, because they have never been in difficult situations. A lot of times I've had to go in and talk to the underwriters and say, "I think this family can make it," and generally it works. At least it has for us—very few of our loans have gone bad.

DAVID DORAN

When the Doran family moved into Lawndale Gardens in 1962, David was six years old. "Everything seems etched into my mind. I could probably tell you what color the doors were on each particular house. What color the mailboxes were painted. I could tell you everything." Doran, now a 911 official, lived in Lawndale Gardens until the mid-1970s.

I believe it was my aunt or uncle that drove us to the house at Lawndale Gardens for the first time. I remember the setting sun illuminated the buildings as we drove up. I was amazed. I thought that the whole place belonged to us, and that these were just different little doors and exits. Later on, I found out that each one of those doors and exits led to other families.

When we went into the parking lot for the very first time, the project seemed huge. It seemed like forever until we got to our apartment, the last house in the first aisle. There was a crabapple tree right outside our front window. The apartment was much different than the place we had lived in. The stuff within the house seemed a little more modern. The walls were freshly painted, there was tile on the floor.

Previous to that, we lived in a two-flat on the West Side. We lived on the first floor, and due to my parents' breakup, it seemed like we were on the lower end of the social-economic pecking order in the neighborhood. When we moved into the projects, my eyes were really opened. The public housing units were very well kept. The lawns, the maintenance, everything was meticulously kept up.

My mom decided that public housing would be the best for us because, well, my father was not really what you would call consistent as far as paying child support. And chances are you're not going to get too many landlords sympathetic to a woman with four kids who doesn't have a man to curb these children and ensure that none of the property is damaged or stolen. So looking back, my mom was pretty bright. She saw this opportunity and she took it.

I never felt ashamed about living in public housing—absolutely not. The project itself brings back so many good memories. In the beginning, when we first moved in, there were still a lot of nuclear families. The fathers did great. They were making money and had brand new cars every year. Yeah, they were living in the projects, but they thought that if you take care of the place you live in and you're happy, then this is your palace. It doesn't make any difference what society feels. As far as being able to go out and earn a buck every day, the possibilities were unlimited.

We went to Spry [the local public elementary school]. Academically I did very well until in sixth grade, when my mom decided she was going to move us to a private school. After that I just couldn't get it together for some reason. I felt like my roots were removed, like I was ripped out of my element. We went to Grace Lutheran School, which was not a bad school, there was nothing wrong with it. But I just never felt comfortable, and that's when I began to feel the difference between us and the other kids that went there. Those kids were the haves, and the kids like myself were the have-nots.

In the project, we were all on the same level. Basically, we were all poor, so it really didn't make any difference. But when I was exposed to these snotty, whining little brats that got everything they wanted—things I had never seen before—it came as a shock. Their families had two cars. My mom didn't even drive. We never had a car, you know.

Later, I went to Harrison High School. Harrison was 85 percent black, maybe 7 percent white, and the rest Hispanic. Basically, I began to feel that because I was white, I was being edged out of all these little programs that

I was trying to get in. I didn't really attribute it to prejudice. I just figured, well, they had the majority, and they basically had control of the school. At that point, I decided, I don't want to be in this pond anymore. Maybe it's time to pick up and find another pond and see what I can do. So I went into the military.

And it was like being home. I mean, I just felt home between the way the project was set up and the way the maintenance section was set up in the Marines. We were people of all different races, colors, creeds, and understandings, and yet we all worked together as a team. We learned from each other. And that was one of the things that was important about people living in public housing. You couldn't be narrow-minded. You just couldn't. There were so many different opinions going back and forth, and there were so many different cultural tidbits that I was exposed to on a daily basis that it would be impossible for me to be a stereotyped white guy. I just couldn't be like that. Sometimes I have difficulty relating to white people.

I got to see how black people were not really different from us. Other than some cultural things they'd do or the foods they'd eat, they weren't that much different. They went to the same school as us, we played ball together, we did a lot of things together. As we were growing up, color was not important.

Elizabeth Wood, mid-1940s (J. S. Fuerst).

Altgeld Gardens, aerial, 1945 (CHA).

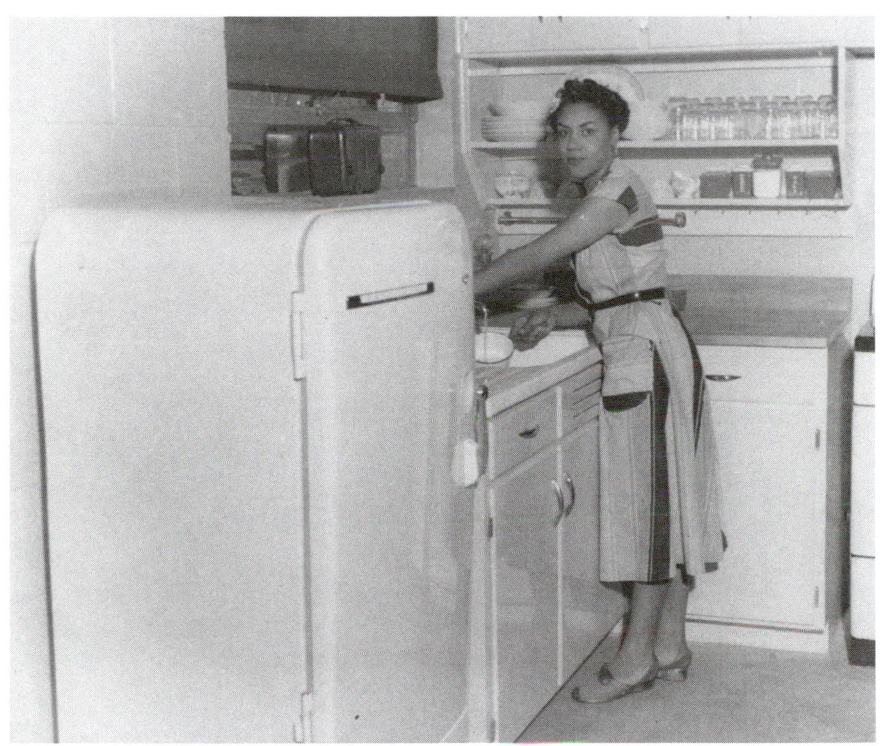

Altgeld Gardens, interior, 1953 (CHA).

Altgeld Gardens, library, 1945 (CHA).

Brooks Homes, 1948 (CHA).

Cabrini Homes, early 1950s (CHA).

Dearborn Homes, mid-1950s (CHA).

Ida B. Wells Homes, 1950 (CHA).

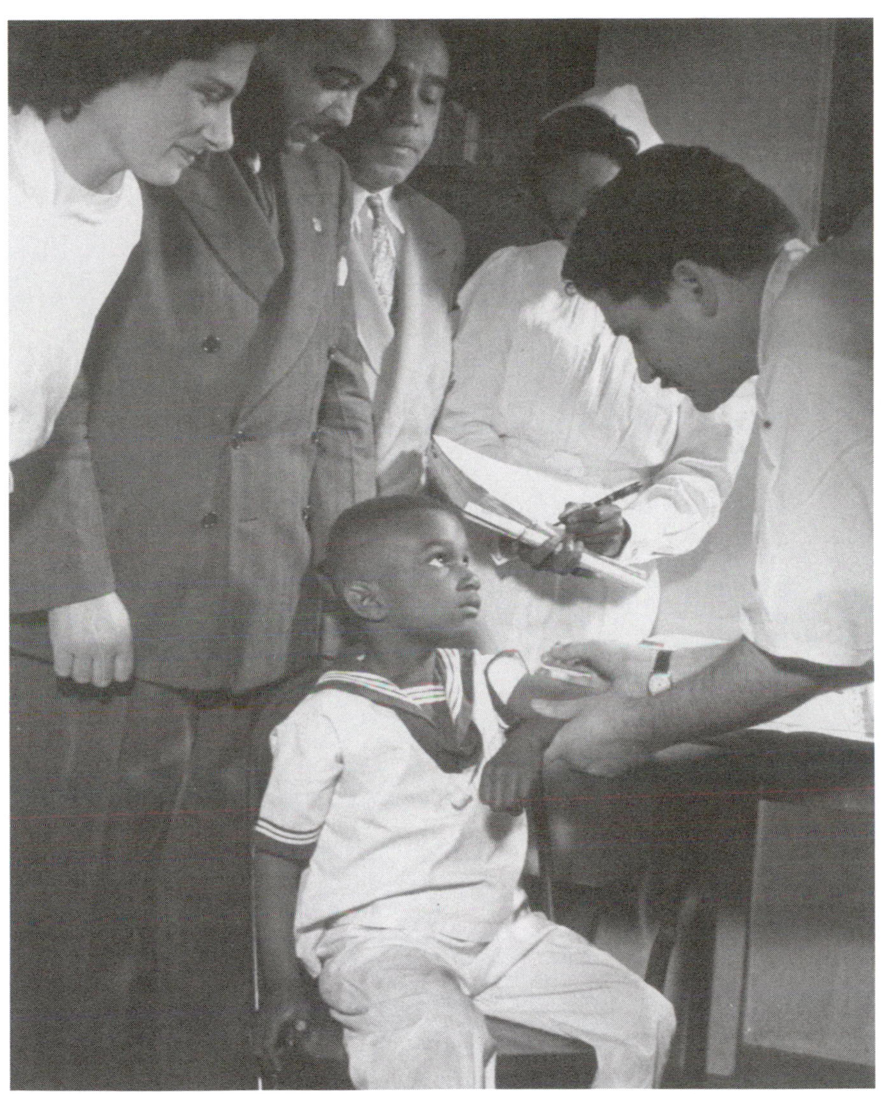

Ida B. Wells Homes, TB inoculation, 1942 (CHA).

Leclaire Courts, 1954 (CHA).

Leclaire Courts, integration, 1952 (CHA).

Leclaire Courts, interior, 1952 (CHA).

Loomis Courts, Loewenberg and Loewenberg, architects, 1949 (CHA).

Lowden Homes, tenant council, late 1950s (CHA).

Stateway Gardens, first tenant receives keys from project manager, June, 1957 (CHA).

Chapter 5

Investments in the Mind: The Importance of Education

Beyond the importance of housing, the former public housing residents interviewed for this book recognized the importance of their educational experiences in shaping their lives. Most of the voices heard in this chapter attended Chicago's public schools; a handful went to private Catholic schools. Respondents remember a positive educational environment and strong values in public schools during the 1940s and 1950s, despite a largely segregated system. Repeatedly, they recollect discipline by school administrators and the effort demanded by parents and teachers. Respondents look back on these expectations as the force that pushed them to achieve an education. An education offered them a chance at higher economic status and better lives.

The lesson expressed by these interviews is that good public housing, by itself, clearly is not enough. The problems of the poor cannot be addressed by a single magic cure. Rather, a "total" approach is the only means of tackling the deprivations that currently block upward mobility. Along with good housing, a responsive public school system tops the list of needs.

A large share of the former tenants interviewed for this book went on to careers in education for at least a portion of their working lives. They, along with others, are discouraged by the loss of discipline and lack of respect among young people in public schools. Parents and the larger community, they believe, must help reinstill these values. Public housing, in its earliest days, had exactly this parental involvement and community respect that contributed to a successful learning environment.

EUGENE FARMER

Eugene Farmer's family moved to Dearborn Homes in 1949, just after he was born. "I went to Wendell Phillips High School and graduated with honors."

Farmer was also an all-state basketball player. After playing basketball at Emporia State University in Kansas and serving in the Army, he returned to Emporia State, where he got a master's degree in education. Today, he's an administrator with the Chicago Board of Education. One of his responsibilities is to oversee the sex education curriculum in five city schools.

We have girls in our schools that are getting pregnant at a very young age. They're getting pregnant at thirteen, twelve—in one case, we had a girl eleven years old. So we're trying to counsel these young girls. If we can get them involved in after-school programs, where they're dealing with math and science, or gymnastics, or whatever the activity may be, they are much less likely to become pregnant. Because usually the sex occurs after school, between four o'clock and six. The parent is working, and the children have got a lot of room there for error.

We also focus on the young boys that are engaging in sex with no control. We have a high level of sexually transmitted diseases among these young girls. So we're trying to bring those young boys and young girls together for counseling. Last year, we had over four hundred females become pregnant at age thirteen or fourteen. And that's only in the area that I deal with, not in the whole city. In the last eight to ten years that I've been involved with this program, we've only made a very small dent in the problem.

As a religious person, I'm strongly against abortion, but if we look at it from the standpoint of thirteen-year-olds having babies, abortion would be the proper procedure. We're talking about twelve- and thirteen-year-olds. That's a child having a child, and a child can't raise that kid. Some of these girls have parents who are alcoholics or on drugs, so in some cases their family can't raise the kid either. The problem is, the girl needs to be with her family as much as possible. If not the parents, then maybe an aunt, a cousin, or another relative. She needs to be in a family setting—not put into an apartment to run it by herself. It's almost an impossible situation. Because now you're putting an irresponsible child into an apartment.

That is one of the reasons why we now have so many problems in public housing. I don't want to put these girls in public housing apartments. They don't know how to take care of bills, and pay rent, and raise that child. There are too many young adults in those apartments.

It wasn't so when we were growing up. Absolutely not. They lowered the standards that were established. When we moved into the projects, you had to be screened—you had to be married. With that you had some control over who lived there, and you did not live there if you were an "undesirable." As time went along, when I was leaving high school to go on to college, we had a change. They were not screening. You did not have to be married. Kids with babies were given apartments.

Before, if you walked on the grass, you had to pay a fine. If the security officer saw anyone out there beyond ten o'clock, they would be questioned and told to leave. The standards of the projects—I'm speaking of the Dearborn Homes now—have been lowered. And because of the influx of teenagers who are moving in with no family structure, you're going to have a chaotic situation. You cannot put a group of undesirable people in one given area. If you still had the original type of families and structure, I would say that Dearborn Homes could be great and very workable. You see that type of setting today in Lake Meadows [a large, predominantly black private apartment complex near Dearborn Homes]. But in the projects, that type of structure is gone. Because of drugs, because of gangs, it would be very difficult to rebuild that structure.

But I'm not saying it's impossible. Here's what I'd do in Dearborn Homes. Once a family moves out, close that apartment. Don't use it again. And when we get down to a certain number of people, pull them all out, place them somewhere else, and then let's go back to day one. Let's bring back that type of institution we had in the 1960s, where you had to be screened. You had to be a family. You had to work.

We can do those things. Put those families back in with that type of structure. Public housing would work if we had families that had a sense of understanding: this is where I live, this is my house. I have to take the responsibility for keeping it clean, neat, graffiti-free. We can do that. But you cannot put in dysfunctional families. Because once you do, it's just laying a foundation for the gangs and drugs.

When we grew up in Dearborn Homes, that whole building raised us. The whole building gave us the hope that if you receive an education, if you do these good things, good things will happen to you. All of my brothers and sisters finished high school. That was an absolute, you had to finish high school. And today, my older sister is a supervisor with Ameritech in Iowa. She's been there for twenty-five years. My little sister lives in Iowa and she works as a sales rep with hospitals. My youngest brother works for the Board of Education. And my brother next to me is a minister in Peoria.

Today, we don't have a community raising our kids, we have gangs raising our kids. That's why it's hard for them to see that light through the tunnel. If the adults would help raise these kids, then yes, I could see hope. My role model was my dad. My dad was a minister, plus he drove a cab. He didn't have to be a basketball player or a football player. He got up every day and went to work. My dad worked and my mother worked. Those two—they were my role models. I wanted to accomplish something in life like them, and I wanted to be looked up to. Basketball was a step for me. It was a tool that I used to accomplish what I wanted. That's what I tell the young kids now. Use what you have, use your ability—it may be in writing or whatever—to accomplish what you want to in life.

The black church plays a great part in the upbringing of kids, but the church is not doing what it could do. I don't see the church reaching out to these young black men out there on the street. The church is like, "You come to me." I think we have to go to them, because we have young brothers out there who don't have any direction. It's very difficult to get them into church. Even if you did, it might make some change, but I don't really feel it would make the drastic change that we're looking for. The church can only do so much. We need something else to go along with the church: centers where kids are able to go, where these boys would be able to play sports, to seek vocational-type training, so they can have something to put their hands on, something they know they can accomplish. We don't have that now. We have to put the tools into the community to do that.

I was in the Million Man March in Washington, D.C. We had over 1.5 million men. I want to make this clear because the press did not quote that right in the paper. I took my son with me, we flew down. It was an experience I will never forget as long as I live. You're talking about 1.5 million black men coming together. There were some white people sneaking in there, too. And we came together for one common cause—to become focused on family. It was about taking charge and bringing up our families like we used to do.

I'll tell you, [Minister Louis] Farrakhan was great, the speech that he gave was great. I don't think any other man could have done what he did. And half the guys I went with believed the same way. But it wasn't about Farrakhan. It wasn't about Reverend Jesse Jackson. It was about men coming together for one common cause—for the betterment of the whole country. Yeah, the American flag flew very high there. No one talked about disgracing the flag. We talked about living together as black and white people on this earth. And in our society we must have that, because divided we will fall.

We must live in this world, in this country, together—blacks and whites in harmony. Dr. Martin Luther King did the first march, and look how far we've come. And we're going to go even farther when, as whites and blacks, we can hold hands and move along those lines, helping each other. We should never look down on a person unless we're going to pick that person up, whether he's black, white, Chinese, Mexican, Puerto Rican, whatever. Because we are all in this together—we bleed the same blood. Let's not forget Vietnam. We all fought in that war. We fought side by side. Why can't we live side by side?

RITA LEWIS-PERRY

Rita Lewis-Perry is a doctor, specializing in geriatric psychiatry, and is affiliated with Ingalls Hospital in Chicago. She and her family moved to Leclaire Courts in 1962, when she was three years old. Today, she lives in South Holland, a Chicago suburb.

Leclaire Courts is a different animal now. I'm sure every project is. At the time we moved in, a lot of people there were working. And believe it or not,

I can specifically remember only one of my very closest friends whose father and mother never lived together. There were a large percentage of two-parent families at that time. But the working families were forced out because their rent was being raised, which is the main reason my family wound up leaving Leclaire Courts. It was the subsidy people who were able to stay.

Through my young adolescence, Leclaire was generally a pretty decent place to live. There were always community things going on. They had the Leclaire Community Center, and they used to have the schools open in the evenings. I remember going there and skating in the gym, playing pool, tennis, Ping-Pong. The kids had a place to go where there was adult supervision and they would be off the streets. I thought Leclaire was an ideal size. The facility was big enough that you had a community, but it wasn't so large that you felt trapped within the community. I remember there being all different types of people there, including Hispanic, white, and black.

The other families seemed fairly solid, though not quite as intellectual as ours. My dad is Jamaican and from a strict upbringing, and our lives were structured. Education was very important. We had all types of encyclopedias. If we didn't have food, we had encyclopedias. So we were exposed to various things, like opera and famous artworks. Our family took care of our lawn. We had it beautiful. We had roses in the front yard, evergreens. There was a clear, obvious difference between us and other families, and it was seen by them. They would pick up on what we were doing and learn from us. They would start taking care of their front yards, making sure that there was no litter in their grass and taking pride in their own.

There were eight children in our family, with me in the middle. The majority of us are fairly successful, and that is very surprising, I think, coming from where we grew up. You just don't hear about an entire family as large as ours with each one being successful in their own way. Let me just start with my oldest sister, Deborah Gilliam Mayes, who is a phenomenon in herself. She runs LaSalle Bank's mortgage Loan Department, and she did that after divorcing her husband at a very young age. She went back to college, raised three kids, and went on to be very successful. She lives in the single-family home development next to Leclaire.

Next is Larry—he ran an auto repair business on the South Side up until his death last January from colon cancer. He was a veteran of Vietnam, and his death, we believe, was related to a significant Agent Orange exposure. My nephew is presently running the business; he kind of followed in his father's mechanical footsteps. Then there's another brother, Randy. He is a master electrician and has wired some of the biggest buildings downtown, and the new O'Hare terminal. Then there's my brother Ronnie, who has been a part owner of a copy machine repair business for many, many years. He is married, with three children, and he recently purchased a home near Leclaire Courts. So I have my sister, my mom, and my brother straddled over a couple of blocks in that area, which is actually a very nice area.

Then there is me, and I am a medical doctor with a specialty in geriatric psychiatry. I just finished a fellowship and started to practice last July. I enjoy what I do very much. I have a teenage daughter in high school who is hoping to be a child psychiatrist. I have a sister under me, Ruth, who was an assistant buyer for Spiegel's for many years. Three years ago, she left work to raise her three boys and now she runs a child-care business out of her home. The next child is Rene. She is an industrial engineer living in Phoenix, Arizona, working for the Intel Corporation. She has one child—not married, but doing very well. Finally, the last child is Robin. She lives in New Jersey and is in the communications field. She's done broadcast news for stations in Chicago such as WGCI.

I went to Northwestern, and after two years of being out of school, I had my daughter. Then I went on to Southern Illinois University for a year and a half of medical preparatory work, and then to medical school at the University of Iowa. It was culture shock for me to go to Northwestern and Iowa. I grew up in very poor circumstances, very poor. I had to struggle all the way through school. I had to be concerned with how was I going to eat the next day, as opposed to reading a book for class. And if books couldn't be the number one concern on my mind, where am I going to fall when it comes to taking an exam? At the top ranks, or am I going to fall below?

Of course I didn't do as well on exams as some of my white counterparts, although I could have. I had to work. I didn't have the time to put into the studies that they did. So why, after struggling so much, shouldn't I be given a slight advantage? That's why I think affirmative action is important. It's a wonderful opportunity for blacks to get their foot in the door at various levels. It came out of a time where the whole thought process was like, "Blacks aren't able to do this, they aren't as capable as whites." When I was growing up, affirmative action was very important. It gave us opportunities we wouldn't otherwise have had.

We've been held at a disadvantage for so long, why not give us a slight advantage and a chance to prove ourselves? Individuals that are not black aren't going to look at it that way, because they, of course, don't want to place that blame on themselves for holding us back, but we have been held back. I think a black can do just as well if they have the mind to do it. I had the mind to get an education to go on and become a doctor. But it was a struggle every single day. Because I had to be concerned about where the money was going to come from. That was first and foremost on my mind.

WINIFRED DeLOACHE

Winifred DeLoache has been a special education teacher and counselor in the Chicago public schools for thirty years. She lives in Flossmoor, a well-to-do, predominantly white suburb south of Chicago. She grew up in Ida B. Wells in the 1940s and 1950s with her mother, a brother, and two sisters.

We were like a big family, the families that were there. I think our parents had the same kinds of ideas and goals for their children, you know. School first. My mother went to Northwestern for three years. Her father was a lawyer. My grandmother was a teacher in Kentucky. That was something that my mother instilled in all of us, that we were going to go to college—even though there was no money there. There were no grants then, none of that kind of help. But it was just, you know, we were going to college. Basically, the families in the Ida B. Wells Home had those kinds of goals for their children. There are many successes from Ida B. Wells. There are many like me that went straight as an arrow and had no problems. The problem kids were, I really must say, in the minority. Because I think going to school was the priority in every family. At least finish high school. Now, there were kids that did not go beyond that, and in many cases it was because they had no desire, or they did not have the family support.

In terms of talking about family, my next-door neighbor could tell me, "Winifred, don't do such and such . . . ," and I would not do it because I knew that she would go back and tell my mother, and I would get the consequences of it. So you respected adults, I don't care who it was. If an adult said something to you, you did what they told you. You didn't necessarily never talk back, but you would do what they said. You just did not disrespect anyone.

When I graduated from high school, in 1951, I got married. The first part of my marriage, we spent in the Ida B. Wells. And then we bought our home out on 82nd and Kimball. And that's where my kids grew up. My daughter was in second grade when we bought the house, and I had my son the following year. I'm Catholic, so they went to St. Felicita's Grammar school, and my son went to high school at St. Ignatius and my daughter went to Academy of Our Lady. Both of my children were honor students.

My son's a trader for the stock exchange. He lives in London. My son went to Northwestern, my daughter to Loyola, and I graduated from Loyola. I graduated in 1973, she started in 1973. See, I went back to school to get my degree. I got my master's from Chicago State. I am a school counselor at the Gillespie School at 93rd and State. I've been there about seven years now. I cannot base every school on my school, but I can say this: I have seen a transition in the children. When I first arrived, there was a different type of child, a different family environment, a different concern about children.

Most of our children [at Gillespie] now come from Lowden Homes [a CHA development on the far South Side]. At one time, Gillespie was considered a very good school. The parents were home owners, and they inspired the children. Now, we have to deal with so many behavior problems. I have kids that come in and talk disrespectful to their parents, and I stop them immediately. I tell them, "No, you do not talk to your parents in my office like this. Now if you talk like that at home, and your parents permit it, fine. But not here. You will respect your parents." No problem. It immediately stops, and they do what I say. It's because they know "Mrs. Loach does not take any nonsense. If she says something, I'm going to have to do what she says, because otherwise I'm going to be in some serious problems. She will get me suspended, or whatever." But, you know, parents thank me for doing it.

I had a student that graduated a couple of years ago, DeLong. Smart as a whip, this boy. I said, "You are, to me, another Malcolm X." I said, "You could be." Because Malcolm X was a tremendously smart man. Not in terms of his philosophy and the Muslim faith. But academically, that man had a brain, a tremendous brain. And this is what I told DeLong. I said, "If I can just get you to channel it in the right direction, you can be whatever you want to be." He'd always laugh at me and say, "Mrs. DeLoache, you just think too much of me." But when you've worked in the system as long as I have, you can see kids and what their potential is and capabilities are.

When it came test time, he missed a test. I said, "Come in, DeLong, and I'll give it to you so you can make it up." Well, DeLong had gotten involved with the street and began to deal drugs. But he came in and worked as much as he could, and then he said, "Mrs. DeLoache, I've got to go."

I knew what he was saying. I couldn't keep him there. I said, "Okay, DeLong, but I hope that you'll come back so that we can finish up the test." Well, he never did, but he graduated, because he had to graduate. I found out this past year that he had been in some trouble; I think he robbed somebody or something. The social worker called me. And I just shared with him, saying, "He was probably doing that to help take care of the family." Because the mother had two or three other kids, you know. He was the provider of the family, and she was, really, *his* child.

I told the social worker, "If he was put in the right environment, he could become something." In fact, I said he needed to be taken away from the mom. In some kind of way allow him to free up his mind. He had all the potential.

That's why we still need programs like affirmative action. There is still that disadvantaged school that will produce a student who needs that boost in order to get them going in the right direction. If they do not have it, then they can't even compete. They can't even begin to compete, because the white schools have prepared students totally differently. Ask a black student, "Do you know *Macbeth*? *King Lear*? Do you know music? Do you know anything about art? Do you know about Monet? Do you know Renoir?" All of these things are introduced at the high school level for white students. Not so for black students. Those kinds of things take them out of the ball game in terms of competing on a regular basis for a position. They need that extra boost in order to make them competitive.

ABDUL ALKALIMAT

Alkalimat, born Gerald McWhirter in 1942, lived in the Frances Cabrini Homes until his family moved to the West Side in 1953. He attended Ottawa University as an undergraduate and started work on his Ph.D. in sociology at Chicago's Roosevelt University in the 1960s.

"That was when they used academic ranking as a basis for the draft. And several of us graduate students who were teaching said, 'What the hell is this?' There was a protest, and I was canned from Roosevelt. Yeah, yeah, I was thrown out. They said, 'You'll never work here again.' But you know, I did work there again, but that's another story . . ."

He is now chair of the Department of African-American Studies at the University of Toledo. An early advocate of Black Studies, Alkalimat in the late 1960s helped establish Atlanta's Institute of the Black World, which would later become the Martin Luther King Jr. Center. He has taught, among other places, at Fisk University, UCLA, the University of Illinois at Urbana-Champaign, and Oxford.

I think Cabrini was an experiment. I have nothing to prove this, but I perceive it as an experiment by CHA to see what would happen if you integrated a community by race, nationality, language, and religion. There were lots of social activities where the residents could interact. And it was a kind of supervised interacting, so that people weren't just left on their own. People were kept within a series of relationships that kept them from polarizing. It prevented conflict that might otherwise have occurred.

But there was also a lot of independence allowed then compared to now. In other words, when you moved into public housing, it wasn't like you were signing a contract with some kind of prison facility, which is the way these housing projects are today. You still had a sense of being in an apartment. It just happened to be a subsidized place the government had set up. So you still had your independence.

Though I remember, in families, people outside the project saying, "Ah, you're living on welfare, kinda." But I think I had a childhood second to none. I remember those years as golden years, frankly. I cherish having grown up in Cabrini. If there were a place like our Cabrini today, if you had that kind of thing, with community rooms, with child care, etc., yeah, I think you could stabilize it without any question. But you would have to have stabilized employment.

There was a real role that parents played in the neighborhoods within the projects. I can remember knowing—when you were going from one little area to another area—who the patriarch or matriarch of that area was. And so there was an informal organized structure: if you were somewhere and you needed some help, you could go to somebody's house. All that was operating, so it was a very safe environment.

But, you know, there was some delinquency. We were cutting school and doing all kinds of stuff. But not anything antisocial to the people in Cabrini. I mean, look, this area was like Disneyland to me. We had a doughnut factory on Chicago Avenue, we had a tamale factory. I lived across the street from a comic book factory. Can you imagine what that was like? We'd sneak in there over the weekends and literally break into the factory. So we had extensive comic book collections.

Cabrini was the center of a kind of left-wing cultural and intellectual activity. The Communist Party had a real base in Cabrini. At the community center, people like Win Stracke, the Pete Seeger of Chicago, would be there regularly—people knew him, and people gathered around him. And there were house parties, where the parents got together and did things like playing charades.

My general impression is that they promoted social awareness and intellectual stimulation, as well as discussions and leadership. These were the people who were the leaders of the community. I'm not talking about somebody that lived in a middle-class neighborhood, who was sort of doing their work by going over into another neighborhood. These were people who lived there, who were part of the community, and emerged as the leaders of the community.

I remember us as being a real enclave, and people really bonded. I mean, we were all in each other's houses. There weren't any subghettos where we lived. On our block, Chestnut, there were Irish, Filipino, Mexican. Some blocks were more diverse than others, but my memory is that it generally was mixed.

When you're assessing integration, you have to ask: Did people work together? Did people go to school together? Did they really live together? And when you look at all three environments in Cabrini, you find real integration. My dad worked with Italians at National Malleable Steel, for instance. On weekends he would be over with them making what they called—what he called—"Dago red." Cabrini was right in the heart of the city. Look, I think of Cabrini as an idyllic, golden, wonderful time.

But you know, I think that to oppose all-black projects is a very dangerous thing to do. To oppose them in a way that denies or stigmatizes the people who live there is a terrible thing. There shouldn't be a pejorative connotation for anybody who grew up in that environment. You know: "We're better and you're obviously limited because you grew up in a segregated environment." If you then ask the question, "Why did the integration stop?" I think it was a lack of will by those in a position to make the decision.

Clearly, living in a multicultural setting with a lot of diversity provides unique opportunities for growth and development. It gives you survival skills and achievement skills that one needs in the kind of world we live in. On the other hand, I can't bring myself to say there's anything wrong with an all-black environment. While we have to uphold the general value of diversity and create as many opportunities for it as possible, at the same time we have to raise everybody's quality of life, which in the next generation or two will involve a lot of people who are living in all-black or, for that matter, all-white settings.

In other words, if you live in an all-black housing project and go to an all-black school, the question is, "Can you get a decent education?" In an all-black school, a poor all-black school, you'd go out and find things like the Algebra Project. You would put additional resources in schools like that so students would have the opportunity to score well on national standardized tests.

Actually, you should go back and look at the way some black schools were under segregation, where you had a concentration of black people who got advanced degrees. Horace Mann Bond did a study and found some high schools throughout the South disproportionately produced the people who went on to college.[23] So let's reproduce those schools. What you'd find is, if you got schools going like that, they would no longer remain all-black and poor. Everybody else would go there, because they want their kids to make those same scores. That's the direction the struggle for integration would have to take.

Ultimately, color discrimination still defines the American experience. To eliminate it, we have to have the kind of commitment we thought we were getting in the 1960s. But, as we know, that period of change lasted for maybe one generation. Shortly after that, the door was slammed shut.

On the surface, everything is wonderful. You can talk about the difference between now and the time when you wouldn't see anybody black working in the stores on State Street. But when you look at fundamental issues of quality of life—if you look at dealings with financial institutions, if you look at health care, at longevity—I mean, just go into almost anything, and the aggregate condition of African Americans is still much worse than white Americans. And that's a function of racist oppression. There is not an instance of institutional behavior where black people are not getting screwed. Take mortgages, take any dealings with banks, any dealings at any financial institutions, any dealings with a fair thing in the government.

The vast majority of black people are still existing under conditions of racist barbarism. That's the only way I can describe the state of race relations in the United States. I don't care what Clarence Thomas thinks. If he walks down the street without his robes on, then he faces the same thing that all black men face relative to the criminal justice system. I mean, it's barbaric.

I would say that one-third of the black community faces chronic problems of unemployment and is acculturated in a marginalized cul-de-sac. The upper one-third, of course, is mainstreamed. And the middle third is bouncing somewhere in between: they're one paycheck away from disaster. I think that's why, for example, you get such turnouts to the Million Man March.

Now the overwhelming majority of the marchers were in this middle one-third. These people in the middle are scared to death and are prepared to go for Farrakhan's rap. Which is something I've been thinking a lot about. I've been thinking about why it is that in the late twentieth century, in an urban postindustrial society, we have such a problem with reason. People may say the march had nothing to do with Farrakhan's message, that they just went to show solidarity, but that's all rhetorical. It also had to do with Farrakhan.

The people who are in control now are rapidly redesigning industrial democracy. In its place, they're developing a much more exclusionary meritocracy, where privatization is turning the public sector over to the private sector to reengineer it for its own interests. We're going into the twenty-first century with people being set back to conditions before the New Deal.

When you had that industrial economy, you had the social basis for stability. You had institutions that you, your family, and your neighborhood were a part of. When I lived in Cabrini, you had a community where everybody was cooperating to keep everybody on track.

I'm just not sure we could replicate that. I think that was a time when all the people—be they black or white—were going through the experience of proletarianization and urbanization, and it was a new experience they were sharing.

In the 1940s, 1950s, and 1960s, with an expanding economy, immigrants, be they from Italy or from Mississippi, could be incorporated, absorbed, into the industrial setting. And therefore they would be brought up to speed with everybody else. The public school could play the role it's historically played in the country, of being an institution to socialize the second generation.

But what happened in the late 1960s—and really hit in the 1970s—is that the Ford model of mass production is replaced by the Toyota system. And the computer comes in. So you get a shift. People are no longer absorbed in that kind of industrial setting. The school is no longer a bridge to industrial employment with fairly reasonable wages. And therefore, the projects begin to shift from being a way station for working people who are on their way to somewhere else. Instead, it becomes a dumping ground for people on welfare. There is no way that federally subsidized housing could have remained a form of subsidy for employed workers in the industrial sector because, in fact, the overall economy was shifting.

Cabrini was an opportunity to experience democracy and the joys of growing up in the multinational, multiracial working class. I lived the poem by Langston Hughes, "Let American be American again." Now we have a completely different situation. The mass employment of the industrial factory period is a thing of the past. However, I still believe that such places as Cabrini can live again. People can have lives full of meaning and purpose even when they don't have a job. Rich people do, so poor people can, too. The main thing is that the society has to redefine rights so that everyone continues to eat, to have a place to stay, education, health care, etc. This is the kind of country worth living in. This is the kind of country I am dedicating my life to build.

MAUDE DAVIS

Maude Davis is retired principal of the George S. Patton Elementary School in Riverdale, a suburb south of Chicago. She moved into Altgeld Gardens in 1949. She currently operates a settlement program in the city.

We have 546 kids in the Patton School. At least four hundred of our children come from Pacesetter Homes, a federally subsidized development but not public housing. Their townhouses remind me very much of Altgeld, but I don't think they have the same appreciation for the housing that we did. I don't see the pride in the houses.

Over there—and it's even true of Altgeld now—there is this concept that low-income housing is for the poor. Low-income housing is for the gangs. Low-income housing is for those who have nothing better to do or no other place to go, who don't want to work. That concept is associated with low-income housing, and even includes these privately operated developments. We didn't have that concept in Altgeld. We felt it was just paradise. We felt this was just the greatest housing that we could live in! There was pride in it.

We never looked at Altgeld as public housing. We would do our little yards and the flowers, and we just thought that was the way people lived. We had the freedom of leaving our doors open at night, or staying out late. I remember sitting on the porch many nights at twelve o'clock, freely talking, freely having fun out there. We would go to the store late at night. We felt very safe in doing those things.

We didn't have a problem with safety. Your neighbors looked out for each other. It was a real friendship, a caring. You felt free to go into your neighbor's house, free to ask your neighbor for anything, because they were always sharing and giving. That was the general feeling out there. It was not one being better than the other. We freely shared toys, whatever we had. Altgeld is where I learned to ride a bike. And it was on someone else's bike. I guess we didn't realize we were poor, we felt we had so much.

Altgeld was divided into thirteen blocks, and during the summer, the baseball teams from each block would play against each other. I was a shortstop at the time, and then I got on the all-star team, which was thrilling for me. And Halloween was always a marvelous time in Altgeld. They would have big bonfires, and the children would put on their costumes, going from house to house, freely. Then we would go back to the children's building and have apple cider and candy. We would just have such a marvelous time.

I'm convinced everybody needs one person. I had my sister, Addie Wyatt. Addie was the one for me, she was the driving force. I'm the rebel of the family. I went astray. After two years at Wilson Junior College, I said, "I'm not going back to school, and you can't make me go." It was Addie who would not let me rest. She and I almost began to dislike each other. She kept bugging me and bugging me: "Go back to school, go back to school."

Once she got me started, she couldn't stop me. I finally went back to finish up. I wasn't too sure what I wanted to do. At one time I was going to be a nurse, but then I chose education, because that was my second love. I loved helping, and I love working with children. The greatest thrill for me was to see Addie cry when I received my master's degree from National College. She was in the audience. I looked, and I could see her crying. I know what Addie went through to get me to that point. You need that one person.

You know, even in Altgeld back then, the girls were always ahead of the boys. I wish I knew the answer to that. In this school, during the first three grades, the boys and girls are equal. In third grade, the boys are doing great. But they seem to fall down in fourth grade, and then it's a downward spiral for them. I don't know why! They don't seem to be as motivated. We're turning them off for some reason and I don't know where and why.

I think one problem is the lack of role models. They need mentors. They need that individual attention. Those that achieve have somebody who latched onto them, who kept telling them that they could make it, who was patient with them as they went through their wilderness period. That's how they make it. If nobody's there for them, if they're not able to relate, we lose them.

They just don't have the male role models in the home, and we don't have enough male role models in the schools, either. They need that. I have one male teacher here, and I lean heavily on him. He's a "today" male, you know, he can relate to today's kids. I turn him on to my boys. I say, "This little boy needs somebody to talk to." I'm using him constantly to relate to my boys. I'm overworking him! [Laughs] But he lets me do that.

The girls don't need as much of that nurturing or that one-to-oneness as the boys do. The boys are influenced by so many other things. Boys are the bulk of our discipline problem. They're the ones that will cut school. They're the ones that will create the problems as far as the gangs, etc. It's my boys.

MARY ROBINSON

Mary Robinson is principal of Harland High School, a public school on the South Side. She lived in Altgeld Gardens from 1945 to 1950, leaving after she graduated from high school. "We were a family of six. There were four children."

As I look at the group from Altgeld as a whole, they did very well. Don't get me wrong, we had kids who did drugs, we had kids who did alcohol, and I'm sure there were kids who would not come to school. But I don't think I was aware of them, because we automatically went to school. My parents had to work, and there was no one to send us off to school, but we knew we had to go. Don't ask how, but we knew. It was there, and you had to go.

As I look back, we had concerned teachers. I remember one English teacher in particular who wanted to give us experiences beyond Altgeld. She had us over to her house, for a luncheon, to give us some experience outside of a housing project. I'm sure that our schools must have been good enough, because many of us were able to explore other educational possibilities. Everybody anticipated getting a college degree of some kind. We had no money, so we went to junior colleges or city colleges or state colleges, but we went somewhere. [Laughs] My brother, who graduated with me, he went to Roosevelt University for a while, went into the service, and later went back. Most of us have gone on and gotten degrees beyond a bachelor's.

At Altgeld, a lot of us were involved with the Wyatt Choral Ensemble. I couldn't sing, by the way [laughs], but I was involved with Addie's Choir. There was a feeling of respect for the elders, whoever they were, that you do not see now. It never occurred to us to be disrespectful to Addie or Claude, even though their ages, I'm sure, were quite close to ours. That's something you don't find anymore, either.

I think there was more of a sense of community when we were in Altgeld. Well, we were probably all very poor in terms of money, but not poor in terms of spirit, ambitions, and anticipation of what the future held for us. I think about all the people who were there with me who became involved in some kind of educational activity so that they could have a better life than their parents. There was a different outlook on housing projects at the time. Now it's a very negative outlook. That was not our feeling when we lived in Altgeld.

You have to look at what was available to us before we got to Altgeld Gardens. When I went to Altgeld, it was a pleasure. We moved from an area that was completely rat-infested. I mean, Altgeld Gardens was a garden for me. [Laughs] Because it was so much better than what we had when we first came to Chicago. So to get to a place that was clean, and where you had access to a backyard and a front without going through a lot of buildings, was ideal for us.

We looked at our housing options a little bit differently from the people who are presently in public housing. At the time we were in Altgeld, there were no options for black renters. Because of the segregation problems here in Chicago, you were contained in a small section of the South Side, or the little area on the West Side. You had no wide range of housing. Today, because there are other options available, there are negative connotations associated with public housing. There were no negative connotations associated with us going into housing at that time because there were no other options.

As a teenager, I could walk all through Altgeld and never feel any fear. I'd come home on many nights from various activities, by myself, and really never felt afraid. And that's something I would not do now!

The Housing Authority then seemed to take pride in Altgeld, they had staff out there to keep it well maintained. If there was a problem, you could pick up a telephone and get immediate service. Everyone developed beautiful yards, and there was pride in the flower shows and that kind of thing. There was a sense of "This is your home, and you keep it, and you keep it well." I don't see that people consider a housing project as their place or their home anymore. It's just a place to sleep, a place to eat. Certainly, there is no pride of ownership. I think they're trying to correct that with these various tenant organizations. The more they get people to become involved and invested in what is happening in that particular community, the better the community will be. Until that happens, you're not going to have the return of housing to what it used to be.

You cannot put that high degree of poverty in one area and expect the community to flourish and become something worthwhile. It's not going to happen. We have some unrealistic ideas about what constitutes a poverty level in the United States. Today, the *Sun-Times* had an article talking about the level of poverty here in the state of Illinois. They said $12,000 was the poverty line. Twelve thousand dollars a year for a family of four. That's ridiculous! They need to raise the amount of money you can have and still live in those housing projects. Because even a family with $20,000 can't afford to go out and buy a home. But they also need to change what constitutes a decent rental payment for Housing Authority apartments. Because when you start charging people seven and eight hundred dollars for a housing project, then the families with any money at all are going to move on. I mean, why live in a housing project when you can find something else for six and seven and eight hundred dollars? If you want to develop a strong housing development, you want to keep those families there. If everybody is barely making it, then you're going to continue to have the problems you have now.

ANANIAS SAMUEL, JR.

Ananias Samuel, an only child, moved with his mother and father into Ida B. Wells in the spring of 1941, when he was three years old. His parents divorced when he was six. "The only input that came into my house was that which my mother brought in," Samuel says. "So I learned the values from her that she wanted me to carry through life." He left Wells in 1955 after graduating from Wendell Phillips High School. He now sells steel products for a Chicago firm.

I've been working since I was fourteen. I worked over at the Fair Store on State and Adams, and from there I went into the military. After three years, I came back to Chicago and started working, wherever I could find work. Went back to the Fair Store, and then I left and drove for the CTA. I became a precinct captain, 6th Precinct, 14th Precinct, Sixth Ward; I worked for the Bureau of Forestry; sold insurance; drove a taxicab; worked at the steel mills. Oh, God, I did a myriad of jobs. It was all interesting. I'd work six, eight months to a year, sometimes longer. Off and on. Of course the steel mill was in and out. You would work for a certain period; they would lay you off. And when they lay you off, you can't just draw compensation. You could, but I wasn't of that ilk, so I went out and got a job. I went back to selling insurance. I worked part-time as a bartender for twenty-three years, at the Brown Derby Lounge at 51st and Indiana. It was kicking. Yes, I still enjoy it.

Well, how many jobs did I say I had? About five hundred? My two sons, they've never known me not to work. I've done jobs where people said I have to have degrees as long as this block here. But I hold a public library card. I will always have a public library card. Anything that you want to learn, anything that you want to do, in life, you can go to the public library, and if you want to commit yourself, you can learn more about it reading a book than anywhere else.

My boys were born in the public library. When they got out of school, the bus would let them off at the public library, and that's where they would stay until I got off of work to pick them up. They got their homework done, they did their research. You get bored, read a book! My sons both graduated from the University of Illinois. One is in insurance and the other is an accountant.

Well, in 1941 Black America was still in the Depression. They said the Depression was over in the 1930s. No, not for Black America. So, in Ida B. Wells, we had a life that most people thought was rich. To move into Ida B. Wells, you were wealthy. You had hot *and* cold running water. You had heat. We had the first Laundromat. It was a great life, and because of segregation, there were no outside influences that came in. This is pretelevision, of course. So the only thing we could listen to, when we were allowed to, was the radio. We were creative, in a sense. By listening to radio, we envisioned what we heard, and we carried that type of creative imagination into our world. If we wanted something, we made it. Because no one had money to buy anything. If you wanted a scooter, you'd find an old roller skate and a two by four; you got some nails; you got a brick; you beat it out and straightened it out; you went up to the gas station; you got some grease and oil; you put a pop bottle top on the top; and you put a milk carton on the back. Whoosh! You're off and gone! Creative! Whatever toy we wanted, we made.

My first three years in school, I went to St. Elizabeth. So Sister Mary Whatever, she beat the heck out of you. I mean—Ooof! You had their knuckles in the back of your hands, it was a form of discipline, but you survived.

It hurt then, but you forget about the pain. The pain goes away, but the memory and what she was directing you to do stuck with you. It wasn't negative—it was positive, because it was a matter of holding your head up, speaking from the diaphragm, looking a person in the eye. "Don't hold your head down," they would teach us. You know, that's where it came from.

I've been involved in the church from the time I can remember. I've been on every board, I was in choir, I taught Sunday school, I was a Bible scholar. All of us all sang together through the Metropolitan Boys Glee Club. All of us sang in the choir, and it was a choir of young men to keep us out of trouble.

Even in the most primitive tribes, a form of segregation takes place in every young man's life. We call them "gangs" today. I guess you could call them "gangs" back then. Well, we were a part of that society, but we sang, we did something constructive. I think being a part of something or of a group is very important. Being a part of anything, like being a part of that backyard [in Ida B. Wells], it still clings to us. All of us want to be a part of something.

I'll say 95 percent of the people that moved into Ida B. Wells in the spring of 1941 had roots in the South. Very strong ties, which meant that nine times out of ten religion played a very important role in their lives. The mind-set of the people was entirely different. Again, that village was there, and we were segregated, so you had to learn from within. And there was someone pushing you out. Today, there's so many outside influences coming in, that as a kid, it's tough.

Now, remember, I was being raised by a single mother. During the summer months, she did not want me to be home all day by myself, so she would send me to my grandmother's in Arkansas. June, July, and August, you know, I'm out of here! En route there, starting at Illinois Central Station, there was a colored section and a white section. When you got on the train, there was a colored car and a white car. When you got to Memphis, the colored bathroom and the white bathroom, all the way through. I experienced that for fifteen years. It became a part of life. It was segregated, we knew it was segregated, and there was nothing we could do about it as kids. It's something you just dealt with.

Today, you can live anywhere. And everyone should be able to live anywhere—everyone. Now, I know some guys say, "I would rather be with blacks." And there are people that are moving to Idaho and northern Montana that say, "I only want to live with whites." I don't want the Aryan Nation. Because of the complexity of the world today, we're going to have to intermix, interrace, inter-everything. If everyone closed their eyes, all things would be perfect. Because we could not distinguish who's black, who's white, who's got a big nose, who's got a little nose. We would just accept someone's helping hand or warm voice or warm embrace or nourishment, or whatever it is, and say, "Thank you."

It is difficult to return to the projects today because the CHA tenant selection and the media have put so much stigma on them that going back into the "projects" now is demoralizing. Then it did not have a stigma. You would kill to get into the projects, as we called it. But now, a kid would feel like, Wow, I ain't going to make it. I'm living in the projects, this is as far as I can go.

When I was in the military, I was with the 61st Military Police Security Escort, over in Europe, and I had extensive training doing quite a few things. I came back and I was working for CTA, and I tell you why I quit CTA. The CTA was starting up their own police. Well, I've got all the training. I've got documents and I've got letters and I can show you all kinds of things. Pooh! I should have been a cinch in the job. Six-one, 185 pounds [slaps body], hard as a rock. I applied for the job. It came down to me and a white guy, forty-seven years old. Why did he get the job? He had been in the union longer than I had. He had been in the union. Now, who was qualified? I was. Who got the job? He did.

They told me, "Oh, well, you know, Mr. Samuel, he's been in the union longer than you."

I said, "I thought you were looking for someone who's qualified to do the job."

"We are, but . . ."

Knowing what I know about management, now, I believe the most qualified person should get the job. I've worked in human resources, my wife's in human resources, she's Vice President of Human Resources for CNA Insurance. In America we've discriminated for long, so long, that it's become a part of us. We hire friends, we hire people who look like somebody we're going to like, we hire all different ways. But when it comes down to someone who can really do the job, there are times that the person that's doing the hiring is not qualified to make that selection. And so he's making his selection based on whatever prejudice or thoughts were put into his head.

At the Million Man March you had a million people coming together, a million black men. Now, in order to really grasp what this means: during our unwanted migration here, 527 years ago, the first thing they did to keep us from being strong, the first thing they did, was to separate us. We could not communicate. As long as you can't communicate, you can't cause no problems. The second thing they did is they made a law. If you taught a black how to write or read, they would kill you. Because they realized black men together, learning how to write and read, knowing the laws, and speaking together, can cause problems. So here you are, five hundred years later. We said, "Black men, unite." Now, anyone that calls himself a man went. And you stood there. Not knowing why you went, or what you were going to see or feel when you got there. But you knew you had to be there.

We got there at 5:30 in the morning. We were standing there just as the sun was coming over the Capitol building. Everyone faced east. And you heard the words "God is great." And at 8:30 in the morning, you had at least four hundred thousand people standing there, in silence. Not the Nation of Islam, not Catholicism, not all the other religions. I don't care whatever—Christians, Jews, people of all religions turned to the east and in unison, stood there and felt something.

I mean, there was harmony. There was no words spoken, but it was harmony. There were no beer bottles on the ground. There was no whiskey bottles, no reefer being smoked. And when we left, the park was as clean as if we just never were there! That silent movement, and no one was saying a word. There was no "Kill whitey." You didn't hear any of that. It was positive, spiritual.

If you bumped against someone, you'd say, "Oh, excuse me." They'd say, "No problem, brother." Remember the word "brother." I have not seen you in five hundred years. [Laughs] So we embrace, we hug, and the tears are flowing. You had to be there. And every time that you hear a story, you will hear one million different stories. Because one million messengers left it. Not just one. It took five hundred years for us to get back together, as one, again. When a million black men get together, oh, my God, call out the Army, because, if you see four of 'em on the corner together, there's going to be a riot! Well, we are paranoid against each other, too. That's because we have not been able to communicate with each other in five hundred years. But we'd say, "Why are we afraid of each other?" And we just embraced. And that was it! No other words need to be said! Because we all felt it.

VONSELL ASHFORD

Vonsell Ashford, a former teacher in the Chicago Public Schools, lives in Hyde Park, an integrated neighborhood on the South Side that is home to the University of Chicago. She formerly lived on the eighth floor of a mid-rise building in the Harold Ickes Homes on the near South Side.

I moved into Ickes in 1956. I believe it was April. I thought I was moving to paradise. The building was new, and they had a beautiful playground for the children. You couldn't ask for a better location, and the place was just marvelous. I had three bedrooms, a nice storage area, and a linen closet. I was twenty-three years old, I had three children, and I was expecting the fourth. I was a real young parent, I was awfully young. But there were some in Ickes that were a little older that had children. And I had wonderful neighbors.

I didn't finish high school, so I worked at different types of factory jobs and things. Well, one day I broke a finger and a thumb, and I said, "Lord, no more broken bones." I went to the back window at Ickes where I lived, and they were tearing up the ground. They were getting ready to build a day care center. I went down to a CHA office, and I said, "I would like to have a job there. What are the qualifications?" Well, they told me I had to have at least a high school education to get the lowest position. They said, "Why don't you get a G.E.D.?" So I got a G.E.D. and I got hired. A little later, the National College of Education came in. They said we could get grants. I said, "Get grants?" I did not think grants would help me. But I filled out my papers for the grant and I got it. So I started going to school, and kept on going till I got a bachelor's degree in early childhood education. I finished in 1978. I was promoted from a child-care aide to an assistant teacher, and then to a teacher.

I lived in Ickes for twenty-three years, in the same apartment. Well, things have so greatly changed, but I want to take you back. Sometimes you have to find what's wrong now by going back. There was accountability when we moved in. There were approximately eight apartments per floor—each person on the floor had to mop and wax the hallway. If your children played on that grass, you'd have a call, and you'd get fined five dollars. Once a year we had an inspection to see if the apartments were kept up: the knobs on the doors, the doorstops still there, and the handles on the refrigerator.

In public housing, the tenants have to be screened. You have to know what's going on. When we applied, they took our name, and then we went over to the office. That's what really stuck in my mind: they wanted a marriage license. They said, "You have to be married." Not just say you're married, but you had to bring your husband with you. We had to be properly married. We were young people, and we were looking for decency.

We took pride in Ickes. If I caught my kids stepping on the grass, I whipped their little behinds. You know, "You've got all this playground. You don't get on the fence, you don't climb on trees. I'm not going to be called down to the office. I don't have five dollars for your misbehavior." Five dollars at that time was nice money. When the children got home from school, they didn't play on the elevator. For people who say you can't have families in elevator buildings, I would say, "You're nuts!" I lived there, how can you tell me people cannot live in elevator buildings? If high-rises are the problem, then what is the problem over there today in Ida B. Wells, where they don't have the elevators? If you choose the right kind of people, you are not going to have problems. If you choose a single mother with no husband, who has no concept of how to handle children and no concept of discipline, then you're going to have problems. You're going to have problems if you don't have accountability.

We got through the 1950s pretty good, then slowly through the 1960s things got worse. What really started destroying things is when the family structure broke down. But the most important thing, I think, really, is the kind of people they were putting in. The CHA wasn't being as careful, and then they switched the criterion for how you pay your rent. Across the hall from you, they paid forty or fifty dollars for the same apartment that you paid five hundred for. A lot of the working people said, "Well, I have to pay this much more, I'm going to move out." And they left. So what was left? The welfare recipients. The young girls who have their babies and get the apartment.

It's not that I didn't like the apartment, I loved my apartment. And some people had gorgeous apartments. The outside might be poor, but you walk into some of those people's homes, I'm telling you, so lavishly furnished, and spotlessly clean. I mean, they just knew how to decorate an apartment. But then you go across the hall, and this person doesn't have a door on the bathroom, the oven door is pulled off, and the sink is broken. Lord knows how. And you'd be saying, "What in the world . . ." Once the family structure broke down, then everything else started crumbling.

JOE THOMPSON

Dr. Joe Thompson grew up in Dearborn Homes and in 1973 graduated from Loyola University Law School. He practiced law for several years with a large Loop law firm, but, unfulfilled by the legal profession, he left to go to medical school. Today, Thompson splits his time between working as an emergency room doctor at Cook County Hospital and practicing law.

Some years ago—about 1984 or 1985—I came back and I just walked through Dearborn Homes. It was eleven-thirty, twelve at night, and I went up to the apartment that I had lived in. The elevators were broken, so I walked up the stairs to see what it's like today. It's horrible, it's terrible. I couldn't imagine anybody living there.

When we moved there in 1950, the building was new. It was as good as any high-rise you would find middle-income individuals living at. The down side of that is as we got older, because there was an elevator, a lot of the children used to use it as a playground. In 1950, I don't remember a single undesirable family. I'd say 60 percent of the families had both parents, and the fathers worked. Even up until 1967, Dearborn was still a decent place to bring up children. But as I grew older, the makeup of the building began to change. You had more and more poor families, with single mothers on welfare.

I believe that you have to have some mix of incomes in public housing. It's very difficult to have individuals exclusively of a lower welfare level living in high-rise housing. To balance out the families with incomes of under $9,000 per year, you have to have families with incomes of up to, say $30,000 per year, kind of moderate-income working families. You cannot put poor people in an area with that much density without giving them hope that they're going to rise above it. They're going to stagnate.

Public housing should never be a permanent place for people to live. If you take individuals, and you say, OK, we'll give you public housing, we'll give you a welfare check, but you've got no education, no hope of getting a job, no hope of moving up, it's like being in quicksand.

I have friends who call Robert Taylor Homes the Soweto of Chicago. It breeds hopelessness. The young kids, they look for an alternative, and too often the alternative is to join a gang and sell crack. We didn't have crack in 1950. Sure, we knew certain people in the neighborhood that used heroin. But we were afraid of drugs in my community. Kids today, they're not afraid of drugs. They think, well, let me use this, it'll make me feel better, and it'll take me away from the misery I see in the projects.

Times were different when I was growing up. My mother and father forced me to attend St. James Grammar School, which is a Catholic school. I think they did so for the discipline I would get, and they felt I would get an overall good education. I think they were correct. The majority of my friends went to Williams public school, and thereafter either to Phillips or Dunbar. My mother forced me to go to De LaSalle, a Catholic high school. So I think they had a lot more insight than I did into what would be best for me. And it's turned out better for me, no doubt about it.

I attended Loyola University, graduating in 1970, and graduated from Loyola Law School in 1973. I practiced with a large firm here in the city for a couple of years, then went back to medical school. Growing up, I always tried to fulfill whatever my mother wanted me to do, and my mother had always wanted me to become a doctor. I studied at Rush Presbyterian Medical School and did a residency in diagnostic radiology. I went to California for a while to practice. I decided I wanted to come back to Chicago, to County Hospital, and did two years in the family practice residency program. I ended up becoming an emergency room physician. I work a couple of nights a week along with my daily law practice.

I believe that much of my success has been due to the general pressures of affirmative action, but I don't think the playing field has been leveled. I believe that corporate America, for the most part, still has a glass ceiling. And whenever you get a minority or a person who is hyperpigmented, they're looked at differently. Certainly many, many minorities are able to overcome this, mostly by their own tenacity. It's a terrible mistake to assume that America is an equal society when it comes to granting its privileges, and I believe the reasons for trying to get rid of affirmative action have an economic basis. With the loss of industrial jobs in our country, there are fewer and fewer opportunities for everyone, and the majority, of course, does not want to see the minorities having those limited positions.

HORTENSE IRWIN BRIGHT

Hortense Irwin Bright is a retired principal of the Lucy Flower High School. "My mother and three sisters moved into Altgeld Gardens in the mid-1940s."

My parents were separated. My father was in France with the U.S. Army. He did not return to the family. We had come up from Vicksburg, Mississippi, and were living at the back of an old mattress factory when Mother found Altgeld Gardens: three bedrooms, a living room, and a kitchen with an upstairs-downstairs layout. For us it was palatial—compared to our shelter on 31st Street. Of course for my mom, who had declared her independence by moving out of the family home in Vicksburg, it meant freedom to be on her own with her kids. She was working at Western Electric on the West Side. I was nine years old at the time.

At Altgeld, there was always something doing. There was the Children's Building: Tuesday and Friday were skating nights, and Saturday night was for dances. Every four blocks there was a recreation room, where we could also have dances. We had social clubs and of course we had chaperones. We had great baseball games. We were fanatic fans.

I stayed at Altgeld until I was sixteen, when I graduated from Carver High. Easily some of the best years of my life were at Altgeld Gardens. The friends I established there and my high school years were extremely happy. I can't think of a better time. But there was a vast difference between elementary and high school. Elementary school was lackluster—however, one bright spot was Ms. Margaret Goss Burroughs, who was my fifth- and seventh-grade teacher. Had it not been for her and for my mother, who was a well-read lady, I might not have been exposed to such a range of cultural and educational experiences.

In high school, the strongest and most memorable teachers were Mr. Rudd, our music and chorus teacher; Mrs. Kingslow, our history and English instructor; Mr. Hines, our math teacher; Mrs. Walters, our biology teacher; and Ms. Hunter, who taught English and speech. During my junior year we had a new chemistry teacher, a young German girl, Ms. Froelich. I remember the fellows thought they could walk all over her because she was so young, but she just shone. She had an air about her, and the boys soon learned she was a force to be reckoned with. We all loved her. There were others who were shining lights in my high school career. Many of them took a personal interest in us; they demanded excellence and made us feel that we were accomplishing something.

These teachers brought a lot into our lives—plays, classical music, museums. In fact, there was a radio program I used to listen to on Saturday mornings, the *Young People's Philharmonic.* We used to do our housework to it. We had great fun. My brother-in-law used to hum almost all of the classical tunes. So that stimulated our interest, too. If I had to guess the reason for the excellence at Carver, it was the dedication of some of the staff, which can make all the difference in the world. In addition to all the frills and educational resources, you need outstanding teachers to make the difference in student performance and achievement.

My mother used to tease me because when I was twelve, which was kind of old to be asking a dumb question like this, I asked her, "Are we rich?" I kind of felt we were, I had a sense of richness. I certainly had no feeling of deprivation. When a child tells me, "I'm poor, I live in a project," that doesn't cut it with me. I know he can make it. I tell the teachers, "If you think the kid can't do it, then he isn't even going to try. And more importantly, you won't attempt to teach the child in such a way as to help him achieve his absolute best!"

Chapter 6

The Building of Character: Religion, Sports, and Music

Beyond education, other important civic institutions had significant influences on the lives of public housing's early tenants. Good housing alone did not create the kind of successful communities managed by the CHA at Altgeld Gardens or Ida B. Wells in the 1940s and 1950s. Churches, recreational clubs, parks with sports opportunities, and cultural outlets all contributed to public housing's success in its early years.

Likewise, religion and the church provided a powerful guiding force that steered the young away from the lures of the street and toward positive community activities. Early CHA residents consistently mention church and faith as essential elements of their upbringing and success. A number of the tenants went into the seminary to become ministers and priests, and for many who became teachers, lawyers, and doctors, religion played a significant role in their lives. In a considerable number of cases, their children or nephews went into church-related work.

According to the interviews of several respondents in this chapter, Addie and Claude Wyatt's church-based programs were responsible for dramatically turning around their lives. Similarly, Bob and Bea Fairfax at Altgeld Gardens channeled their religious beliefs into community-based organizations such as labor unions, monthly newspapers, and the Boy Scouts to improve the life of tenants.

Another indication of the meaning of religious life to these tenants was their participation in the Million Man March of 1995. Most described the event as a powerful display of community and religion, with as much emphasis on togetherness as on faith.

For many, organized sports teams provided a forum for growth and opportunity. The CHA encouraged recreational baseball and basketball leagues as part of its community-building mission. Like ministers and priests, coaches provided crucial leadership and guidance to residents at an early age. Many of the tenants interviewed here were able to attend college and earn degrees because of the scholarships they received for their excellence in sports, including Eugene Farmer, Wilson Frost, Ananias Samuel, Arnold Weddington, and Richard Townsell. Finally, Barbara Jones won two Olympic gold medals in track and field, a remarkable achievement that she attributes primarily to her coach, Ms. Alyce Holden [then Alyce Holmes], a director at Ida B. Wells's Madden Park.

Like sports, music and the arts offered structured learning while fostering self-expression, providing upward mobility for some. Jazz pianist Ramsey Lewis is included here, and prominent soul artist (later Cook County Commissioner) Jerry "The Iceman" Butler is also profiled.

The sum of these activities and faiths supported a remarkable community in public housing's early years. Catalytic activities nurtured in public housing residents self-esteem, respect, discipline, and accomplishment—all values that served these interviewees well later in life.

CLAUDE AND ADDIE WYATT

Addie Wyatt and her husband, Claude, were leaders of a youth choral group. They are both reverends, and for the last forty-four years have been ministers at Vernon Park Church of God in Chicago. Addie is also a longtime leader and organizer for the United Packinghouse Workers. They lived for ten years at Altgeld Gardens, on the city's far South Side, during the mid-1940s and early 1950s.

Addie: The children and families at Altgeld were so isolated because transportation was very poor. Very few had automobiles, so when you got out there, you were out there. As a result, young people were getting into different things that we didn't like. Being clergy, we wanted to help. We were both involved in the musical field, so we started a youth choir called the Wyatt Choral Ensemble, which became known all over the city.

We would have all the children come into our living room. We'd take the living room furniture and move it into the kitchen, and the young people would sit all over the floor, up the stairs, and in the courtyard—and we would sing together. They would come over, sometimes every day. They'd come over at night—sometimes until midnight. Those who were in trouble, you know, they would come over and we would pray with them and talk with them. We would take anybody in—didn't care who you were—but you had to change.

There was one young man lying on the sidewalk one day, cursing God—drunk, lit up—and we talked to him and began working with him, as we did with the others. He had dropped out of grammar school, and he didn't know which way to go. Well, he started going back to school—correspondence school—in our living room. Twenty years later he got his Ph.D. He married a young woman from one of our congregations who also got her Ph.D.

Claude: His story is beautiful. That was Alvin Lewis, Dr. Alvin Lewis, formerly executive director of our own Vernon Park Church of God. His story is beautiful. And then there's Dr. Everett Jackson. We found him in a hallway on Thanksgiving morning. He didn't have a place to stay, and he came over to talk with me and that's when I began to work with him. He received several degrees and a Doctor of Divinity. Now he's teaching at the seminary at North Park College. He came up out of Altgeld Gardens.

The Wyatt Choral Ensemble had a conduct code and a dress code. When kids went to school and got into trouble with the principal, they would call us, because to be in the ensemble you had to be a respectable person. We would take anybody and we didn't care who you were.

Claude: Now, one day when we had our little group rehearsing in the community center, Miss Elizabeth Wood and some of the people from the Housing Authority came out and saw us. When she heard the choir singing, she said, "This is great." We were an asset to Altgeld Gardens, and she recognized that. So Miss Wood honored us. We loved Elizabeth Wood! She made us feel as though we were really doing something. She would invite us downtown to bring the choral group and give us trophies. This made the young people feel like they were somebody.

Claude: Well, Altgeld really was sort of choice. It was the baby doll of all the projects, from my point of view. They were constantly working, repairing, they kept the streets up. It was a real showplace. We had five rooms in our house—three bedrooms, living room, kitchen, and the utility room. Most important, we didn't have to go into a big building. I was so excited when I first moved in there. I would put my key in the front door, go out through the back, come around to the front door again, and walk in and go through—again. I couldn't believe it.

Addie: Child care was an everyday crisis for us until they opened up the nurseries and the child-care services out there. When we first moved in, the government was running around trying to get women to come into the war industry, so they provided child care. That gave us a new lease on life. Child care at the community center did so much for our children. Before that, they went from one neighbor's house and one friend's house to another. Every morning, you had to find somebody to keep the child. You'd leave screaming children and never know if the kid got his lunch.

Of course, when we lived there, this was the greatest community we had seen and we were just delighted. People on our block were striving to improve themselves. I don't know how many were striving to get out of there, because we weren't. We had just found this heavenly place. We loved it and wanted to stay.

See, Altgeld changed. At first, Altgeld was not just low-income families. They required you to work in a defense plant. That was the only way you could get in there. So there were people who had earning power. But after the war, it changed over to low-income. People stayed until most became disqualified for having too much income. My preference always has been to not concentrate too many people in the same economic category together.

Claude: The only reason we moved from Altgeld Gardens is that Addie got a job as an organizer with the Packinghouse Union, and we were making more money.

Addie: Let me tell you. We have since owned two lovely homes, but we never had the pride in either one of them that we had in Altgeld Gardens. In Altgeld we had a home to live in. It was wonderful.

Claude: One of the tragic things about Altgeld was that we got very little help from Roseland Community Hospital. [Roseland is the neighborhood, then all-white, to the west of Altgeld.] Unless it was really, really serious, they didn't take you in.

Addie: For instance, when our niece, Diane, was born, my sister-in-law was in labor and we ran over to try to get her to the hospital. We had planned to go all the way from Altgeld to the Cook County Hospital [on the near West Side]. But she kept saying, "It's here, it's here." I said, "Not yet, not yet, just hold on till we get there." And then I took a peek and saw this little beautiful head and I said, "Oh, my God."

So we had no choice but to go to Roseland Hospital. It was December 31, and so cold. They took her in there and cut the cord and then pushed her out in the hall without adequate clothing. This mother was out there shivering. They left her out there until the patrolmen changed shifts and could then take us over to County Hospital. We put our coats on top of her and went with her all the way to County Hospital.

Claude: Now, there was a man who lived across the street from me, just a little bit older, and he was very ill. His wife didn't have any way to get him to County Hospital, and she couldn't take him to Roseland. They would not take him in—they'd just give him some medicine and send him back home.

So every week I would have to drive from Altgeld Gardens all the way to Cook County Hospital and wait and then bring them back. I did that for a whole year. That Christmas, Addie and I didn't know what we were going to do because we didn't have any money. A lady knocked on our door and walked in and said, "Mr. Wyatt, I want to thank you for helping my husband and me. You're just so wonderful, here's an envelope." I opened it up and inside it was about fifty dollars. That was a lot of money then. Oh, my goodness, that was our Christmas.

Claude: We always asked the question, "Why did they bring us way all the way out here [to Altgeld]?" But we never really thought at the time in terms of being discriminated against. Because it was all black folks. We weren't even sensitive to that. Just give me decent housing, give me decent health, give me a decent job, and give a good education for my kids and don't worry about it. We were only sensitive to having a comfortable place to live, you know. Whereas today we are a little wiser.

ALVIN LEWIS

Alvin Lewis was a down-and-outer and living in Altgeld Gardens when he met Claude and Addie Wyatt at age fifteen. He was "saved" by the Wyatts, who helped him turn his life around. Twelve years later he received a Ph.D. from Kansas State University and became a minister of a large congregation in Kansas. He was a minister at the Vernon Park Church of God in Chicago from 1992 to 1999, and today he preaches in Jackson, Mississippi.

I moved to Altgeld in January 1951, when I was around sixteen years old, from the West Side of Chicago. At that time there were ten children in my family; I was number four. Altgeld was certainly a step up, because the house that we had lived in had only two bedrooms. We were sleeping in the kitchen, in the living room—it was close quarters. When we moved in, we thought we had moved to the North Side, so to speak. Altgeld had hot water, showers, a nice bathroom. We only had to share two in a room. It had an upstairs and a downstairs. In those days, the CHA had some pretty strict requirements in terms of what your kids did, how you kept your yard, how clean you kept the house. Although there were ten children living in our house, you couldn't tell, because my dad insisted we keep a clean house.

My dad was very strict when it came to a clean house. He periodically did labor, but we also grew up on welfare. He had heart trouble, so by and large he was incapacitated. When he could work, he would work. Since I was nine years old, I've always worked, with one exception, and I've never depended upon my family. In those days you could get scrap metal, rags, paper—those are the little hustles we had on the side.

Just before we moved to Altgeld, I ended up in Montifiore [a reform school], basically because of truancy and rebellion. I just had no desire to go to school. In those days I was a big kid; when I reached six feet, the school authorities didn't bother me. I left Montifiore and started running around with a friend, a guy named Roosevelt Wilson. Roosevelt made a change in his life and became clean-cut, so I asked him what had happened and he said he had been "saved." That was the term he used. He told me, "I found some good people that helped me out and took me in." So Roosevelt took me to a prayer meeting. He told me it was a party—I will never forget that. That's when my life was changed, in July 1953. That's when I met the Wyatts.

That conversion experience was the keystone experience of my life. Addie Wyatt had a community choir, and she allowed us to get in. That was risky, because we grew up your typical thugs, you know. I was from the West Side, and West Side people always get a bad rap. But from the choir I went back to school, and on to college and graduate school and seminary and all that. In 1953, that's when I had my mind together for the first time, I knew what I wanted to do. I felt a call to the ministry, but I didn't take it lightly. I felt as a minister, I needed to prepare, and that was one of my motivating factors. I've always been insatiably curious about everything—I think I inherited that from my mother. My mother has always been a real inspiration.

I finished up high school and enrolled in Northern Baptist Theological College in 1959. I got married that year—met my wife at a youth convention in Gary. We became friends, and about a year later we got married. We've been together thirty-seven years. When we first got married, we moved to 310 West 73rd Street and stayed there until 1960, when we moved into Princeton Park [a private, semi-subsidized housing development on the South Side]. In those days, they were very strict at Princeton Park. They would only allow a certain class of people to get in there. You had to have an income; I don't know of any welfare families that lived in Princeton Park. Since then, I've always moved into communities where you have blacks and whites. It's not because I believe black communities are inferior. I was always a mobile person, and I thought it would be easier to sell a house if it was attractive to both blacks and whites.

I do not believe that affirmative action gives special privilege to a particular group simply because of their color. I think we give special considerations to people because of their history, because, by and large, the privileged people of our society have been white. They are the ones who have had the privileges and the opportunities for the better jobs. The programs set in place under Lyndon Johnson are just as valid today as when they were instituted. People like myself would not have had the opportunity to attend certain schools and take advantage of certain programs unless it had been made possible through the government. We have to look at who really controls the resources and who is in charge of the political system. It is still slanted—the power base is not in the hands of blacks.

It's not reverse discrimination when you're only talking about letting a few black people in the room. If I'm going to have a hundred people in the room and I let five blacks in, to me that is not taking anything from white people, because you've still got ninety-five whites in that room. Without some kind of affirmative action, a lot of our people would still be on the outside looking in.

EVERETT JACKSON

Everett Jackson moved to Altgeld Gardens with his mother in 1944. He is now a professor at North Park Theological Seminary in Chicago, though he followed a rather unorthodox path in getting there. A self-described "underachiever" in high school, Jackson dropped out in his senior year and joined the Army. After serving for three years, Jackson returned to Chicago in 1956. "I had been discharged with mustering-out pay," he remembers. "I had several thousand dollars, and so I got back into the drug scene, I got back into the scene of heavy drinking. I was what was known in those days as a kind of pool hustler." Only later did he begin college, after he, too, was "saved" by Claude and Addie Wyatt.

We were one of the first families to move into Altgeld. It was quite a shift from what I had known. I spent the very early part of my life on the West Side of Chicago after my mother and I moved from Philadelphia, where I was born. Then we moved to the near South Side. My mother worked for one of the plants close to Altgeld Gardens. And so when the housing opened up at Altgeld, there were many people who worked in that vicinity who chose to move in. There was a distinct difference from what we see in public housing today. At that time, people were very much open to the idea of looking out for each other's children. When I was in the neighborhood, everybody knew each other.

Altgeld Gardens in those days was, to some extent, like the neighborhood that I live in now, Wilmette [a wealthy and predominantly white North Shore suburb]. At that time, we sort of thought of Altgeld Gardens as being a suburban area. It was very clean, everybody took care of their properties, people were very cognizant of being neighborly. Of course, those apartments were not what we typically think of in terms of housing projects.

Well, I dropped out of high school, and shortly after, I went into the military. I stayed in for three years and developed some attitudes that were sort of hostile. I got into drugs and alcohol, and developed a propensity to be hostile toward authority. I decided that I wasn't going to take any pushing around, particularly from white folks. I was court-martialed three times, but I guess the stockade finally did me some good, because by the time I was discharged, I had become a disciplined soldier.

Unfortunately, when I came out, the discipline I had learned in the military declined for a bit. I got back into the drug scene. I began to frequent the pool rooms and make money and sometimes lose a lot of money. For about a year I bummed around. I was homeless, really, sleeping in automobiles, sleeping in hallways, riding the streetcar all night. I didn't have the money to go home and pay rent.

There was a local minister who used to come around the pool room. He'd come around the dice games and try to talk to me. I had never seen a minister who would come around pool rooms and dice games or taverns to seek someone out. I was rather impressed by him—his name was Claude Wyatt.

On Thanksgiving Day I went to his home, and he fed me. He was a fantastic man, very generous, with a large heart. He took me in. That evening we went to what was known in those days as a "cottage meeting." A cottage meeting is a prayer meeting, but it moves from home to home rather than being in a church. That evening I decided that I would try this religion that he had told me about. After that, he introduced me to his church, and I became a member. They bought clothes for me, they treated me like the prodigal son. They set me up in the home of one of the church families, and I lived there until I was able to get on my feet.

He got me a job where he worked, at a packinghouse company, then I got a job at Lake Meadows [a private apartment complex] on the near South Side, doing menial work. Then I enrolled in Wilson Junior College, and after a year, I transferred to Roosevelt University to get my bachelor's degree. And I discovered that I was beginning to enjoy life. I got my first master's degree at Northern Illinois University in DeKalb, in secondary and professional education, and they offered me a teaching assistantship. So, after twenty years, I was still in school getting additional degrees. Some of my friends began to say to me, "Man, you're becoming a professional student." And perhaps I was, but I was enjoying learning.

During this time I became, I think, quite a successful minister. I had gone to Freeport, Illinois, which has about twenty-five thousand people. I built a new church, got the people in, got them stabilized. But I decided I wanted to go back and get some more education. I met a fellow who was a professor at Garrett Theological Seminary up in Evanston. I caught his eye, and he tried to persuade me to leave DeKalb and come to Garrett on a full scholarship, free ride. A year later, I took him up on his offer.

If I had not gotten the solid foundation of affirmation and support—the support that my mother gave me by having a firm hand and letting me know that it was important to get a good education—then perhaps I'd never have had the limited success that I've had. I had the discipline instilled by my mother and through the military. And in order to develop discipline, people have to have some sense of self-esteem, of worthiness, of value.

People should make individual choices as to whether or not they live in integrated or all-black neighborhoods. I don't think anyone should try to dictate where people live. I think part of the question is whether blacks who become successful should move out into other areas. And I say, if other people have done it, why shouldn't African Americans do it?

I'm very careful about the use of the term "integrated living." I choose not to use the term "integrated," but "desegregated." Because the notion of integration carries with it not only access but also acceptance and social intercourse—things that don't necessarily happen, even when African Americans are living in desegregated neighborhoods. When I was growing up, there was a saying that was very popular, that went like this: "In the South white folks don't care how close you get as long as you don't get too big. But in the North they don't care how big you get as long as you don't get too close." As long as those two ways of thinking are in operation, you can't possibly have integrated living. Desegregated living is more accurate.

There certainly is a rationale for black people wanting to live together, and some of it is not so much on a conscious level. Some of it is what one of our African-American Congressmen refers to as "subterranean racism." There are certain subterranean feelings of inferiority, inadequacy, that remain in much of the black community. This has come about over three hundred years of racism and discrimination. And so if the larger community has developed feelings of supremacy, the opposite of that has taken place in much of the black community.

ROSCOE KING

A member of the Wyatt Choral Ensemble, Roscoe King lived in Altgeld Gardens from 1945 until going into the Army in 1952. For thirty-five years, he has worked for the city of Chicago as a Sanitation Department truck driver. For several years he was chairman of the Friends of the Parks, a citywide, nonpartisan watchdog group that keeps an eye on the Chicago Park District.

Addie Wyatt's sister, Audrey, I was crazy about her. By going to see Audrey, that's how I met Claude and Addie Wyatt. They invited me to choir rehearsal. When I joined their chorus, the police were looking for me. They were arresting people, and I didn't have anyplace to go. I joined their chorus right in front of the police.

When I was a young fellow, I didn't have a good reputation, you know. I was gang-banging, reefer-selling, and all that. Claude was going to let me go, but Addie told those people who demanded that she throw me out or they'd remove their children, "Well, you'll just have to take the children out." She let me stay, and that changed my life. That's why I love her so.

In my peer group none of us used hard stuff, but we all drank wine, smoked marijuana. Our parents never knew we did these things. But then Addie Wyatt came into our lives, and she had us involved in church and good things that took all that other stuff away. Addie and Claude Wyatt were the biggest influence on young people that came out of Altgeld. I used to go to their house and sit there until twelve or one at night, and they would read the Bible to me, trying to straighten me out.

I remember Alvin Lewis. He was a grammar school dropout. We didn't socialize with Alvin. Right now, Alvin has a Ph.D. He and his wife go all over the country, teaching about husband-and-wife relationships. Here is a man that Addie and Claude Wyatt exposed to the church and turned around. He's just a history by himself. He came from a welfare family. He has a brother in the penitentiary. And now he's one of the greatest guys I know.

Out at Altgeld, the only thing you had were the people you knew right there. At the time, Roseland [a neighboring white area] didn't want Negroes. Once in Roseland, I went with a friend to get a bowl of chili, and the man gave it to us in a paper cup. He wouldn't give us chili in a bowl. I've never forgotten that. Those things have always stayed with me. The [Ninth Ward] alderman, Reginald DuBois, was a racist from his heart. He didn't want any more public housing. He said Negroes ought to move to Robbins, where they belonged. I remember going on a political picnic in the Ninth Ward, and they had a race riot out there at the picnic. They had to put us all on the bus, because the whites were drunk and they wanted to fight. My daddy never backed away from a fight. He thought the best thing to do was stay and fight. Those things happen.

One thing that came out of Altgeld was community pride. See, the project wasn't a ghetto. It was affordable housing—that's exactly what it was. When we lived in Altgeld, we had pride. There was a pride in yourself, and a pride in your neighborhood. We had block clubs—every block was organized. The CHA had a Block Beautiful contest.

When we lived in Altgeld, we never locked our back door. We didn't even think about breaking into people's homes. We went from house to house, we had teenage canteens, we had Boy Scouts, we had the chorus, we had a lot of fellows from all walks of life—just a whole lot of good people who came from all over Chicago. The first time I ever had a room of my own and a front yard and a backyard was at Altgeld. You had to take care of your lawn, and you had to maintain your house. It was not "Altgeld was a slum"—it was a good community.

I think at the time CHA was part of the family. The people on the Housing Board came to Altgeld—we knew them. Oscar Brown [Altgeld's manager] brought Miss America—Bess Myerson—to Altgeld. Paul Robeson came to Altgeld. And Miss Wood was very much a part of that. Miss Wood knew Addie, she would call Addie. They honored Addie one year and made her Woman of the Year.

We read about the cancer fright in Altgeld and how many people are afraid they'll die of cancer. Do you remember when they removed asbestos a couple of years ago? Every house in Altgeld was loaded with that garbage. I lived there for eight years and didn't know anything about it. The Sanitary District put that big sludge plant across the street from Altgeld, and that smell is still there. As far as I'm concerned, and I mean this from my heart, the people who live in Altgeld should be relocated, and the entire thing should be tested for toxic waste, and it should be removed.

I'll tell you how many have passed. The Dennis family: Heavy-Duty Dennis, Lola, Hatti, Sis Dennis. Four people in one family died of cancer, all under the age of fifty. Bob Fairfax, our scoutmaster—he died of cancer. John Wald died of cancer. Louis Garcia died of cancer. Mickey Cameron, Addie's brother, died of cancer. Her sister Edna died of cancer. Altgeld was the only community in the world that had several Congressmen whose wives died of cancer. You go down the list: Henry Black, Kevin Black—they died of cancer. They lived at Altgeld ten or twelve years. Charles Hudson, Helen

Hudson, Ralph Hudson—they lived there eight years—all died of cancer. Altgeld was built on wasteland. It's not housing's fault.

I've had a wonderful life. I've learned a lot. I've learned how to respect people. I hope that people have learned how to respect me. I've just been blessed. I had a good mom, a good dad, and Addie and Claude have really been a very big part of my life. They straightened me out. I've been very fortunate.

BILL "BUTTERBALL" CRANE

Bill Crane grew up in the Ida B. Wells Homes. There he developed a lifelong fascination with radio and electronics. A radio engineer and disc jockey for WVON, Crane was close friends with the late Leonard Chess, legendary owner of Chess Records, perhaps Chicago's most famous blues recording label. In honor of his friendship with Chess, who was Jewish, Crane wears a necklace with a large Star of David. "Leonard wasn't walking around on a spiritual trip," says Crane. "He lived it. He lived by the word. He never jived anybody. And that's what made me really admire him." He is now a supervising engineer at WGN in Chicago.

At Ida B. Wells, I built shortwave receivers and antennas, and I'd listen to stations from all over the world. I knew that with antennas, the higher they are and the further they are from surrounding objects, the better they'll receive. So I had to climb the roof. I was about twelve or thirteen when I got my ham license. I would climb out the third-floor window, stand on the ledge, jump up and grab the rain gutter, and then flip myself up on the roof! If I missed, I would have broken my neck. I mean, when I think about it, it was foolish!

Anyway, the assistant principal at Doolittle Elementary knew that I was messing with radios, so she went up in the attic at school and found test tubes and little science projects that the other kids weren't using, and she gave those to me. I got a little mortar and pestle, a little test-tube stand, and even a little burner that used some kind of solid-state fuel. I mean, she trusted me with these adult things. This was a white lady by the name of Mrs. Skleronsky. And this is why I never had any prejudice.

There was a teacher at Doolittle School, Miss Blanche Smith, who really helped me, too. She saw that I could do outstanding work. In fact, I skipped a couple grades in elementary school. Miss Smith was very nice. On Saturdays, I would go over and help her rake the yard or do whatever she wanted me to do. I enjoyed talking with her. She made sense, and she kind of picked my brain. [Laughs] She made me feel grown-up.

I came out of grammar school at age twelve and finished high school when I was sixteen, but I couldn't get a job anywhere. Hallicrafters Corporation made shortwave equipment, and they knew I was good at that, but they wouldn't hire me. So a guy showed me pictures of Navy electronics and talked me into going in the Navy. I waited till I was seventeen, and then I joined.

The Navy was quite rewarding. The Navy liked crack people. If you were good, you were *there*. I got sent to Norfolk, Virginia, to radioman's school, and since I knew Morse code, I aced that school. I scored so high they heard about me over at the Commander of Surface Force, Atlantic Fleet, where all the high brass and all the sharp radio operators worked. That's where they sent me to communicate with the fleet. I was just a little black boy, seventeen years old, sitting down with these older guys, twenty-five and thirty, and I could outdo them! The Navy was good to me. Every time I had the time and rank to go for another test, I went for it, and I got the stripe. In fact, I made First Class Petty Officer in less than four years. It generally takes people two enlistments to make that. Before I left the Navy I extended my time so I could go to Teletype repair school.

When I came out of the Navy, I worked for the Chicago police as a Teletype operator. But they put me on a midnight shift, so I found a job at RCA, working on the two-way radios for cabs and fire departments. Around 1964, when I was twenty-five, there was a radio station starting up out in Chicago Heights and they needed some engineers out there. I heard about it and was hired immediately because I knew transmitters.

So that started me in radio. I wired up studios, wired up the audio consoles, and I was the sign-on engineer there. One day the announcer came in drunk. He couldn't go on the air, so *I* went on the air. I played records and I clowned around. Well, they put me on the air full-time. After about a year, Leonard Chess heard me, and he says, "Hey, man, you want to make some money, why don't you come back from the country?" In fact, you know how Leonard cursed up a storm . . .

But before I took the job with Leonard, I went to WYNR in the city, and then some people in Detroit heard about me. They offered me the sky, so I went to Detroit. But in Detroit, the guy was asking me for kickback money, saying, "Now look, we've got to have some of your hustle." So I left Detroit, and called Leonard. I said, "Do you still want me?"

He says, "Yeah, you in trouble?"

I said, "No."

He says, "You need some money?"

I said, "No."

He says, "Well, bring your butt in here!" I called him on a Friday, and by Monday I was on the air!

He treated me like a son. In fact, I had jurisdiction over Marshall, his son. Marshall saw my motorcycle, and he had to have one. He got a motorcycle, and Leonard was scared to death about it. He says, "Look, you get that bike from Marshall and teach him how to ride it. I want you to check out that machine and make sure it's perfect. I don't want him dead!" And he cursed me up and down.

I respect Leonard so much that when our twins were born, I named them Leonard and Lynette. Well, I blew his mind. Leonard was just overwhelmed. He says, "Hey, bring your wife down here, I want to see her." So I brought her down. He says, "Look, I want to give you some money for these kids, and I want you to put this in the bank." He says, "But I don't trust this nigger, he might walk off and leave you!" [Laughs] That's the way he talked. And I took no offense. He was like, "Hey, you name these kids after me and I'm going to take care of them, and if you act the damn fool, I'm going to show you." That's the way he was.

Now, as for me and the spiritual trip. I woke up, and I started seeing things exactly the way Leonard was talking. And then I spoke with other Jewish people that I've met through the years, and it dawned on me, "Hey, these people accepted me as *Mishpochah*." They treated me as family, they kept harm and danger away from me, and it just blew my mind. All these other fools I dealt with, they talked one way and acted another. But these people went out of their way for me. And then I found some other friends that were Jewish, and they were also Christ believers. Now, this is called a Messianic Jew. So this is the group that I am with. There I was, a young black guy trying to make it, and normally a white guy would stab me in the back! The Jews never did!

I have three children, two girls and a boy. My oldest girl wouldn't go to college, even though I offered her the chance. She took ordinary jobs and is taking care of herself very well. The younger daughter, the twin, got her master's degree and then went off to Texas in an old jalopy that I wouldn't have driven to Gary. She is now a school principal. The other twin, Leonard, went into the Marine Corps, got an honorable discharge, and is now doing heavy construction jobs in Norfolk, Virginia. He is doing dangerous work, about as crazy as I was, but making very good money. I'm a senior engineer at WGN, where I've been for many years. We live in South Shore, where I've rigged up a minor radio station in my house. I'm still married to the same woman, and she has never worked other than taking care of the kids and the house. In my opinion, women need to be in the home and take care of the children. We wouldn't have half the garbage that we do today running around the streets. I'm just thankful that I have been able to take care of my family.

WALTER BLOCKER

Walter Blocker was the second black insurance salesman hired by Allstate, and now he runs his own agency. He moved into the Ida B. Wells Homes in 1941 with his mother, stepfather, and sister when he was seven years old. He moved out during his senior year in high school.

I was raised in the Apostolic Church of God, the Pentecostal church. I had no choice—had to be in church. My mother didn't send me—my mother took me. Let's put it this way, I was not happy in the church as a child. I'm the first college graduate in my family, and I was the first college graduate out of that church. The minister, he was a very charismatic man and a very smart man, but I don't think he had a formal eighth-grade education. As a matter of fact, he had been a tough man, he had been on the street. And in some ways that's good, because tough men quite often are leaders.

But I suffered in that church because I needed a much greater degree of intellectual thought, and it wasn't there. One of my favorite descriptions of my pastor's sermon was that no matter what the topic, after the first five minutes it was the same sermon. And I just couldn't hold on to that. There was no nutrient there. But my mother was very devout, and so it didn't matter what I thought. I had to be in church.

It wasn't until I was about sixteen years of age that I got involved in the Young Men's Christian Association over on 38th and Wabash. We had a club there that met on Sunday afternoons. That became my liberation, my ultimate escape from church prison, because I was given permission to leave church early to attend this service. After I finally finished high school, I had the privilege of not attending church—and I didn't. It was a long time before I went back to church, at least twelve years.

Well, I went searching because my hunger for God has been constant. In my twenties, I could not make any sense of it, so I dismissed it. I said, "I can't figure it out, and so I'm not going to try." My life has been lived largely on what they call a secular humanist basis. But at a deeper level, that was never good enough.

I'm sixty now, and I had the great pleasure and privilege and opportunity and blessing about five years ago to meet a young lady who was very spiritual, very religious, and who slowly but surely, God working through her, brought me back to the church. It was almost like trying to break a bronco, I mean a bucking bronco. And I had the great good fortune to encounter a man by the name of Jeremiah Wright, Jr., who is the pastor of Trinity United Church of Christ.

I found out that what I needed was a trilogy, or a trinity, so to speak: I needed spirituality, intellectuality, and identity. I needed Afrocentricity. And Jeremiah, in his very God-blessed way, has brought those three things together, so that I could finally hear the message clear enough to come closer.

I always dismissed the Jesus story, and that still does not connect for me intellectually. But with my heart it connects, because I now understand that God has to be presented to most human beings on an anthropomorphic basis. Now, I'm very comfortable. I love the Jesus story now. I love it.

I am on a high today because I am unashamedly black and unapologetically Christian. That is the motto of our church, Trinity United Church of Christ. We had a revival this week with sermons all week long and into the final meetings on Sunday. At the six o'clock service on Sunday—

we have three services on Sunday—we had an unexpected guest: Stevie Wonder. When Stevie Wonder was announced, the church went crazy. He was asked to sing, and he said no, he just came to worship. But the spirit of God was there, and the pastor preached so eloquently, so powerfully, the church just literally ignited. Stevie caught the wave, and came down and sang the Lord's Prayer in his inimitable style, and the church was just—they were frenzied.

So I'm on a high, you understand, I'm on a high.

I majored in education at Illinois State, but also in English and social science, and that was because of my mother. My mother was working as a school clerk at the time. She told me, "Walter, you ought to major in something you can get a job with." Because earlier, when I went to Navy Pier [the University of Illinois at Chicago], I had kind of thought about business administration. Somewhere deep in my heart I always knew business was where I was supposed to be. But not having proper influences, or direction, I didn't know how to deal with that wall of racism.

So I became a teacher. I taught at Lucy Flower High School on the West Side, when it was an all-girls' school. It was mostly white when I went there, and I was the first black male to come there, kind of like a Jackie Robinson. But after seven years of teaching day, night, evenings, summers, and not being able to make enough money to support my family, I decided to go into insurance. I was the second black hired as a salesman by Allstate Insurance Company. The first black was George Gray, who I met and who then recommended me to the company.

My ex-wife is a schoolteacher. I met her my first year out of college, and we married a year later. She reared our two children for the first ten years, and then, through my encouragement and her determination, she went to school to finish her degree. She's been teaching the last eight, nine years. I'm very proud of Carol Blocker. Though we are divorced, she is still my wife. She's still my wife.

My daughter, I affectionately call her a "drug pusher." She was working for the family business, but a pharmaceutical company came along and offered her double the salary and a new car, so off she went. She's married, doesn't have children yet, but I'm hoping. My son, Eric, is my business partner, my right arm. God has blessed me, and I give thanks every day.

The way Ida B. Wells was organized, there were well-defined communities within the whole. In many cases the buildings were arranged around an inner court. As a matter of fact, I call it "the compound." In those compounds I think there were forty-four families. And everybody had a back window from the kitchen looking out on the court. So, the court, literally, became like a stage where you could look out and see your children playing.

I think almost every family consisted of a mother and a father. I can't remember if there were more than three or four instances where there was a single mother. Now that wasn't an accident. People had been screened to create that sociology and that condition. That made for a very interesting community, because, by and large, the males were in control of the community. You did not have any of the lawlessness from teenage boys that has now become a hallmark of public housing; the young boys were not in control of the community. There was no child out of control in that compound.

There was a phenomenon which occurred in public housing that, even at my young age, I understood. The concept of public housing was flawed because it did not deal with fundamental sociology. You have a community, and now you have people who begin to prosper. So what do you do? Ignorantly, stupidly, and almost criminally, you force all of the most prosperous people out as soon as their income reaches a certain level.

What has happened in the past thirty years—and it's happening in the ghetto—the best and the brightest leave. Which means they leave the old people, and the dumb ones, and the criminal-minded, and the psychopaths, and what have you. So what does that do except just destroy a community? The only way a community can be vital, just like our bodies, is that it must be recycled. The young people who come up have to replace the older people, you know what I'm saying? It's an organism.

So now, in terms of chemistry, what do you have? You have a weakening of this solution till you get none but the worst. Who in the world could have concocted anything like that? [Claps his hands] Unless they didn't really care. The smart white people who were involved in that could not have missed that point. Or if they did, then some ignoramus overruled them, because that was the worst thing you could do.

RAMSEY LEWIS

Slender and elegantly dressed, Ramsey Lewis might be pegged as a corporate executive securely ensconced in some corner office. In fact, he's one of the most influential jazz pianists of his generation. He moved to the Frances Cabrini Homes in 1947, while in sixth grade, and left when he was a junior in high school.

It was many years later, after I left Cabrini, that I really realized I had come from a lower economic background. If you notice, I didn't say poor. I think poor is a state of mind, and we never felt anything less than very good inside and very good about each other.

We used to listen to a lot of radio, and occasionally we'd go to the movies. But it was nothing compared to turning on the TV and seeing all the advertisements and how the rest of the world looked compared to us. We had what we needed. We had plenty of food to eat, we had plenty of clothes to wear, and our house was warm. My dad worked, my mother worked, and we figured that's the way it should be. Everybody's front yard was grass and flowers, and usually people had vegetables and things like that in the back. Those houses were relatively new, and people were very respectful of each other. People up the block would go and tell your mother if you were saying bad things. If you were throwing rocks, somebody would say, "I'm going to tell your mother on you!"

When we were at Cabrini, we never saw it as our permanent home, we saw it as a stepping-stone. After four years, we moved on. In my family, all of the kids—my older sister, Reverend Jackson, and my younger sister, Gloria—we all went to college. I took a leave of absence to try my hand at music and didn't get back, but my two sisters finished. To this day I don't know how my parents did it—my father doing maintenance work, and Mom doing domestic work—but we all got to college.

I think one thing that didn't make it seem oppressive then was that the families were not stacked on top of each other. The buildings were only two stories high, and there was plenty of sunshine. I mean, you could see the sky.

I attended Wells High School, at Augusta and Ashland. It was an integrated high school at the time. We had a marching band, a concert band, a symphony orchestra, ballet, modern dance, and three or four different choruses. A few of us got together and had a jazz band, and we had all the different clubs—the Latin Club, the Chess Club, etc. Wells is still there, but it's totally changed now.

I think if you look at public housing more like a community, then you're doing something. If you just put in some buildings without other support systems, you create real problems. You put too many people of low income—and therefore, of like habits—together, and they feed off each other. There aren't enough role models involved. There aren't enough professionals or craftsmen coming in and out of the neighborhood, and there's no incentive for small business to go in and say, "I think I'll put a grocery store here, I think I'll put a cleaners there." You need to go a step further and get in touch with the religious institutions in the neighborhood and say, "Hey, we're thinking about doing this thing. Can we get your support and get your input?"

Society has to be there to help people move from one place to another, to help them get a start. I've always found it interesting to read magazines and see on television people who come along and say, "Why should they get anything when we don't get the same thing?" It tells me that these people have blinders on. They don't read history.

What happens to a group of people—whether they're pink, orange, or green—if they're systematically held in slavery, and then systematically offered no education? I've met people, they're wonderful people: it's just, when you socialize and have a drink, and start talking about political issues, they'll get into this trickle-down theory. We get into this "My parents pulled themselves up by the bootstraps. How come your parents didn't?" And, on the face of it, I wouldn't say these people are racist, but they espouse racist attitudes.

The church was a pillar of our community. The majority of people in our neighborhood went to one of three or four churches that were within several blocks. We went to Wayman AMC Church, which still exists in Cabrini. Dad, in addition to working forty, fifty, and sixty hours a week, was the choir director at our church. I was the piano player, and Mom sang in the choir. We were in church all day Sunday, and then, sometimes during the week, we'd visit other churches to sing. So we were totally immersed in church music and the church group.

I think the church is very important to our communities, and the music in our churches has always attracted people. When we were going to Wayman, we had a youth church, as we would refer to it, and a youth choir. Not all the members started out necessarily God-fearing, but they would do these things, and before long, a lot of them were pulled in. We've been going through a period where our churches are not held in high enough esteem by young folk, and our society shows that.

They still get a great number of young people. My older sister, Reverend Lucille Jackson, is principal of a religious school at her church. On some Sunday mornings, at the service they'll call on the students and say, "These kids have all gotten A's. We want these kids to stand up." And those kids put their chests out, and the other kids think, "Well, I can do that, too!"

BARBARA JONES SLATER AND LEON JONES

At the age of fifteen, Barbara Jones won the gold medal in the hundred-meter dash at the 1952 Helsinki Olympics. "I'm in the Guinness Book of World Records *now," she says. "I'm the only one so far to win at fifteen." She won again in Rome in 1960. Barbara Jones Slater now lives in Atlanta, while her father, Leon Jones, lived on Chicago's South Side until his death in the late 1990s. The interview was conducted in his home.*

Leon: During the war years I worked at the Dodge plant, and after 1942, I went out to a Union Carbide plant and worked there until I retired—about thirty years. Never missed a day. They had a beautiful relationship with employees and a retirement plan, of course, and they gave me paid-up insurance for death.

In the Ida B. Wells project, we had four stories. In the 506 building, where we lived, we kept it clean. It was like this was our home, all four floors. We understood one another, we had a camaraderie, we all lived in that area, we knew everyone. In the high-rises, because there are so many people, people don't really trust one another, you know, they're fearful of one another.

We went to Ida B. Wells because it was a haven for us. The rent was cheaper, it was clean, and everything was brand new. When we first moved in, the administration interviewed everyone, and they took only the choice people. We had social workers, and they'd come out and look in the halls—any defect, you'd have to correct it. But after a while, the people who were choice moved out. After they moved out, the Authority relaxed their regulations and standards, because they wanted to fill up the houses. When we could get out of there, we did.

Everybody knew Miss Butler [a CHA housing official]. When Miss Butler walked in, if you had roaches in your house, Miss Butler would say, "Ok, we're going to have exterminators." And then she came back next month, and if you still had roaches, you had to move. Because whatever you were doing, you were dirty—you were causing these roaches. So Miss Butler would now have to exterminate the whole building because of your filth. It made people straighten up and fly right.

Miss Butler would see you walking down the street, and if you were acting up or cursing or doing anything you weren't supposed to, and you saw Miss Butler, oh, you'd straighten up and fly right. It was her expectations—if you expect the best, you receive the best. That's what I'm talking about as far as Wells being a little village. Everybody knew everyone else.

Barbara: Growing up, my whole life centered around my family. My mother did not work, because my father preferred her to stay home and take care of us. We weren't latchkey kids. I went to Holy Angels Elementary School. After school, we took off our uniforms, did our chores, and went over to Madden Park, where I ran track.

That's how Ms. Holmes [today Alyce Holden, see interview], the track coach at Madden Park, knew me. I used to run and play football and basketball out in the park playground. Well, Ms. Holmes saw me running and asked if I wanted to join her track team, and I said "yes." I loved winning, I just didn't like practicing. But to show you that extended family again, when I would stay home and not practice, she'd knock on the door, and my daddy or mom would answer the door. She'd say, "Barbara here?"

"Oh, yes, she's right there."

I'd be hiding, and she'd walk right over and say, "We're going to practice." And that was the type of person she was. She expected the best from you and didn't settle for less, and because of that I had to practice constantly.

I'll never forget one meet at Madden Park. We only had T-shirts that said "Madden Park." Our sweats were blue jeans and tennis shoes. This girl from another team walks over—she had heard about me. She was a white athlete, and her daddy was her coach. And she didn't have any competition, so they came to Madden Park to compete against me. She walked in with her starting block, sweatsuit, spikes, everything—the works. When I saw all of this paraphernalia, I thought I couldn't beat her. So Ms. Holmes said, "If you let this girl beat you because she's wearing a sweatsuit and she's wearing yellow spikes and this, I'll never speak to you again!" And I said, "But she's got . . ." She says, "That has nothing to do with it. It's talent, and you have it! You can do it!"

Ms. Holmes was like that. And I beat her! With all of her gear. Her father whipped her, because she lost.

She brought Jesse Owens in to talk to us, to show us that we were just as good as anybody else, even though we lived in the projects. We could go to the Olympics, but we'd have to work harder. The Madden Park District, however, could not afford to send anyone to the Olympics. Ms. Holmes introduced Mabel Landry and me to the CYO [Catholic Youth Organization] coach. That meant we would not run for her anymore, we would be running for CYO. In 1952, CYO took us to the National Juniors track meet.

Well CYO was mixed, so, you know, I didn't know anything about segregation. See, my family, they didn't raise me telling me about black and white, they raised me talking about good and bad. The friends around the house, they were calling me a tomboy because in those days, you just didn't see girls running. Girls were always wearing gloves and being feminine and ladylike. My father asked, "Do you want to do it?"

I said, "Yes."

He said, "Then do it."

And I did it! You see, the peer pressure didn't stop me, because I had parents there, and Ms. Holmes, to offset that.

At the 1952 Olympic tryouts in Philadelphia, I came in third in the hundred meters, and that qualified me. And so we went to Helsinki in a B-29 plane. It took us a day and a half to get there. Oh, the Finns were wonderful people. It was twenty-four hours of light and I had never encountered that before. When I woke up at two in the morning, there was a carnival. I got up and went down to the carnival, and this was the day I was supposed to compete. I was just enjoying myself on the Ferris wheel, and walking around, just having myself a ball! May Fags and Flora Patterson came looking for me. Because people were wondering where I was. I was not in the Olympic Village. So they brought me back. Fortunately I broke a world's record.

Everything that I learned as a child, I incorporated in my life. It's things like that make the difference in how you feel about life, you know. Life is beautiful, it's just the choices you make and the attitudes you have about life. If you believe, you can do it. As they say, "If you can believe, you will achieve." And I believe.

In 1956, I hurt my knee and they took me to California to heal it, for the Australia Olympics. But my leg wouldn't heal, and they called me a "has-been." No one tells me I'm a "has-been" unless I say it! In Rome, in 1960, I won another Gold medal. [All laugh] Yeah, and that's when Wilma Rudolph received three.

Well, Mayor Daley, Senior, he said, "When you graduate, come on back, and you've got a job." That helped a lot. I don't care what anyone says about Mayor Daley, he took care of his people. He took care of his athletes, he took care of his ministers, he took care of everybody to make this city work. And I think that's why it worked.

I have two girls. Tracy, who graduated from Moorehouse College in Atlanta, is working with AT&T in sales management. My second daughter is in nursing. We followed our children, and that's why I'm in Atlanta now. Before that, we moved from Chicago to Michigan City, Indiana. I was a schoolteacher there, and I had about five, six activities—counseling and student representative sponsor, band, etc. And because I made high demands of these children, I had fifteen of those kids go to college, most of them given scholarships.

Ms. Holmes, she's retired, but she's still a ball of fire! She still square dances. She didn't live in Wells, but you would have thought she did, because she was there day and night. She's remarried, and her name is Holden, but I have never called her anything but Holmes. She never did have children. I guess we were her children.

ALYCE HOLDEN AND LORETTA MARTIN

Alyce Holmes Holden and Loretta Martin reminisced about Madden Park, the recreation center that served Ida B. Wells. Though Holden is now in her eighties, she still possesses plenty of the vigor that she brought to her life as a track coach and activities coordinator at Madden Park in the 1940s, 1950s, and 1960s. Following her success with the track program, she became the Chicago Park District's first African-American supervisor in 1957. Martin, who grew up in Ida B. Wells, followed her mentor Holden into physical education. She later became a guidance counselor and administrator in the Chicago public schools.

Alyce: I started as a gym teacher at Phillips Elementary. Mr. Bristol, who was supervisor at Madden Park, came to me and said, "I hear you really handle those kids over there at Phillips." I said, "Well, I'm dedicated to them, I love them, and I will see that they do the right thing."

He said, "That's just what I need."

Well, I went over to Madden Park and stayed twenty years. I had a beautiful relationship with the families in Ida B. Wells. I could go to houses and find the kids that I wanted to practice, and the parents would get them on out there. I didn't have to run around and chase them to get them to come. Then when we would have our shows and activities, the parents would all be lined up.

Loretta: At Madden, we had all types of activities. We had dance, basketball, volleyball, swimming, softball, gymnastics—I did all of that. We had speech and drama, too—all of us thought we were actresses and actors. I had a very happy childhood. It was like growing up in a small town.

Alyce: But Loretta, those families whose fathers didn't work—we worked and helped them. We helped, and then they'd go around and help wash the windows at Madden Park. I mean, no one was sitting down and saying, "I don't want a job because I'm too lazy." We didn't know anything about feeling inferior.

Loretta: We came from the projects, and we didn't know that we were supposed to be poor. There weren't many children who didn't make it. Even those that didn't go to college were successful. I'll tell a person in a minute, "Yes, I'm a project product, but I think in order to understand, you have to have been in it." We know how to struggle for the best. When I graduated from college, I said to Alyce, "Oh, I owe you so much." She said, "You don't owe me anything, you just turn around and help somebody else." That's the way I pay her back, is to turn around and do the same thing for others. Alyce reached over and helped us cross over the bridge, and we all feel that it's our turn to help someone else to cross over the bridge.

I worked at Lake Meadows Park under Alyce to pay for college, then I worked at Wendell Phillips High School for many years, as a teacher and then as a guidance counselor. And we had very good control over our kids. But then the Board of Education did something called teacher integration. They took many of the black teachers from schools like Phillips and made them go to the North Side and teach in white schools. And they brought many young white female teachers into our schools who were really afraid of our children.

They were afraid to tell the boys to take their hats off. Where a black teacher would sound very much like their mother and say, "Boy, take that hat off your head, you know better than that," and snatch it off, a white teacher would say, "Would you please take your hat off?" They'd look at her and keep going. And that's when we lost control of our children. We were raised with the understanding that discipline was part of our culture. We believe in disciplining our children. But what I learned at Phillips was that the white teachers did not want to discipline the children. They don't want the confrontation. But children demand discipline, and if you don't give it to them, they will give you something you don't want.

RICHARD TOWNSELL

Richard Townsell and his mother moved into Leclaire Courts in the 1960s from the West Side of Chicago. During high school, he became actively involved in a church where he met a peer group that had a considerable influence on his life. In 1986 he graduated from Northwestern University, where he starred on the wrestling team. He placed fifth in the U.S. Olympic tryouts in 1992. "I lost to the number one guy by one point, and he got a bronze medal at the 1992 Olympics. So I was that close."

When I was a sophomore in high school, a friend of mine who lived in North Lawndale [a West Side neighborhood] was trying to get me to come to this church because there was a group of athletes that had a Bible study. The church had a weight machine, too, so they would lift weights and then go to Bible study. I was a wrestler and a football player, so I started going there to lift weights. But I also began to learn what the church really should be about—understanding social justice and economic problems. The church became a big influence in my life from about my sophomore year on.

But even prior to that, I had a very good peer group. We weren't into drinking or smoking or gangs. We were involved in school and sports. Sam Mendenhall [see interview], David Smith, John Walker—we did everything together. We played football, basketball. And I saw Sam's dad, David's dad—they weren't role models per se, but I saw a mother and a father in that house, so I could aspire to that.

If there was somebody that I wanted to be like, it was probably Sam Mendenhall's brother, Larry. He was a valedictorian in eighth grade and a valedictorian in high school. When I saw him getting attention for his academic pursuits, my grades really took off. It wasn't because I was crazy about school; I wanted the attention. It was like, "This guy is getting attention for being smart, OK. Let me change my thing so I can get that same kind of attention."

But I was a troublemaker at times, I had my share of scrapes. My teachers, they could tell you stories, pro and con. I used to fight—I wasn't a bully or an instigator, but I stood up for myself, and I also stood up for other people's rights. Some guy in the neighborhood, a bully, was messing with Sam, and I went to his house and told him if he messed with Sam, I was going to deal with him. I was concerned about other people being trampled on, and since these were my friends, we stuck together.

My friend Tony went to Dunbar High School [a vocational high school quite a distance from Leclaire Courts], and that's why I went to Dunbar. It turned out to be an amazing experience because of the values and the teachers. You knew that the teachers truly cared for you. I had very strong male teachers in high school—these guys were tough. Henry Thompson was my wrestling coach—he was like my surrogate dad. I had a shop teacher for four years, a strong teacher, by the name of Michael Williams, who is still at Dunbar. In terms of graduates who go to college, Dunbar wasn't the best. But the sense of pride that I gained, the sense of accomplishment, really pushed me through Northwestern.

At Northwestern, I think there were times when I settled for certain grades because I was so tired from practice, traveling, and focusing on trying to be an All-American wrestler. But I don't think I could have been at

Northwestern without the discipline that wrestling brought me. So it was a double-edged sword.

I graduated from Northwestern in December of 1986, and then I came to work for the Lawndale Community Church. I left to teach at Evanston High from 1988 to 1992, and then I came back to work for the Lawndale Christian Development Corporation, which is associated with the church. The organization was established in 1987, and I've been the Executive Director since 1992. We do affordable housing and economic development; we do rehab and new construction as well. We're not a big developer, we're more focused on this particular area. This year we're going to build fifty-two single-family homes. And we have a three-and-one-half-million-dollar tax credit deal for rehabbing forty-eight apartments, which should be finished this month.

ARNOLD WEDDINGTON

Arnold Weddington grew up in Ida B. Wells. He was an avid baseball fan and player, and for many years he coached Little League teams. Baseball was a very important part of his life. He spent much of his career at GTE, rising to the executive ranks. In 1990, he took early retirement and opened up an electronics repair shop. He lives in a middle-class neighborhood of single-family homes on the South Side.

I recently went back down to Ida B. Wells and could not even relate to it. I could not remember anything ever looking that way. When I was a child, it was just a wonderful place to be. All of my friends now still are from Ida B. Wells—all of them. Even though I have work relationships, I don't consider any of them close friends.

The people that come from Ida B. Wells were like your brother and sister. And their parents were like your mother and father. Everyone was Mr. and Mrs., and if you were caught doing something wrong, you might get whupped once by the person that caught you and then you were going to get it when you got home. It is nothing like today, or even when I was raising my children.

At Ida B. Wells we always talked in terms of a backyard. In each backyard, there were forty families, more or less. And each one was like a small village. Everybody knew everybody, and everybody was close, you know. We all got along, one way or the other. In my own backyard, I had so many role models. There was Dillard Harris. He had a brother named Acey, who everybody liked. And there was Dwayne Denive and Ricky Denive—I think he opened a McDonald's. Dwayne had a big job with the school board. And then Mr. Moore—he started teaching me how to play baseball when I was eight years old. I believe that the learning of baseball—the discipline—was very instrumental in shaping the person that I am today.

When we played our ball games, our parents would be out there with picnics, laying out blankets. The whole family would be there. It was like we were playing in the major leagues. I played baseball until I was twenty-one years old. Kirby Puckett, who later played with the Minnesota Twins, played on my baseball team. He used to sit on the porch with all the other kids waiting to go play ball, just one of the kids on the team.

In Ida B. Wells, when I grew up, we thought we were rich. We never envisioned ourselves as being poor people. As a child I believed we were more fortunate than many people because of where we lived and the way we lived. You have to realize Ida B. Wells was brand spanking new and had all new stoves and refrigerators, and grass and flowers. People planted flowers, they shined floors, and kept the windows clean. Everybody worked at it. They kept it beautiful.

They should have used Ida B. Wells as a model and they should have done it that way forever. See, you have to understand, Ida B. Wells used to have the park, the field house, all kinds of activities. We even had a drum instructor, Mr. Cole. I won't forget Mr. Cole. I think my brother and I got in the drum chorus when I was ten or eleven years old. You know, I never knew whether Mr. Cole was a musician or not, but he knew how to drill us. He was really something.

We had so many different kinds of organizations: baseball teams, track and field, swimming. We had everything at Ida B. Wells. And now if you go down there, what do they have? They don't even have a field house. The last time I went down there to look at 653 37th Place, I had tears in my eyes. I couldn't believe it.

Now the drugs are out there to a point where instead of progressing, people are actually slipping backward. You have people that live right in that community with their kids up on the street selling drugs. The kids are taking over these homes. Of course, it's people my age, grown people, elderly people, they're the ones buying drugs from these kids. The kids are smart enough not to use drugs—they just sell them.

It's hard to say what's gone wrong, but I believe it's the lack of religion. When we were coming up, you had Bible study and Sunday school. I remember two or three churches in our neighborhood—Grace Community, Golden Angels. That's where everybody went to Sunday school. That was something you didn't think about missing—we had to go to church. My mother used to teach a Bible class for the kids.

Back then the parents were involved in so many things, but you don't see that today. It's more selfish. Now everyone is on their own. I believe it comes from the slavery mentality: where you get the crabs in the barrel, and when you get one coming out, all the others try to pull him down. Too often, blacks who do elevate themselves, they forget where they came from. Like blacks who oppose affirmative action—why are they against it? Because they want to stand out. They don't want people of their color up there with them, you know. They're prima donnas.

But if they just took a good look back, what would they see? In my department at GTE, there were only two blacks in an organization of 150. Only two blacks! And some of my working peers were illiterate, but they had those jobs because they knew the right people. If you look at industrial America, you still have all the blacks and all the Hispanics working in the factories on the low level, and all the whites in the management positions. It's so obvious.

SAM MENDENHALL

Sam Mendenhall moved into Leclaire Courts in 1966, when he was two years old, and lived there with his parents until 1982. He then served in the U.S. Army from 1982 to 1985. He returned to live at Leclaire from 1985 to 1988, while he earned his bachelor's degree from the University of Illinois at Chicago. After graduating from the University of Illinois Law School in 1991, Sam joined the law firm of Winston & Strawn, where he is currently a partner in the firm's Litigation Department. He ran unsuccessfully for Congress in 1995.

I saw Leclaire go from a lower-middle-class area to one in which poverty is stacked on poverty. Not the way it is in high-rises, but nevertheless concentrated poverty. You show me a society where there is a concentration of poverty, and I'll show you one on its way to decay and destruction.

One way to combat this decay and destruction is to restore the family. Another is for those of us who make it out to come back and help the children left behind. In 1991, I graduated from law school and went back to Leclaire and started a Cub Scout troop. I ran the troop for six years. I did this not only to give back, but to be a positive role model. We have to have more positive role models. The only time these kids see lawyers is as public defenders. These kids saw me wear a tie every day and then switch into my Scout uniform. So now a lot of the kids are saying, "I want to be a lawyer or I want to be an accountant or I want to be a doctor." I always tell them, "That's fine and dandy, but first let's be good, productive citizens."

We talk about role models like Michael Jordan or Colin Powell. But if my student or Cub Scout had a problem, he couldn't call Michael Jordan or Colin Powell. But he could always call me and say, "Mr. Mendenhall, I'm having a bad day. My mom and dad are arguing about this or that. I can't study. Can you help me?" And as a Scout leader and friend, I tried to help. But of course it goes beyond that. We have to have guys like my dad, who went to work every day for forty-two years—and he had only a sixth-grade education. He was one of the most respected men in Leclaire. There's no way I would have been anything without my dad. Bringing it full circle, we have to restore the family, have more people who make it, give back and serve as father substitutes to help raise these at-risk boys and girls to be productive citizens.

I think public housing as we knew it at Leclaire is good and workable. Scattered-site housing is not practical or workable. The reason why they are touting scattered-site housing now is to get the people out of the Cabrini-Green area because that land is so valuable, some of the most prime real estate in the city. The key to improving these projects like Leclaire or Cabrini is to remove the 25 percent of tenants who are bringing the other 75 percent down.

Chapter 7

And the Band Played On and On . . . and Then Off Key: Residents Who Stayed in CHA

Ten of the people in this study of public housing's early tenants were still CHA residents at the time of their interview, though some have since moved out. Most had lived in the projects for thirty or forty years. They have seen both public housing's heyday and its decline.

More so than most of the former residents, these current CHA tenants have had a firsthand view of the factors that have caused the projects' dilapidated state. Unlike many newer residents, they have retired or continue to work at modest jobs with low incomes, thus ensuring their need for public housing. Despite the deterioration of conditions in the projects today, they remain because public housing is their home and they wish to see it retained and improved.

These tenants believe that the high number of families in extreme poverty in public housing today is due to negligent management. They watched the Housing Authority gradually lower the tenant selection standards until nonworking families became the majority of tenants. They also point to changes in rent policies, first mandated by Congress in 1969 with the "Brooke Amendment," named after Senator Edward Brooke of Massachusetts. This well-intentioned but ultimately counterproductive policy set the rent at 30 percent of a tenant's income (up to a limit), reducing incentives to earn more money. In 1982, the limit was removed and the 30 percent rule was applied to all income. Many working families immediately faced a massive increase in their rents and left. As working-class families exited and were replaced by nonworking families, a vicious cycle began. Reduced rental income meant less money for maintenance, which resulted in further deterioration of conditions, which in turn chased out those with options. Several of those interviewed in earlier chapters indicated they might have stayed in public housing if their rents had not increased astronomically in 1982.

The administration of the CHA under Charles Swibel (CHA Chairman from 1964 to 1981) did little to arrest the downward slide. Instead, Swibel used his position to become one of the city's power brokers while failing to stem the decay at the CHA. In 1995, the federal Department of Housing and Urban Development (HUD) took over the CHA's top management. The change meant a shift in policy, as new plans were drawn up to demolish as many units as possible with minimal plans to rebuild.

Few interviewees approve of the demolition of public housing in Chicago. The people whose voices are heard here know firsthand the need for affordable, decent housing for the working poor. To these tenants, renovation, not demolition, of the CHA's thousands of units seems the way to go, along with a reformed management. Renovation, repair, and proper maintenance, they say, are essential to make public housing viable once again and to remove its stigma as the modern-day slum.

Likewise, present tenants support eviction of disruptive tenants. They acknowledge the harshness of such an action, but they affirm that social discipline and tenant responsibility are essential to saving the entire concept of public housing. They remember the 1940s and 1950s at Altgeld Gardens, Leclaire Courts, and Cabrini Homes, when tenants were screened and when those who didn't live by the rules were asked to leave. Back then, the rules had to be lived up to: rent had to be paid on time, trash not properly disposed of resulted in fines, and damage to apartments had to be paid for. Beyond these vital regulations, tenants recalled rules that were equally followed. Tenants did not walk on the grass, children were not allowed to play around the elevators, and project officials received courteous respect. These memories reflect the CHA's careful management and heartfelt attitude toward tenants under the leadership of Elizabeth Wood. Enlightened but firm management based on mutual respect between tenant and landlord is the key to good low-income housing, and such a relationship is sorely lacking today.

Yet, in spite of the present problems that the current tenants find so disruptive, a number of these longtime residents have preferred to stay. Public housing is home for them. Policy makers and future administrators desperately need to hear their voices and heed their concerns.

HATTIE CALVIN

Hattie Calvin moved to Cabrini-Green when she was nine years old, and she still lives there. "My mother applied for public housing when Old Man Daley was Mayor. That's how she got in, through him." Calvin is an administrative assistant at the Cook County Board of Elections.

Why should I move out of Cabrini? I'm centrally located for any- and everything. I can walk to work whether it's hot or cold. And the view? I'm on the fourth floor, but at nighttime, if I go up to a higher floor and look out, it's the most beautiful scenery in the world. It's a better view than from one of those high-rises downtown. Look at Cabrini. I'm sitting right in the Gold Coast on the most valuable land in the world. We're surrounded by areas that are being built up every day. I know there was a time when you couldn't get white folks to come through there. But now the yuppies—the white folks, or people of color that don't want to be black—they want the location. They're coming back into the city now. This has been coming for years. They have deliberately neglected the buildings at Cabrini. Management has been running it like that because they were playing into someone's hand.

I would be against any attempt to tear down public housing, because what are you going to do with all of these people that cannot afford market-rate rent? Where are they going to go with their families? Society has not prepared some of these families. They have let them just sit and linger and given them no help to get out of the situation that they're in. That's what welfare was there for, and now Newt Gingrich is getting ready to cut everything he can.

But it is true that some families need to be moved out so the buildings can be improved for those that want something better. Where do they go? That's hard to say. I feel sorry for some of the teenagers that are caught up in this because they have no love. Some of their parents are caught up in drugs. I feel more sorry for the babies, because they're caught up in the whole turmoil and they're innocent. But for the parents that are into these drugs, into gangs with their children—they need to go. Where are they going to put them? I don't know. I have no solution to that. But they need to move them so families that do want something can go ahead and live their lives in decent, safe places.

When we moved in, I would guess about half the families were female-headed. But there were very few undesirable families. Certainly nothing like the number we have now. To bring Cabrini back to what it was, you would have to clear out about a fourth of the families who live here. If the CHA would come in and do what they were supposed to do and move the undesirables out, the project would be in a condition where they wouldn't have to knock it down.

There used to be a time when the kids here could go outside and play softball, basketball, football, jump rope, hopscotch, and things like that. They can't do it now because you never know when someone is going to start shooting. They used to have a place over at 911 Hudson in the basement for the young kids and teenagers. On Fridays and Saturday nights, we could go there and have parties. But there aren't things like that anymore. You can't have them because you never know if someone's going to come in and get hurt. You and CHA are liable for that. So they have no recreation for children nowadays that will really benefit them.

We have a lot of young men in these developments that are trying to do OK—and who are doing OK—who are not recognized. They only recognize the ones that are into drugs, into gangs. And that leaves the ones doing something positive completely out of the picture.

HALLIE AMEY

Hallie Amey has lived in Wentworth Gardens, a low-rise development just south of Comiskey Park, since 1950. For many years she was head of the Local Advisory Committee (LAC). She is a past president of Wentworth's Resident Management Corporation and is a commissioner of the Chicago Housing Authority.

My daughters would like to drag me away from this project—don't think they wouldn't. They are forever on that, but I told them I'm quite satisfied right now. I feel that I was blessed to have been able to bring up four girls and get them to the place where they can support themselves.

My baby was only four months old at the time my husband passed in 1958. And I was able to stay right here at Wentworth, work for a while, volunteer, and keep up with my children in school. Everybody went on to college, and I'm very grateful. Three of my daughters are teaching and the fourth daughter, the oldest one, works for the Internal Revenue Service. I feel I owe it to the community to stay and help, because this was my teaching to them.

As you can see, the apartments here are just like they were when they were first built. Even though millions of dollars have come into CHA, there's been little modernization, little rehabbing, nothing at Wentworth. Over the years, all the money was squandered by the people in authority. Wasted. That's why I definitely think tenant management is OK. We certainly couldn't do worse than the CHA over the last thirty years.

When Elizabeth Wood was around, it wasn't necessary. But the changeover came in housing when they stopped really exercising rules and regulations. It had something to do with Legal Assistance lawyers accusing the Housing Authority of being too rigid. That's when the real breakdown started. When they changed the rent scale, that's what took a lot of our good families away. Lots of working parents had no desire to move—and many of them have even tried to come back—but they took the rent up so high there just wasn't no way. Rent was going up to six, seven, eight, nine hundred dollars, and people just moved away.

Up to that time, everybody was on their toes. If a family had unruly kids and they were reported, they had to go into the office immediately—and if its kids showed up in the office too many times, that family was moved out. Those were the days when yards were kept up. In fact, if you didn't keep your yard up, you were fined. There were no ifs, ands, or buts about it, you were fined. And that was good, very good. You know, we didn't realize it then, but you do now when you look at the situation, with so many single parents not caring what happens to their surroundings, not trying to keep it clean or trying to beautify their yards. You've just got a handful of people who will do that.

I don't care for sending families to outlying areas, as they do with the new federal program. Now, if there's someone who really had made their choice to go out there, I guess it would be OK, but I surely wouldn't want to go out there. Most definitely not. In general, I don't approve of this kind of scattering the site program.

HELEN PRESTON

Helen Preston moved to Leclaire in January 1951 with her husband and three children. In the 1980s, Leclaire came to national attention when HUD Secretary Jack Kemp oversaw and encouraged the establishment of a resident management corporation at the project. Kemp saw resident management as a cure for the ills of public housing, and touted Leclaire as one of its most inspiring examples.

Preston was elected secretary of the board of the Resident Management Corporation at Leclaire in 1991. She resigned from the board in 1994. Soon after this interview was conducted in 1996, she moved out of the development. In the spring of 1996, the CHA dissolved Leclaire's resident management corporation and resumed management of the development. The CHA took action amid charges of embezzlement and mismanagement.

I moved to Leclaire Courts from the South Side, from the neighborhood where Lake Meadows is now. My mother and father owned a home in that area, and at that time [1951], land clearance came into Chicago and you were displaced, moved out. When I moved into Leclaire, we were the only black family in the row that I lived in. Winston Kennedy [see interview] was the manager then. I have to say this about him: he was an Irish person, and he was a very good person. At first he lived in Leclaire, but I think the people started taking their problems to him after work hours and he moved. Still, he was the best manager.

There was a fairness when you came into this place. They asked you how you found out about it and why you would want to live here. And they told you straight up, "If you have objections to intermingling with other races, then don't fill out an application." And that's how my children grew up. There were whites, blacks, Hispanics, all nationalities—almost like a melting pot.

At the time, they screened you thoroughly before you came in. They checked out your background, they made sure that you were compatible with people who were already living here and that your wants were the same as theirs.

Everybody that moved in here had a husband, and I don't remember anybody not working. That's the point. When we first moved in here, all the fathers had jobs. They came home to their families. In some families, both the mother and father worked.

During the time that my children were growing up in Leclaire, every family wanted to amount to something. They were very conscientious, very outgoing, and very community-oriented. The kids used to get together—black and white—and they would play together. They would be in and out of each other's house. If you were black, so what? If you were white, so what?

But I've seen things change so much. I'm too old to be out here now. I think I've outgrown myself. Because I can see things happening in the city of Chicago and here at Leclaire that I don't like.

For three years, I was the secretary of the Leclaire Courts Resident Management Corporation. I feel like tenant management can work. But it has to be people that are dedicated to keeping it tenant-managed, not reverting back to HUD or CHA management.

Now, I know that HUD gives the money to CHA, and CHA disburses the money to the development, and when you become tenant-managed, the money still has to trickle down to you. So you only have a certain amount, and you are supposed to put this money into keeping the housing up. But so many things have fallen by the wayside. The newer tenants do not keep the property up as though it were their own. A lot of these people use it like transit. They do not regard it as something that has to be taken care of while they're living there, and this is what bothers me.

I left the board because I became dissatisfied with the way they were conducting business. When a board is elected, there's going to be favoritism, even if it's just from the people that work for you. If you happen to say I need a such-and-such, and you're on the board, the worker figures right away, I will protect my job by doing this for them. Damn the fact that someone else needed something done in their house.

Tenant management, as far as I'm concerned, means paying attention to the needs of the tenants. In order to do that, you have to be organized, and you have to know and be in touch with every tenant. You have to have monthly meetings so you know what their needs are.

Last year I almost had a stroke from Leclaire Courts. I worked for twenty-five years for the post office and never had a headache, never had high blood pressure. But I retired and got involved in management here. My daughter had to rush me to the hospital because I was so worried about Leclaire Courts. I felt like we were being shafted. I still do. I feel like the people at Leclaire right now are being taken for a sleigh ride by the resident management operation. My children said, "Get out of it, Mother, it's not worth it."

MARGARET WILSON

Margaret Wilson, her husband, and their five small children moved into the Cabrini-Green development on Chicago's near North Side in early 1962. When they moved in, Cabrini-Green was a vibrant, racially integrated community. Wilson and her husband still live in the row houses in Cabrini. She now serves the area as the chief administrative assistant to 27th Ward Alderman Walter Burnett, Jr.

When we moved to Cabrini, it was very nice. You had very good neighbors. To me, they were the most sophisticated people in Chicago. I never saw so many community organizations. I think everybody must have known Mayor Daley personally, that's the way it appeared. They used to call off the politicians' names, and I'd think, my God, what kind of people are they, hollering to all these politicians? I had never seen a community where the churches were so involved. You had St. Matthew's Methodist Church, Holy Family Lutheran, Saint Phillip's, Saint Dominick's, and Saint Joseph's.

So we thought we had made a very good choice. We had moved in with people who sincerely cared about their community. There was something going on all the time. They were concerned with keeping it up, preserving it, they were interested in the school issues, you name it. I thought it was the best thing in the world. And they had opportunities and activities for children. I was able to put my two little ones in the nursery school for half a day and free myself up. I was just elated.

When we moved in, almost everybody on my street was married. I don't remember what brought about the change. Families began to move out, that's one thing. They did better, and then they moved. I think maybe in the 1970s or the late 1960s they passed a rule where you had to pay 30 percent of your income for rent. Then they relaxed the rule on letting in single women. The men were working then. Because in my mind's eye I don't remember seeing a great many men in the daytime. It was mostly ladies. We would be out washing and hanging our clothes, you know, typical Americans. Of course there were always some people that were undesirable, but they were minuscule, you know.

Don't let anybody fool you about Cabrini. Even with all of the negativism that you hear, this was a very special place. They may not realize how special and how different it was, but it was for me. I was born and bred on the South Side of Chicago. Over here on the North Side, I was introduced intimately to the other ethnic groups, whereas on the South Side I just knew them, you know. Cabrini was a very different place. My family—my children—were raised in this atmosphere, and even after the other nationalities began to leave Cabrini, they still interacted with people other than black folk.

Of course, the people I knew, a lot of them moved. And they've been replaced by new people and their children. People have different standards of living, different morals, you know, standards and principles. For instance, you don't throw garbage on the ground. The majority of the original tenants felt the same about the community. Now, the new people, the younger people, they are different. The CHA stopped screening. So many of my friends have left. I don't know what happened.

My husband and I have five children, and they are all doing well. My husband was in the tailoring business for many years. Two of the children are in the clothing business—one in Texas and one in California. One of our sons works for Whole Foods. When I came here, we refused to live in a high-rise building. That was just totally unacceptable. And I tell you why, a very simple reason: with five children, you've got to wait for the elevator. No, that was unacceptable to us. But something needs to be done about it. It just ruptures my heart to look at this building being torn down when it could have been rehabbed and renovated, to get people off the streets. You've got to work with every family in there. But the undesirables, after you have tried everything, would just have to go.

When my kids were in school, we were fighting for better schools so that everybody, all Americans, would receive a good education. And then everybody can go apply for a job and the best person will win. That is the way we saw it when my children were young. We were concerned with getting them prepared and getting them ready to compete with other people around the globe. I think as Americans this is what we have to do. I don't think it really makes any difference if it's green over here or red over there. The schools should be the same. I don't think they will ever have a completely integrated society. I think that a lot of people will always want to live together because of cultural ties. But everybody should have the same education—equal education is the key.

I became involved with the government in 1965, when I went to work for the War on Poverty, with the Chicago Committee on Urban Opportunity. My interest really wasn't political. I saw the opportunity where the government was going to come in and do some fantastic things, and they did a lot of things that nobody knows anything about. Let me give you an example. It was not structured—we had to structure the program as we went along. That was very exciting, because we were able to create structure as we saw the need for it. They had a group of employees called community representatives. I was originally hired as one. You worked in the community where you lived, because the belief was that you knew your community better than any stranger. And that was true. We really did. So it was much easier to knock on Mrs. Jones's door and say, "Mrs. Jones, how are you? Is there anything we can do for you today? Is there anything that you need?" We could try to connect Mrs. Jones with those things that she needed, because we knew Mrs. Jones.

It was one of the most exciting things I've ever done in my life. I loved it all. I was there eighteen years. Yes, yes, it was exciting. It was total family involvement. You have all these single parents, and we know you. And we'd go in there and actually help. We'd help this lady get her children in nursery. See, the program was broken down into different components: education, housing, health, social welfare, employment. All of those things that concerned a total family. We saw to it that you were referred to the right service or we got that person to your house. We worked so hard, but we didn't know how to market ourselves and let everybody know what we were doing.

I had several passions. Housing was one, along with education and employment. I was able to satisfy most of those passions at the Committee on Urban Opportunity. I left in 1974 and went to the Concentrated Employment Program because it was a brand new program. It only operated on the West Side, but I was able to help my people over here by having them change their address so that I could refer them to the different—maybe I should have you take that off [the tape recorder] [laughs]—to the different training programs and employment programs. It was exciting. We were able to do so many things that you folks in the public never heard about, never dreamed of.

ROSITA HENRY

Since 1990, Rosita Henry has been president of the Lawndale Gardens Local Advisory Council. She moved into Lawndale Gardens, a low-rise, 125-unit development on the West Side, in 1971.

I used to stand in my door sometimes in the evening after the sun had gone down, when it would be dusk, and I would look out over the grass on the boulevard, and it would almost look like velvet. We were very proud—not in a boastful way—but we were very concerned about our yards. If someone else's yard had been trimmed and cut, we would be busy trying to do ours so it would be even. It was a friendly kind of competition. We were responsible for the front and the backyards, and the maintenance of the lawn, and also shoveling the snow. That was our responsibility.

This was what they gave me twenty-four years ago. [She holds up a small handbook.] "For Your Home," that was the name of it, written by the CHA. I took this very seriously, and I've always valued my dwelling place. But I don't find people now that do. They're given an opportunity to have shelter over their head, but they don't value their dwelling place. Today, I feel that the residents that need to stay go too fast, and the ones that need to go stay. Today, they have a lot of unauthorized people coming in. I call them "lootees."

Let me say this, and I'm saying this as a heart of mercy. Many of the people that have come across my path have asked, "Is public housing for everyone?" And the answer is "It is not for everyone." If you can't come and follow some rules and regulations and honor the lease, you can't stay. Now, it's just that simple.

Even back twenty-four years ago, there was a gang problem—some people with antisocial behavior. I'd always felt like that could have been curtailed if the rules had been enforced. Management, even back then, was beginning to relax the rules and regulations. And then, as now, I feel a part of the problem could be solved if management was taken seriously. Because far too many residents don't take management seriously and management doesn't take residents seriously. There needs to be a concerted effort made to rejoin in a partnership, you know, with all people involved. People wanting to raise their children in a better situation and just demanding that there are certain things that have got to be changed for us to live. Residents have to do their part. Certainly the face of public housing does not have to stay the way it is. I have hope that it can be reversed. The media has made it a negative thing, and people have bought into it. But it can be reversed.

I always felt like public housing management, first and foremost, should have been realtor and landlord. I understand, down through the years, that there have been some situations where people needed social programs. But it's been always my thought that management were the landlords and they should be landlords. I was very impressed twenty-four years ago with the screening process that they had. I remember even to this day the way they screened people.

I appreciate Lawndale Gardens. It's not the best, but it's not the worst. There's a lot of pluses here. Transportation-wise, we can catch a bus on any one of those corners there—California or Blue Island—and go anywhere in the city. And we have an El train right up the way. We don't have to worry about broken-down elevators. There are so many pluses here that I can't see why they've just let this place almost go to rack and ruin.

If housing is going to endure—and I've begged, and I have pleaded and I've exhorted [bangs table]—this should be a model. You could come in here with a team of workers, bring these buildings up to code, and then use this as a springboard. It would be all of our success: the Housing Authority, the residents. This is doable, it's rentable. But this place has been neglected until it squeezes your heart.

My thoughts are that with the economy changing the way it is, public housing is needed more than ever. When we were coming up, public housing was just a stepping-stone to get yourself situated. Well, that has changed. There are some people that have moved into public housing, and that's where they'll stay. They'll be renters, they're not going to be home owners.

If I can say that I am well rounded, it's because of my experience. When I was growing up, we were the first black family that lived on the 1300 block of Spaulding right off Douglas Boulevard. My grade school was 95 percent Jewish youngsters. They learned from me and I learned from them. And I went over to Harrison Street forty-five years ago, and it was mainly some Baltics and Italians. If we're going to isolate ourselves, I don't think that we can really learn from each other. So I just hope that we will always have multiracial communities.

Yes, I'm forever trying to reach out. And you know what? I'm giving back. This is my dwelling place, and I'm giving back. This position [of LAC president] does not pay me anything. I would like to retire from this, but I don't want to leave them in the lurch. It's 10 percent of the people who do 90 percent of the work. Period. I can't say that I have five people who work with me. I cannot say that. And I may—on that premise—I may run again for president of this area. Because I don't want the work that's happened on my watch to drown.

EDNA McNEAL

Edna McNeal has lived in Wentworth Gardens for fifty-eight years. She worked for twenty-five years as a matron in the Museum of Science and Industry. In spite of the deteriorating conditions at Wentworth, she does not want to move.

I moved into Wentworth Gardens in March 1945 with my husband and three kids, and I'm still here. My husband, who worked for the CTA until he retired, died six years ago. Wentworth Gardens was one of the best projects on the South Side. We had trees growing, we had swings for the children and benches for the elderly if we wished to sit outside. We had janitors that kept the place beautiful. I wasn't afraid to walk any time of day and night.

I didn't walk around too much, didn't have time to visit, because I had my three kids plus two more after we were at Wentworth. I had to cook for my husband, I had to clean the house and do the laundry. Also, I had a job. For twenty-four years I worked at the Museum of Science and Industry, and loved it. I was a matron taking care of the people, you know, the guards and the administrators. I took people around the museum. It was such a nice place to work. They didn't pay much, but it went a long ways. We were just one happy family.

My husband did all the shopping. I miss him so much. I never had to go anywhere unless I wanted to go. He did all my shopping, down to my dresses, shoes, and things. If I saw something in the paper that I liked, I could just show it to him and tell him what store it was in. He went and got it for me. Now I have to do my own shopping and it's hard for me. Then I didn't have to do anything but take care of my job, my home, and my kids.

But now there are gangs out there. There is shooting at nighttime. I'm even afraid to go out and take my little walk to the Progressive Baptist Church on 39th Street. I'll be eighty-five, if I live, next June 30.

HAZEL JOHNSON

Though early residents considered Altgeld Chicago's "garden spot," there was no getting around the fact that the development was built in one of the most heavily industrialized districts in the nation. It is surrounded by chemical plants, steel plants, garbage dumps, and a sewage treatment facility that assaults the senses when the wind blows in the wrong direction.

Over the years, Altgeld residents began noticing an astonishingly high incidence of cancer in their community. In 1979, Hazel Johnson founded a group, People for Community Recovery, to do something about it. Johnson has led the fight that closed a nearby hazardous waste incinerator, and successfully pressed for the creation of a health clinic at Altgeld. Her work has received national attention, and she's probably one of the few Americans to receive an award at the White House from both Presidents George Bush and Bill Clinton.

My husband died in 1969 of lung cancer. It seems like somebody in everybody's family has had cancer. Lung cancer and breast cancer are the biggest thing out here. And quite a few people that died of lung cancer didn't even smoke. We have the highest rate of cancer in the city of Chicago. I would say 60 percent of the people within Altgeld have had cancer or have died of it. We've also had a lot of miscarriages. And don't talk about the asthma.

Altgeld Gardens was built on a landfill. And now we're finding out that the Housing Authority stored used transformers out here—transformers with PCBs—and they had leakages. We're fighting to get CHA to remove the PCBs from the site.

I've tried to get the city to relocate some of the people, but we weren't too successful, because they were saying they didn't have the funding for it. They also might close Altgeld Gardens—shut it down. The majority of the people in Altgeld are willing to move. But I guarantee that everybody wouldn't want to. This is some people's roots, and they don't want to leave.

Let me say this: I am a sixty-two-year-old woman, and right now, I don't want to leave this community, because I know just about everybody. I moved to Altgeld in 1962, on March 18. It was my husband and myself. We had six kids at the time. And the neighbors were real nice and friendly. We didn't have very much delinquency or drugs. It's just in the recent years that we started to have a lot of that.

But even now, I feel secure out here. I wouldn't feel comfortable walking in Hyde Park or anywhere else at two or three or four o'clock in the morning. But out here, a lot of people know me, and I'd feel comfortable walking at that time of night. But if the Housing Authority would relocate us, I'd say, "Good!" I would go along with it.

MYRTLE MORRISON

Myrtle Morrison moved into Wentworth Gardens when she was eleven, and has remained there for over fifty years. She has three children and is now bringing up a grandson. She would like to move but does not know where else she could be as well known, and therefore as safe, as at Wentworth.

I moved into Wentworth Gardens in December 1946, with my mother, my father, and my grandmother. There were eight children. We had four bedrooms. My father died in 1953, and my mother in 1987. My father worked at Container Corporation for many years, right up until he died. My mother didn't work, and I had a number of younger brothers, so my mother received Social Security until they were eighteen, after which she received public assistance.

I had my first child when I was twenty-three, and moved into my own apartment in Wentworth. My mother kept the other apartment for many years. I had three children, all with the same father. But we never got married. He did, however, help to support the kids.

Living at Wentworth was wonderful. You never had to keep your doors locked. It was like having an extended family. Other families cared about what you did. There was always a mother and father image around. It was great compared to what it is today. We learned a lot. There was respect for ourselves, our friends, and our neighbors. Our neighbors were wonderful. But at that time everybody was thoroughly screened. They got school reports and police reports. I know I was screened even though I had lived there for years.

We worked as a group. Let's say we decided to get out and plant in the springtime. You would start digging in your yard. Pretty soon your neighbor would be digging. Then it seemed like the lady next door to him would come out, and so it would go. Everybody would help everybody. And there wasn't much for maintenance to do because we did it all ourselves, except clean up the grounds and see that the garbage was emptied.

The place started going bad right after 1980, when they stopped being choosy about the tenants they were accepting. It can't be good until they make people liable for what they do. You can't destroy people's property and get away with it. You can't throw debris or garbage anywhere you please. In the old days, the janitors picked it up and traced you and you paid a fine. You couldn't abuse your neighbors or loiter in the hallways. Those were the good old days.

You know, in the beginning we had a good many professionals and working families who moved in. But then they moved in these young girls. Kids who were having kids, kids who were much more irresponsible. They felt that they were away from home influences and did not have to abide by parents' rules. So they would move in with no structure, and the next thing, the boyfriend would move in, et cetera.

The worst thing that happened at Wentworth was the 30 percent rule, which made people pay 30 percent of whatever they earned for rent. All the working families moved away. These families should have been blended in.

I'm not saying that because you are on public assistance you don't have the right to live somewhere, but I think if you put them all in one place, it spoils everything.

Originally, they were going to have Wentworth a mixed project, with people of all incomes and races. I think it is better this way. We have people in this project that haven't been anywhere else in the city. Just like there are people in Bridgeport who have their ideas about blacks, and they've never been out of Bridgeport. I think it's important that people be brought together.

They talk about resident management corporations [RMCs] as helping. But the real thing is that we have to work together. You know, united we stand, divided we fall. We can sit at this big table and have big meetings and accomplish nothing. You have all the officers bickering, nothing happens, and one says yes and the other says no. I'm sitting back and I'm watching these RMCs knock themselves out. When my mother was living, I used to go to all the meetings. I used to enjoy going to meetings because there were constructive suggestions and cooperation with the CHA. Now I only go to the chorale meetings. These RMC business meetings are just too discouraging.

My oldest son works in a packing plant in Des Moines, Iowa. He lives in a mixed neighborhood. My only daughter, she lives on the North Side. She is a physical therapist and a quote reporter at the Board of Options. My son Mark is a career service person at the Abbott School right in this neighborhood.

Right now I have a question as to whether I should move. I have a limited income, and I am concerned about moving into another neighborhood. I know the dangers here and I know the drugs. I can stay here because they respect me like I respect them. But it is still dangerous.

This is a good place—a three-story walk-up with lots of benefits. If the neighbors would share instead of being for themselves, it could be better. But in fact, I think that almost half of the tenants should be evicted in order to make this a good project. But only half.

Conclusion: The Rebirth of Public Housing

The most significant theme that emanates from the lives detailed in this book is the vital importance of positive "community" in shaping life experiences. The community found between 1940 and 1960 in Chicago's public housing projects fostered a togetherness, a sharing, and a caring. The families involved were poor, working-class, and upward-striving—families who sought the American Dream and worked hard to attain it. The public housing developments built in the 1940s and early 1950s provided a nurturing environment for several generations, and the successes of these families deserve not only recognition but also understanding, so that these positive accomplishments might again influence public policy.

It may seem utopian to propose a rebirth of public housing at a time when many urban public housing projects are being demolished. Around the country, dozens of projects and thousands of units are slated for demolition or have already been torn down. In Washington, the Clinton and Bush administrations have essentially ignored the widely acknowledged housing affordability crisis in the United States. Instead, former U.S. Department of Housing and Urban Development (HUD) Secretary Andrew Cuomo spoke approvingly of the number of projects that have been razed. The media pay little attention to the current affordable housing crisis, let alone the need for more public housing.

The current effort emanating from Washington—called the HOPE VI program—calls for tearing down the worst projects and replacing a fraction of the units lost with lower-density, mixed-income, racially integrated projects. In practice, the fraction replaced is small and the pace is slow. Although fifty thousand units have been authorized, only thirteen thousand new units have been built in the program's first six years—a drop in the bucket of what's needed.

Still, the HOPE VI program—at least in theory—calls for a return to many of the policies identified in this book. The developments are designed as new communities and not just houses. Residents will include some working-poor and middle-income families, though at some projects about half of all units will be reserved for "market-rate" families, which in Chicago means the middle class and above. Local housing authorities are expected to work with other municipal agencies, such as school boards and park districts, to ensure a total effort in providing services. Although HUD describes this approach as innovative, most of the elements of this program are merely reviving a practice that was standard operating procedure in Chicago and at other outstanding local housing authorities in the 1940s and 1950s.

However, the HOPE VI program also makes two assumptions about public housing that are challenged by the testimony of former residents. First, the new program assumes that high-rise (and some low-rise) public housing projects are either physical monstrosities or so dilapidated as to be uneconomical to renovate. Therefore, the program concludes, the solution is to tear down most high-rise projects and allow residents to disperse. But the problem is not the buildings—it is their management. The public housing outcomes we see today are caused by decades of ineffective local management, inflexible rules imposed by HUD, and grossly inadequate funding from Congress. While some local managers have indeed failed, HUD has leaped to the general conclusion that private firms are more capable of administering public housing developments. This ignores the many successes of the past, in Chicago and other cities, where committed administrators achieved exceptionally high standards. Rather than blindly condemning public-sector management, HUD should look to the continued success of local housing authorities in New York City, Milwaukee, Seattle, St. Paul, Cambridge (Massachusetts), and Greensboro (North Carolina) for models on how to administer public housing.

Second, while those interviewed for this book wanted a return to a much higher portion of working-class tenants, they did not see the need for the higher-income "mix" that HOPE VI presents as a panacea for public housing. Mixing incomes is a good idea as long as it addresses real housing needs, but the mix currently contemplated in Chicago goes much too far in favoring the middle class at the expense of the lower-income working class. The CHA, for example, is in the process of tearing down the Cabrini-Green project and replacing it with new housing, 50 percent of which is to be "market-rate" (townhouses priced at $350,000–$400,000), 20 percent "affordable" for middle-class families (earning $50,000–$100,000), and 30 percent for "former public housing residents." The stable but struggling working class—restaurant workers, hospital aides, store clerks, cleaning staff—gets nothing in this definition of mixed income. Further, this mix is condescending to the working poor. They do not need market-rate families living next door to have a stable neighborhood.

The limited efforts of HOPE VI and the demolition of large amounts of public housing come at a time when there is a tremendous need for affordable housing in America. Surveys by HUD show millions of families with "worst-case" housing needs who are paying over 50 percent of their income for rent, or live doubled up, or live in substandard conditions. This group includes several million struggling but deserving, upward-striving, working-class families—the same group that constituted the population of the original Chicago projects. In Chicago, the numbers with "worst-case" needs in the 1990s have been estimated from 80,000 to 130,000 families, and as of 2002, the city still suffers from an affordable housing crisis.[24] Yet HUD is sanctioning the destruction of thousands of apartments—many of which could be saved. Obviously, this is no answer to the nation's pressing needs.

Any effort to resurrect public housing must recognize the revulsion that has developed among the American public as a result of the intense concentration of poverty in projects. However, the high proportion of the "underclass" in public housing is the direct result of the decline in standards of occupancy. Since the 1970s, inflexible and intrusive rules for tenant selection emanating from HUD have discouraged local administrators, leaving them little choice but to operate projects as housing of last resort, one step away from the homeless shelter. Public housing in too many big cities is operated as the warehouse for families who have serious social problems and who need drug treatment, health care, job training, and basic educational skills. But the program was not designed to deal with this overwhelming level of need. These families require intensive social services, delivered under the direction of community-based social service agencies funded by federal, state, and local government. Public housing, if it is to be both physically and politically viable, must positively serve the working poor, not negatively serve as a warehouse for the underclass.

This book offers the 1940–1960 period in public housing as a model for a viable future. In Chicago, under the leadership of Elizabeth Wood, public housing thrived, producing good housing, good neighborhoods, and a strong sense of community. Those fortunate enough to live in the CHA's projects in this period developed positive values and went on to make significant contributions to society. The sum total of the interviews of the former tenants in this book tells a remarkable and essentially unknown story. They *loved* public housing. If the policies of this period can be reinstated under new, capable leadership, then public housing can once again provide benefits for the millions of working poor who desperately need and deserve access to better housing.

DESIGN AND SIZE

Some observers believe that the problem with public housing is its poverty-oriented design. While some developments clearly lack positive aesthetics, former residents made few, if any, adverse comments on the design of the units or on their structures. For most families, public housing was extremely attractive because it was a considerable improvement over their former housing. Most remembered delight at being in a home with central heat, hot water, and a bedroom for each child. Their memories centered on good neighbors, regular maintenance, and attractive landscaping, not the physical shape of their buildings.

Despite the tenants' apparent lack of concern with design, there is no question that after 1950 a primary problem in the acceptance of public housing by potential working-class applicants was the uniformity of design, a fact that contributed to their poverty-oriented look. The sterile designs demanded by the federal government not only kept costs low but also kept public housing noncompetitive with the private market. Since most low-income working Americans see themselves not as poor but as middle class, they were unwilling to move into what looks like "housing for the poor."

Elizabeth Wood recognized this limitation, and in 1948, when a state- and city-funded housing program was introduced (which did not have the restrictive limitations of the federal program), she obtained the services of prominent architects, including Skidmore, Owings and Merrill, Harry Weese, and Keck and Keck (as explained in John Ducey's interview). As a result, the CHA built a number of outstanding smaller, mid-rise, "vest-pocket" projects of around 150 to 300 units that won architectural awards. Archer, Prairie, Ogden, Maplewood, Harrison, and Loomis Courts—all of which are between six and fourteen stories high—were for many years considered highly desirable. Such mid-rise projects could be used today as the cornerstone for redeveloping the many vacant (or nearly vacant) blocks in cities.

The general public simplistically criticizes high-rises as negative and assumes that low-income families cannot or should not live in tall buildings. However, the former residents recognize that high-rises by themselves are not the real cause of the problem. While many indicated dismay with abysmal conditions at projects like the massive Robert Taylor Homes, they understood that the present conditions are the result of the admission and management practices of the Housing Authority. Not surprisingly, a number of former tenants are now living in high-rises in other areas. More significantly, high-rise buildings filled largely with low-income families are currently being operated with great success by both public and private management. (See Afterword for more discussion of successful high-rise, low-income buildings.)

Along with the current invective against high-rises is the denunciation of the size of U.S. public housing. Many maintain that low-income working families must be scattered and should not live together in large numbers. In no case, the current wisdom suggests, should there be subsidized housing projects of even two hundred or three hundred units. This thinking ignores the CHA's past successes and makes it difficult to re-create the strong sense of community that existed in the large-scale housing in which former tenants thrived. Not one former tenant criticized, or even mentioned, size as a factor in the quality of project life. In fact, they referred to large developments like Wells or Altgeld as "nurturing." They often narrowed their description to a single "block" or village, showing that tenants on their own—like residents of most neighborhoods—divided larger developments into livable spaces. Joseph Shuldiner, a former top official at HUD and former Executive Director of the CHA, succinctly expressed the idea that design has been overemphasized in accounts of public housing: "We need to be creating viable communities of inclusion and not worry so much about the design of the buildings. We need to manage the property as a socially responsible landlord and perform the little things that mean so much."

RACE AND LOCATION

From the start of the public housing program, race and location have been critical political issues. In the 1940s and 1950s, Chicago's white aldermen, supported by their constituency, sought to preserve residential segregation in the city and blocked public housing sites in their neighborhoods. As a result, nearly all postwar projects were built in black areas. In 1966, a class-action lawsuit charged the CHA with discrimination in site selection. In the case *CHA* v. *Gautreaux* (1969), civil rights lawyers won a victory important in principle but Pyrrhic in practice. The *Gautreaux* remedy imposed severe restrictions upon the location and design of public housing, dictating that no new developments could be built in black areas until seven hundred units had been built in white areas. White politicians continued to use the multiple tools at their disposal to block any substantial construction of public housing in white areas. By the 1970s, aldermen could point to the dismal conditions and extremely poor tenants in public housing to play on the not altogether unfounded fears of home owners—white and black—that the CHA would fill any new projects primarily with many dysfunctional families on welfare. As a result, no housing was built in white areas, and therefore none could be built in black ones. Since 1969 public housing construction in Chicago has dwindled to a trickle.

The *Gautreaux* solution also demanded "scattered sites" as the best approach to locating new public housing developments. This policy, it was believed, offered both the possibility of racially integrating white neighborhoods and overcoming public antipathy to large-scale public housing. But the assumption that only scattered sites can work ignores the positive aspects of the early CHA projects as well as projects in other American and European cities. The scattered-site approach also assumes that the best way to serve the black poor is to move them into dispersed sites in outlying white areas or in the suburbs. But many former tenants suggest that they want to remain closely connected to African-American neighborhoods and live near the churches, family, and community organizations on which they depend.

They did agree that all Americans should have the freedom to move and live wherever they choose, and those African Americans who want to move to the suburbs certainly should be able to do so without barriers. Still, most resisted the idea of a large-scale relocation of current public housing residents to the suburbs.

Finally, the scattered-site approach, with its insistence on integration over all other values, hinders the revitalization of vast stretches of black neighborhoods now blighted with dilapidated houses and vacant lots. The increasing suburbanization of African Americans since the 1980s, coupled with aggressive enforcement of housing codes, has resulted in the wholesale abandonment and clearance of large sections of Chicago's older black neighborhoods. These areas are ripe for the development of good new public housing, along with parks and community facilities. However, the courts have ruled that new projects must first go in white areas, where readily available tracts of significant size are scarce or prohibitively expensive. The Housing Authority is left with the difficult task of finding available land and then overcoming fears of race and class in white neighborhoods. Only a reformed and resuscitated Authority can overcome these obstacles, restore confidence in public housing, and convince nervous neighborhoods that new projects can work. If a community were made aware that the tenants of a new project would be essentially working class, with a not dissimilar family composition and only somewhat lower income than that of the surrounding neighborhood, difficulties might be largely eliminated.

COMMUNITY BUILDING, RELIGION, AND SPORTS

More than mere buildings, the early public housing projects were real communities, with a shared sense of family. This cannot be overemphasized. Administrators in the early years worked hard to ensure that public housing communities radiated "togetherness." Tenants understood and responded positively. Many interviews in this book provide an instance of a parent-like figure in the community who offered guidance, mentoring, encouragement, or discipline. Bert Ellis recalled: "If somebody else's mom saw you doing something, she just picked up the phone, and when you got home you had to answer to that. . . . It was a community that raised children, and there was care." Tenants often referred to other tenants as "my extended family." This close relationship was affirmed by the regular summer reunions of former tenants of Wells, Altgeld, and Wentworth that continue to this day.

This community-building blueprint worked. Interviewees described not only their personal successes but also those of their friends and neighbors. Many of the respondents cited CHA encouragement as instrumental in their positive development and their desire to give back to and participate in the community. The domino effect of these activities led tenants to feel as if those in the public housing village were looking after them. Other catalytic agents in the community—churches, clubs, and sports teams—also provided specific opportunities for the young to grow and excel. Although many of the interviewees here led undistinguished lives, the number of success stories was significant. These include high political positions, tenured professorships, business and professional awards—notable achievements in contrast with the current perception of public housing residents.

The attachment of these former tenants to community and church was graphically manifested in the number who attended the Million Man March in Washington, D.C., in 1995. There was little consensus among the interviews about the views of Minister Louis Farrakhan or Reverend Jesse Jackson. But there was an overwhelming endorsement of the March as a demonstration of community. A large mass of African-American men standing together in harmony—no violence, no trashing, no anger—simply black men rejoicing in the safe embrace of many others just like them. These were men who cared enough about themselves and the next guy to show up at the Capitol and display solidarity. For many, the last time they had experienced anything like this was back in the projects in the 1940s and 1950s.

QUALITY OF STAFF AND REGULATIONS

If cities are sincere about redeveloping public housing projects so needy working-class families can participate, they will have to develop a cadre of Housing Authority employees who exhibit the same dedication and sense of mission that existed in the early years of the CHA and other local housing authorities. There is no question about the difficulties of developing such a group, particularly in a period when the nation's political leadership has done little to promote government as a positive career for young people.

In the early days of the CHA, staff was respected. Tenants lauded the janitors and managers who both enforced rules and involved themselves routinely and positively in the lives of the tenants. The managers interviewed here were obviously devoted to the idea that public housing is a fundamental good. One can jump from the dignity of Oscar Brown to the steadfastness of Ruth Sable to the caring sternness of Muriel Chadwick to the rule-bending humanity of Daisy Brumfield. "Yes," Brumfield says ironically after thirty-five years of outstanding service, "the CHA should have fired me long ago." These administrators cared about public housing and cared about people.

The administrations that succeeded Elizabeth Wood did not share her zeal for good housing or her intense concern for tenants. Through indifference more than incompetence, they converted the public housing into a modern-day poorhouse by making the CHA the provider of the city's housing of last resort. HUD in Washington, limited by a less-than-friendly Congress, imposed further restrictions on local housing authorities that made creative thinking and caring management difficult, if not impossible. The formula for good public housing is not complicated, yet little discussion of a "back-to-basics" approach is heard. Committed management, enforceable rules, good screening, and stable, working-class tenants are the key to positive public housing outcomes.

Some observers have offered tenant management as the panacea to public housing's woes, and this cure has been embraced by both Republican and Democratic administrations. Despite its supporters, tenant management has proven ineffective in most cases. Almost none of the respondents who had lived under a tenant management system had anything positive to say about it. The best that was said was by Hallie Amey, who commented that while Elizabeth Wood's administration required no tenant management, the utter incompetence and lack of caring of the subsequent administrations made tenant management at least a viable alternative. However, both Helen Preston and Myrtle Morrison lived under various tenant management schemes and were unhappy with these administrations. Deborah Gilliam Mayes, a bank executive who lived under tenant management, said, "The basic management decisions should be made by professionals who know the housing business" and not by part-time tenant managers. Phyllis Offord, Leclaire Courts resident and supervisor at a nearby settlement house, remarked, "Resident management was set up by the government to fail." At Leclaire, tenant management failed. Other cities—St. Louis, Boston, Washington—have experienced similar problems.[25]

Apart from tenant management or ownership, a more basic question is whether public housing should be managed by public or private entities. Since the 1980s there has been a backlash against the public sector and a strong push toward privatization of any public operation, including hospitals, schools, transportation, even parks and prisons. Although there are few direct comments in the interviews on private versus public operation, there clearly was a respect and admiration for the CHA's public operation in its early years. Similar managerial success was evident in other cities during this period, and New York City has sustained generally respected public management to the present. Further, all over Western Europe there has been managerial and operational success in subsidized housing. In Paris alone, a city of two million people, two thousand units of affordable housing for low- and moderate-income families are built *each year*. By comparison, in Chicago a total of only two thousand "scattered site" public housing units have been built *since the 1970s*. The idea that public-sector management is inherently inefficient ignores the many examples of solid government efficiency, past and present.[26]

TENANT SELECTION

The most important proposal for recovering public housing's former success is a return to the careful screening of tenants. This is the most consistent battle cry of both current and former residents. Originally, public housing was for working-poor families who came from the bottom third of the income scale. People struggling, yes, and occasionally unemployed, with a modest portion receiving public assistance, but striving for better. Countless former residents spoke approvingly of the rigorous screening process of the CHA's early years. Interviews and inspections by CHA staff made a significant impression on applicants even before they were admitted to public housing. Families waited eagerly to see if their housekeeping and general standards met the demands of the CHA. These original tenants understood and approved of such monitoring. Careful tenant selection techniques were not unique to Chicago. Other cities experienced similar success in the early years of the program. Boston under Ellis Ash; Washington, D.C., under John Ihlder; Pittsburgh under Alfred Tronzo; Baltimore under Oliver Winston; and Cleveland under Ernie Bohn achieved positive results. More important, the New York City Housing Authority, with 160,000 units of subsidized housing, continues to receive high marks for its enlightened management.

The CHA's early progressive administrators set income limits for admission to public housing to ensure that the working poor received priority. They were also concerned that public housing not become a modern-day poorhouse and raised these limits periodically, recognizing the need to retain upward-striving, working-class role models. But in the late 1960s, Congress enacted the Brooke Amendment, requiring public housing residents to pay 25 percent of their income for rent (later raised to 30 percent and known as the "30% rule"). For the working class, this policy meant a rent hike with each pay increase. Similarly, in the 1970s and 1980s Congress forced local housing authorities to give preference in admissions to the poorest of the poor. Once fully implemented, these policies had a devastating impact on public housing across the country, turning many projects from beloved parts of the community into warehouses shunned by outsiders. Gordon Cavanaugh, a former head of the Philadelphia Housing Authority, explained, "Most experienced leaders in public housing knew the unsoundness of the federal policies which brought public housing to this [current] state, mainly overarching admissions priority for the poorest of the poor, protection for badly behaved tenants over peace and quiet for the whole . . . and imposing a rent system that penalized employment."[27] The view from below is similar to this view from above. The interviews in this book confirm that these changes in tenant selection policies were an important reason why many working-class families left public housing.

The former tenants also say one reason for the success of the early projects was the high proportion of two-parent families. As they recollect, almost all the families seemed to have a mother and father, and only a small percentage were female-headed families. Actually, about 30 percent of the CHA's tenants in the 1950s were from female-headed families, and roughly a third of interviewees were also from such families. Nevertheless, most respondents recalled a far smaller proportion. In all likelihood, they arrived at this perception because the families, whole or broken, seemed to be solid families. Still, public housing in this period was essentially a working-class community, not unlike other Chicago neighborhoods at the time. Today, of course, the number of single-parent families of all classes is far greater, and certainly public policy must recognize the significant social changes that have taken place since the 1940s. Indeed, respondents did not seek policies that rejected families on the basis of marital status. Instead, tenant selection, they argued, should be limited to upward-striving, low-income families—single-parent or two-parent—who have demonstrated the capacity to live by community standards and who can benefit from good, affordable housing.

The future of public housing is dependent on the policy choices in tenant selection. Given the current conditions in public housing in Chicago and in most other large urban cities, three stark alternatives are available:

1. Housing authorities can continue the present policy of taking applicants from the waiting list on a first-come, first-served basis with virtually no screening, with continued preference for extremely poor families, and with limited power to evict problem tenants. Existing projects will deteriorate further until destruction becomes inevitable, followed by HUD-sponsored "mixed-income" redevelopment. This publicly funded gentrification will drastically reduce the number of public housing units while providing far too little for the working class. Ultimately, this path means essentially the end of public housing in the United States.
2. Housing authorities could continue to accept the problem cases and evict few, while the federal government provided tenants with a massive new input of resources and social services, including improved police protection, health care, job training, and vastly improved schools. Assuming these extra services are politically feasible (a doubtful proposition in the short term), this solution would largely humanize the existing "poorhouse" nature of public housing. Under this scenario, public housing would remain a stigmatized program exclusively for the very poor.
3. The most realistic alternative is to evict a significant portion of tenants who have proved destructive and reinstate the screening processes that were in effect in the early days of public housing. The former and current residents interviewed here argue for the eviction of a substantial number of tenants—somewhere between 10 percent and 30 percent—who have proven to be disruptive and dangerous to project life. The removal of this fraction who have failed to demonstrate an ability to live up to acceptable community standards must be done humanely and with a large-scale infusion of social services. But no other single step would go further in restoring social order in project life.[28] Although this may seem draconian, it is clearly far less disruptive than the current practice of evicting all tenants and demolishing entire buildings, a policy that, amazingly, seems to call forth less public obloquy.

The draconian course of action is the one recommended by former residents—those with firsthand experience to understand the problems of public housing. This solution would also require the reforms discussed earlier—new leadership, enforcement of standards, and substantial rehabilitation of long-neglected developments. Admittedly the most difficult component of reform centers on the eviction of a significant portion of tenants, since that action will undoubtedly meet with serious opposition from the courts, civil libertarians, and the media. As Daniel Wuenschel, Executive Director of the Cambridge (Massachusetts) Housing Authority, explained: "Housing authorities, more often than not, encounter judges unwilling to grant evictions of tenants for 'just cause' and even non-payment of rent because they erroneously conceive of public housing as 'housing of last resort.' How many times have public housing attorneys heard judges say, 'If I grant you this eviction, where are this mother and her children to go?'"[29] Certainly, families should not be displaced without careful attention to finding alternative housing. But public housing authorities cannot continue to bear the burden of serving seriously deprived families in a poorhouse setting. Admittedly, eviction is a painful proposition, but one that acknowledges the limitations of a housing program. Public housing unaided cannot possibly address the multitude of societal needs, but it should not be dragged down by a lack of basic services like early childhood education, health care, job training, and drug rehabilitation. If true social justice is to be achieved, each of these efforts demands governmental attention. A strong, viable public housing program for those who could benefit should not be held hostage to this overall societal neglect.

THE REAL SOLUTION: A RETURN TO THE POLICIES OF YESTERDAY

If public housing is to work in the United States, there must be a return to the positive attitude that characterized the Elizabeth Wood administration of the CHA. Her administration was cost-efficient, intelligent, and, although selective, remarkably humane. New policies would look much like the old ones. To carry out this dramatic change, the government, the media, and the courts must cooperate. The process must be executed with humanity but with firmness, and it must be recognized that this "surgery" is necessary if public housing is to be saved. We must avoid repeating a self-defeating cycle whereby inadequate administration is followed by public condemnation that in turn leads to destructive occupancy and ultimate destruction of the program.

Of course, an important component of any reform must be extensive physical renovation of existing projects. Unfortunately, the CHA and many other housing authorities have allowed conditions to deteriorate considerably. This long-term neglect by public officials may make it necessary to demolish *some* of the structures but rebuild them with a *similar* number of units. This is what is done in France and England, countries with similar economic ills, where projects are rebuilt with equivalent amounts of housing.

It was recognized at the outset of the public housing program that low-income families required better schools, better health services, and a generally fuller life in which religion and sports played an important role. This thinking went into making the successful villages that the Chicago Housing Authority once administered. Stories like those heard from Bertrand Ellis, Edgar Johnson, and Abdul Alkalimat do not invent the past. They remember a time when the projects were the safe, caring havens they were intended to be. Let us return to a past that succeeded, and embrace the compassionate vision of Elizabeth Wood for public housing in Chicago and elsewhere in the United States. There is no question that the challenges are enormous, and even some enlightened housing authority executives from around the country believe it is an uphill battle. But it must be done if we care about working families that face a chronic shortage of good, affordable housing.

Afterword

Despite this book's recital of the positive history of public housing, many readers will remain skeptical that the program's earlier achievements can be replicated today. This attitude is buttressed by the current policy of tearing down high-rise projects. With the blessing of (and funding from) the federal government, Chicago is in the middle of the largest housing demolition program in history, with plans to tear down all fifty-one of its high-rise public housing buildings. Numerous buildings at projects like the Robert Taylor Homes, Henry Horner Homes, and Cabrini-Green have already come down. St. Louis started the trend in the early 1970s with Pruitt-Igoe; Baltimore has already won the race to be the first city to rid itself entirely of high-rise public housing. Extrapolating from conditions at the most infamous projects, policy makers have readily jumped to the erroneous conclusion that high-rise public housing cannot work for low-income urban families, and to the spurious conclusion that it is economically impossible to rehabilitate them. Urban planners argue that high-rises are a failure and that low-rise, row-house, and walk-up buildings on scattered sites are the only appropriate housing for the low-income urban masses.

This policy ignores numerous high-rise buildings that today serve low-income families quite well, belying the idea that either design or income alone holds the key to housing the working poor. Three projects in Chicago are examples of what publicly subsidized housing could be. The first is a privately operated, heavily subsidized building called Long Grove House. This 448-unit development would be a welcome neighbor in even the most up-scale neighborhoods. In all aspects, Long Grove House is an outstanding success, challenging the current consensus on what makes a housing project "work."

At twenty-nine stories, Long Grove House is nearly twice the height of the Robert Taylor Homes. Located at 20th and Michigan Avenues on

Chicago's near South Side, it sits only four blocks from several less-than-successful Chicago Housing Authority public housing projects. Completed in 1968, Long Grove was for many years a bright light in an otherwise struggling neighborhood. The 1990s have seen new development in the area, and Mayor Richard M. Daley lives six blocks to the north, in the new Dearborn Park development. Since 1995, gentrification has redeveloped neighboring warehouses and former factories into upscale housing.

Long Grove's 448 families are nearly all low-income, mostly working poor. Roughly 80 percent of families are female-headed, and roughly 30 percent are on welfare, according to the development's long-time manager. The average household income is around $20,000, slightly above the poverty level but well below Chicago's median family income of $60,000. Ninety-eight percent of residents are African American. The typical resident of the building is exactly the kind of hardworking, struggling mother for whom housing assistance makes the difference between poverty and stability for herself and her children. Conversations with residents immediately reveal their high levels of satisfaction with Long Grove. One mother, a special education teacher at a private school, explained that she could not possibly find affordable housing for her three boys in Chicago's private market; yet at Long Grove she has lived for the past ten years in a three-bedroom apartment with a view of Lake Michigan. Another tenant, recently off welfare, can walk to her new job at the nearby Chicago *Defender*. Residents expressed genuine approval of conditions and few complaints about life at Long Grove. Safety, they said, was not a serious concern. As a result, turnover has been extremely low—less than 3 percent in 2001—and the waiting list for new applicants has been essentially closed for two years.

Part of the reason for this tenant satisfaction is that Long Grove is simply an attractive environment all around. While entirely typical of late 1960s designs—modernist concrete with a Miesian influence—the building is clean and up-to-date in every sense. The entrance lobby has a modern, glass-partitioned lobby with polished stone floors. A day care center occupies a large space on the ground floor, along with a well-equipped exercise room. Rental apartments are mostly one or two bedrooms, with some three-bedroom units. All have wall-to-wall carpeting, recently upgraded windows, modern kitchens, air-conditioning, and well-lighted hallways. Outside are a well-kept lawn and flower garden. In short, the building is entirely indistinguishable from the typical rental high-rise buildings that stretch along Chicago's lakefront from Hyde Park to Edgewater.

How does this building with all the supposed strikes against it—high-rise, segregated, full of single-parent and welfare families—provide not just good but outstanding housing? Several reasons are apparent, all of which can point to the failures of other aspects of federal housing policy rather than the design of the building or the incomes of its tenants. First, strong management is a crucial factor in the success at Long Grove. Its manager has been in property management with the Habitat Corporation (the building's owner), for twenty-eight years. She lives in the building, adding a reassuring presence. The manager explained that she has had only a handful of "problem" tenants in her tenure, and five families were evicted last year. But in each case she had the resources and support to pursue the often lengthy court battles to evict, ensuring the long-run viability of the project. Similarly, maintenance is astonishingly good at the building. Residents said maintenance concerns were handled within hours, not days. Screening has also helped sustain a healthy environment, though only 10 percent of applicants fail to make it through the application process. The manager is not creaming the crop (as evidenced by the significant portion of welfare families) but merely enforcing the rules.

A second crucial element of success at Long Grove has been a sufficient level of resources. In the parlance of federal programs, Long Grove started out as a "221(d)(3)" project—subsidized by a low-interest federal loan that allowed rents to be set at affordable levels. In 1995, Long Grove received federal subsidies to preserve it as a subsidized project—its owners might otherwise have converted it to market-rate apartments. Currently, 85 percent of the building's units (381 out of 448) are subsidized under the "Section 8" program. Under this program, building owners are guaranteed a specific rent; tenants pay 32 percent of their income for rent, and HUD pays the rest. As a result of these subsidies, Long Grove House receives roughly $460 per apartment per month in subsidies ($2.5 million a year) from HUD. When subsidies are combined with the tenants' contribution, Long Grove has the financial resources necessary to hire an experienced management team, to ensure prompt maintenance, and to plan for long-range upgrades.

Another development demonstrating that high-rise buildings work is one of the CHA's own. In the early 1990s, the CHA used federal funds to extensively rehabilitate two seventeen-story high-rises with 282 units and created Lake Parc Place, now one of its most desirable communities. Despite its 1950s architecture and its horrible condition in the 1980s, the project was saved by an infusion of funds. The careful rehabilitation of the two high-rises included new kitchens, new landscaping, and new management. The development reopened in 1992 with careful screening of residents and effective maintenance. As a result, it has remained an attractive, viable development since then. Roughly 40 percent of residents are "moderate-income" (with incomes between $25,000 and $40,000 per year), and 30 percent are working poor earning less than $25,000. Finally, about 30 percent receive some form of public assistance. Significantly, the substantial number of elderly families and married couples with no children helps bring the average number of youths per unit down to roughly 1.5—a more manageable figure than at some high-rise projects, where young people outnumber adults two to one.

But fundamentally, caring management, increased security, and a healthy rent-paying tenant base keep the buildings in good condition. Attractive but solid wrought-iron fences indicate both safety and care, as do the well-monitored entrances. Tenants are organized, but not in a way that paralyzes action. While the development is a resident-managed corporation, tenants do not in effect run the complex and do not overly interfere with the ability of the professional managers to do their jobs. As a result, Lake Parc has a healthy relationship between tenants and management. Finally, employed tenants pay a slightly higher rent. While Lake Parc gets far less subsidy than Long Grove House—only about $220 per unit per month—when combined with tenant rent, the income is sufficient to sustain a well-maintained and pleasant building. Conversations with residents suggest high levels of satisfaction. The Lake Parc success story has received surprisingly little media coverage—few know that the CHA has actually renovated a high-rise and made it work.[30]

A third example of a successful publicly subsidized building occupied by low-income and moderate-income families is Archer Courts. This 147-unit building was constructed in 1950 and operated successfully by the CHA for roughly forty years. Most years, it served a mix of Chinese-American, African-American, and white tenants (see the interview with Pat Harris, a former manager). Unfortunately, the CHA neglected maintenance and security problems in the 1990s, allowed the building to go somewhat to seed, and felt compelled to sell the building for $650,000 (little more than $4,400 per unit) to the Chicago Community Development Corporation, a private firm. The CCDC initiated a $6.5 million makeover ($44,000 per unit) that included not only interior renovations and additional community space, but also an exterior glass curtain-wall that enclosed formerly open balconies. The glass transformed the building's facade and created a highly attractive appearance that has received several awards for architectural ingenuity.[31] Three-quarters of tenants who were residents before the makeover are still residents; since then, turnover is about 7 percent a year. Tenants are roughly 60 percent Chinese-American and 40 percent African-American. Clearly, a mid-rise or high-rise building can be renovated to serve low-income families of all races. The only question is why the CHA believed it had to sell Archer Courts to a private corporation when Lake Parc's success showed it could do the job itself. Perhaps the answer lies in the more generous subsidies received under the Section 8 program, which provides Archer Courts roughly $500 per unit per month, more than $800,000 per year.

These examples could easily be replicated at the CHA's other high-rise public housing developments, especially if public housing received the same generous Section 8 subsidies as Long Grove House and Archer Courts. Instead, the CHA buys into the simplistic argument that it is the buildings—and not their management—that have been the root cause of problems. Former residents of Dearborn Homes and Ickes Homes (both mid-rise projects) emphasized that they had found nothing inherently oppressive or destructive of family values in the design of elevator buildings. Instead, they were deeply concerned with admitting the right kind of tenants and maintaining standards.

With good management, with sufficient funding, and with reasonable screening, publicly high-rise public housing for low-income, female-headed families can be sanctuaries, not penitentiaries. The late Philip Klutznick, former head of the Federal Public Housing Administration, an outstanding builder of private housing, and later U.S. Secretary of Commerce, explained in 1990 that design is less important than management: "It is not whether buildings are high-rise or low-rise that determines whether the building functions well or not. Buildings are not the enemies. It is bad management that permits the poor type of tenants to continue in occupancy. High-rises properly tenanted and maintained are perfectly adequate for low- and moderate-income families. In a country so lacking in housing for low- and moderate-income families it is almost criminal to tear down buildings that are repairable."[32]

Notes

1. Most discussion of public housing in the media suggests that congregate projects operated by public authorities cannot function well. Yet, a major 1992 survey of public housing found only 6 percent of projects "severely distressed." While considerable deterioration may have been allowed to occur since 1992, it remains clear that public housing of both the low-rise and high-rise variety is still an eminently usable program. See U.S. National Commission on Severely Distressed Public Housing, *The Final Report of the National Commission on Severely Distressed Public Housing: A Report to the Congress and the Secretary of Housing and Urban Development* (Washington, DC: U.S. Government Printing Office, 1992).

2. Alex Kotlowitz, *There Are No Children Here: The Story of Two Boys Growing Up in the Other America* (New York: Doubleday, 1991); Nicholas Lemann, *The Promised Land: The Great Black Migration and How It Changed America* (New York: Vintage, 1991); Frederick Wiseman, *Public Housing* (Cambridge, MA: Zipporah Films, 1997).

3. Studs Terkel, *Hard Times: An Oral History of the Great Depression* (New York: Pantheon, 1970), 383.

4. The CHA's administrative costs compared favorably with those of other local housing authorities as well as of private projects. See J. S. Fuerst, "Housing Management Costs Compared for 16 Public and Private Projects," *American City* (May 1950).

5. For more history on relations between the City Council, Mayor Richard J. Daley, and the CHA, see Martin Meyerson and Edward Banfield, *Politics, Planning and the Public Interest: The Case of Public Housing in Chicago* (Glencoe, IL: Free Press, 1955); Arnold Hirsch, *Making the Second Ghetto: Race and Housing in Chicago, 1940–1960* (Chicago: University of Chicago Press, 1998); and Adam Cohen and Elizabeth Taylor, *American Pharaoh: Mayor Richard J. Daley* (Boston: Little, Brown, 2000).

6. For Wood's speech, see J. S. Fuerst, *Public Housing in Europe and America* (London: Croom Helm, 1974), 157–158.

7. See Arnold Hirsch, "Massive Resistance in the Urban North: Trumbull Park, Chicago, 1953–1966," *Journal of American History* (September 1995): 522–550.

8. On the CHA's management efficiency, see J. S. Fuerst, "Housing Management Costs Compared for 16 Public and Private Projects."

9. In fact, it was Mayor Martin Kennelly who pushed most aggressively for the hiring of Richard J. Daley's second cousin in 1953. At the time, Daley was chairman of the Cook County Democratic organization, and Kennelly had hoped his intervention on behalf of Daley's relative would convince the leader of Cook County's Democrats to support his bid for a third term as Mayor. Daley, however, did not support Kennelly, and won the nomination and the mayoral election in 1955. See Arnold Hirsch, *Making the Second Ghetto*, 234.

10. The Public Housing Association was a private housing reform organization in Chicago that strongly supported public housing.

11. Lake Meadows is a large apartment complex built in the late 1940s as an early form of "urban renewal." Thousands of homes were demolished to make way for the complex.

12. For a recent history of Park Forest, see Gregory C. Randall, *America's Original G.I. Town: Park Forest, Illinois* (Baltimore: Johns Hopkins University Press, 2000).

13. Frank London Brown, *Trumbull Park: A Novel* (Chicago: Regnery, 1959).

14. The "30 percent rule" refers to the 1969 Brooke Amendment, which made rents in public housing a function of a tenant's income. Initially, rent was set at 25 percent of income, later raised to 30 percent. From 1970 to 1982, the CHA placed a cap on the amount of rent in an effort to keep working-class families in public housing. But in 1982, in a misguided effort to increase rent revenues, HUD forced the CHA to require all tenants to pay 30 percent of their income as rent. For some working tenants, the 1982 change meant a massive increase in rent. For rental rates from 1965 to 1984, see series Chicago Housing Authority, *Annual Statistical Report*, available at the Chicago Public Library, Municipal Reference Collection.

15. The Public Housing Administration (PHA) was absorbed into the newly created Department of Housing and Urban Development (HUD) in 1966.

16. The CHA had discretionary power to evict following a 1951 federal district court case, *CHA* v. *Elizabeth Ivory* (341 Ill. App. 282). In 1967, after several unfavorable court decisions concerning evictions, HUD issued new regulations that instructed local housing authorities to institute extensive new tenant rights, including tenant review of evictions and a lengthy appeals process. See J. S. Fuerst and Roy Petty, "Due Process—How Much Is Enough?" *The Public Interest* (Spring 1985): 96–110; Robyn Minter Smyers, "High Noon in Public Housing: The Showdown Between Due Process Rights and Good Management Practices in the War on Drugs and Crime," *Urban Lawyer* (Summer 1998): 573–613.

17. During the 1990s, the *Gautreaux* program, named after an important court case against the CHA in 1969, helped move roughly two thousand former public housing families into suburban areas. While most of the people interviewed for this book speak negatively about the program, it should be noted that at least one substantial study found the program had a positive impact on lives. See Leonard Rubinowitz and James E. Rosenbaum, *Crossing the Class and Color Lines: From Public Housing to White Suburbia* (Chicago: University of Chicago Press, 2000).

18. Surviving CHA *Annual Statistical Reports* from the late 1940s suggest that roughly 70 precent of families at Wells were "two-parent" families, and between 25 and 30 percent relied on some form of public aid. See CHA, *Annual Statistical Report, 1949.*

19. For more on the significant problems with cancer at Altgeld Gardens, see Heather M. Little, "Toxin Shock," *Chicago Tribune*, January 15, 1995.

20. See CHA, *Annual Statistical Reports*, for data on income by project.

21. In 1952 and 1953, Congress required all public housing residents to sign a loyalty oath. Following a Supreme Court ruling in 1954, the oath became "voluntary." In 1956, the CHA dropped the oath altogether.

22. Midway Gardens, at 60th Avenue and Cottage Grove Boulevard, is a seventeen-story high-rise built in 1953 by the nonprofit Chicago Dwellings Association with subsidies from the state of Illinois. It was Chicago's first "middle-income" project and has been occupied predominantly by African Americans since its opening.

23. Horace Mann Bond, *Black American Scholars: A Study of Their Beginnings* (Detroit: Balamp Publications, 1972).

24. U.S. Department of Housing and Urban Development, "A Report on Worst Case Housing Needs in 1999: New Opportunity Amid Continuing Challenges" (2001). Evidence from the 2000 census is mixed on whether the problem is getting worse or better. See David Mendell, "The Boom Decade: Census Data Show Chicago Area Rode Wave of Economic Prosperity in '90s," *Chicago Tribune*, May 15, 2002; and *Chicago Matters: Housing*, a radio and television series produced by WBEZ, WTTW, and the Chicago Housing Trust (2002).

25. See J. S. Fuerst, "Tenant Management in Low Rent Public Housing," *Social Service Review* (June 1988): 337–344.

26. It is beyond the scope of this book to discuss the other forms of subsidized congregate housing that have provided good, decent housing for Americans. Programs such as HUD's Section 236 and Section 221(d)(3) subsidies have provided numerous examples of successful projects that have been well managed. Of course, critics can always find buildings that have been neglected by poor managers, but that is as true in the private sector as in the subsidized one. For an overview of subsidized housing, see R. Allen Hays, *The Federal Government and Urban Housing: Ideology and Change in Public Policy* (Albany: State University of New York Press, 1995).

27. Letter from Gordon Cavanaugh, Reno and Cavanaugh, PLLC, to J. S. Fuerst, September 6, 2001.

28. Clearly, defining a new set of "community standards," likely written into law or regulation, will be necessary to implement a restoration of social order in public housing. Deciding where to draw lines of acceptable behavior will not be an easy task and will require concerted political energy and community input. It is worth repeating, however, that the former residents interviewed here believe the bar should be far higher than it is today.

29. Letter from Daniel J. Wuenschel, Executive Director of the Cambridge (Massachusetts) Housing Authority, to J. S. Fuerst, August 21, 2001.

30. For more information on the Lake Parc success, see James E. Rosenbaum, Linda K. Stroh, and Cathy A. Flynn, "Lake Parc Place: A Study in Mixed-Income Housing," *Housing Policy Debate* 9, no. 4 (1988).

31. See Gwenda Blair, "Out of the Ashes, Cinderella," *New York Times*, January 2, 2003.

32. See J. S. Fuerst and Roy Petty, "High-Rise Housing for Low-Income Families," *The Public Interest* (Spring 1991): 121.

Further Reading

PUBLIC HOUSING IN CHICAGO

Bowly, Devereux. *The Poorhouse: Subsidized Housing in Chicago, 1895–1976.* Carbondale: Southern Illinois University Press, 1981.

Brown, Frank London. *Trumbull Park: A Novel.* Chicago: Regnery, 1959.

Cohen, Adam, and Elizabeth Taylor. *American Pharaoh: Mayor Richard J. Daley: His Battle for Chicago and the Nation.* Boston: Little, Brown, 2000.

Hirsch, Arnold. *Making the Second Ghetto: Race and Housing in Chicago.* Chicago: University of Chicago Press, 1983; reissued 1997.

Hunt, D. Bradford. "What Went Wrong with Public Housing in Chicago? A History of the Chicago Housing Authority, 1933–1982." Ph.D. Dissertation, University of California at Berkeley, 2000.

Kotlowitz, Alex. *There Are No Children Here: The Story of Two Boys Growing Up in the Other America.* New York: Doubleday, 1991.

Lemann, Nicholas. *The Promised Land: The Great Black Migration and How It Changed America.* New York: Vintage, 1991.

Meyerson, Martin, and Edward Banfield. *Politics, Planning, and the Public Interest: The Case of Public Housing in Chicago.* Glencoe, IL: Free Press, 1955.

Polikoff, Alexander. *Housing the Poor: The Case for Heroism.* Cambridge, MA: Ballinger, 1978.

Rubinowitz, Leonard S., and James E. Rosenbaum. *Crossing the Class and Color Lines: From Public Housing to White Suburbia.* Chicago: University of Chicago Press, 2000.

Venkatesh, Sudhir. *American Project: The Rise and Fall of a Modern Ghetto.* Cambridge, MA: Harvard University Press, 2000.

Whitaker, David T. *Cabrini-Green in Words and Pictures.* Chicago: W3 Chicago, 2000.

PUBLIC HOUSING IN AMERICA

Baumann, John F., Roger Biles, and Kristin M. Szylvian. *From Tenements to the Taylor Homes: In Search of an Urban Housing Policy in Twentieth Century America.* University Park: Pennsylvania State University Press, 2000.

Bratt, Rachel. *Rebuilding a Low-Income Housing Policy.* Philadelphia: Temple University Press, 1989.

Freedman, Leonard. *Public Housing: The Politics of Poverty.* New York: Holt, Rinehart, and Winston, 1969.

Hays, R. Allen. *The Federal Government and Urban Housing: Ideology and Change in Public Policy.* 2nd ed. Albany: State University of New York Press, 1995.

Radford, Gail. *Modern Housing for America.* Chicago: University of Chicago Press, 1996.

PUBLIC HOUSING IN OTHER AMERICAN CITIES

Bauman, John. *Public Housing, Race, and Renewal: Urban Planning in Philadelphia, 1920–1974.* Philadelphia: Temple University Press, 1987.

Meehan, Eugene. *The Quality of Federal Policymaking.* Columbia: University of Missouri Press, 1979.

Plunz, Richard. *A History of Housing in New York City: Dwelling Type and Social Change in the American Metropolis.* New York: Columbia University Press, 1990.

PUBLIC HOUSING IN OTHER COUNTRIES

Fuerst, J. S., ed. *Public Housing in Europe and America.* New York: Wiley, 1974.

Harloe, Michael. *The People's Home?: Social Rented Housing in Europe and America.* Oxford: Blackwell, 1995.

Karn, Valerie, and Harold Wolman. *Comparing Housing Systems: Housing Performance and Housing Policy in the United States and Britain.* New York: Oxford University Press, 1992.

Index

ABLA project, 24, 33
abortion, 126
affirmative action: former public housing residents supporting, 52, 81, 85, 96, 103, 130, 132, 147, 156, 175–76; Ida B. Wells residents not needing, 54; as not dealing with people after they're in, 44; at University of Illinois Dental School, 110, 112
African Americans. *See* black Americans
Afrocentricity, 164
Airport Homes, 5
Alexander, Gwendolyn Duncan, 105–6
Algebra Project, 135
Alkalimat, Abdul (Gerald McWhirter), 133–37, 204
Altgeld-Carver Alumni Society, 92
Altgeld Gardens: aerial view of, *see photo essay*; as affordable housing, 160; annual picnics at, 92; baseball teams at, 137, 148; Bright as resident of, 147–49; as built on landfill, 190; CHA board members coming to, 160; child care at, 153; Children's Building at, 148; Davis as resident of, 137–38; decline of, 35; defense workers at, 12, 93, 154; as engine for upward mobility, 2, 76; environmental hazards at, 94, 160–61, 190; Bob and Bea Fairfax helping improve life at, 151; flowers at, 58, 59, 92, 115, 137, 140; Greenlee as resident of, 58–59; Harris as resident of, 34–35; Ida B. Wells Homes compared with, 12; as isolated, 116, 152; Jackson as resident of, 156–59; Johnson as resident of, 189–90; King as resident of, 159–61; kitchen interior, *see photo essay*; Lewis as resident of, 155–56; library, 78, *see photo essay*; Moore as resident of, 92–94; reunions at, 198; Robinson as resident of, 138–40; rules at, 77; satellite police department at, 116; screening applicants for, 76–77, 180; Shaw as resident of, 114–16; Erman and Dorothy Sing as residents of, 76–79; as suburban, 157; vegetable gardens near, 115; Claude and Addie Wyatt as residents of, 151, 152–55
Amey, Hallie, 182–83, 200
Archer Courts, 34, 35, 102, 196, 208
arts: structured learning in, 152. *See also* music
Ash, Ellis, 201
Ashburn Homes, 22–23
Ashford, Vonsell, 144–46
Associated Negro Heritage Library, 118
Associated Negro Press, 118

Audy Home, 87
Austin, Margaret, 89–92

Back of the Yards neighborhood, 71
Barnett, Claude, 118
Becker, Ben, 16
Benjamin, Claude, 5
Bennett, Johnny, 60
Berrios, Joseph, 66–68
Bild, Sidney and Bernice, 103–5
Black, Henry, 160
Black, Kevin, 160
black Americans: aggregate condition as worse than whites, 135–36; giving back to the community, 69; integration as low priority for, 102; living in black neighborhoods, 37, 44, 49–50, 59–60, 82, 83, 102, 116, 118, 121, 134–35, 156, 159, 197–98; male role models, 44, 50, 107, 127, 138, 176; migrations to Chicago, 57, 101; as not controlling their communities, 85; students needing something extra, 66; suburbanization of, 198; women as able to get jobs, 81. *See also* middle-class blacks; race
Black Belt: abandonment of, 198; borders crumbling, 101; establishment of, 101; "kitchenette" apartments in, 1, 101; middle class moving out of, 72; public housing projects in, 102; segregation restricting blacks to, 139
Block Beautiful contest, 160
block clubs, 160
Blocker, Carol, 165
Blocker, Walter, 163–66
Bohn, Ernie, 201
Bond, Horace Mann, 135
Bowen, Charles, 90
Brady, Nelvia, 68–70
Bright, Hortense Irwin, 147–49
Brooke Amendment (30 percent rule) (1969), 30, 179, 185, 191, 201, 212n.14
Brooks Homes, *see photo essay*
Brown, Oscar, Sr., 10–12; at Altgeld Gardens, 11, 160; dignity of, 199; at Ida B. Wells Homes, 4, 10–12, 52–53
Brumfield, Daisy: as CHA manager, 29–32; as inspiration for this work, 6; rule-bending humanity of, 199; and Shepherd, 36
Buck, Tom, 19
Bullock, Larry, 113
Burroughs, Margaret Goss, 148
Bush, George, 190, 193
Butler, Jerry, 60–63, 152
Butler, Miss, 169

Cabrini Extension, 105
Cabrini-Green: Berrios as resident of, 66–68; Calvin as resident of, 180–82; creation of, 105; demolition of, 194, 205; high-rises at, 49; as integrated, 185; value of land of, 177, 181; William Green Homes, 105, 107; Wilson as resident of, 185–86. *See also* Cabrini Homes
Cabrini Homes: administration building as center of activities at, 105; Alexander as resident of, 105–6; Alkalimat as resident of, 133–34, 136; Butler as resident of, 60–61; decline of, 105–6, 107, 121; in early 1950s, *see photo essay*; as engine for upward mobility, 2; flowers at, 167; as in the heart of the city, 106, 134; as integrated, 4–5, 60, 101, 106, 120, 133, 134; left-wing cultural activity at, 134; Lewis as resident of, 166–67; as low-rise, 61; as a model, 119; as an oasis, 107; Pugh as resident of, 106–8; screening of applicants at, 180; Willuweit as resident of, 119–21
Calvin, Hattie, 180–82
Cameron, Mickey, 160
Campbell, Clifford, 54
cancer, 94, 160–61, 190
Carter, Vivian, 61
Carver High School, 92, 115, 148
Cavanaugh, Gordon, 201
CHA. *See* Chicago Housing Authority
Chadwick, Muriel, 32–34, 199

CHA v. Elizabeth Ivory (1951), 212n.16
CHA v. Gautreaux (1969), 37, 50, 103, 197, 212n.17
Chess, Leonard, 161, 162–63
Chess Records, 161
Chicago Committee on Urban Development, 186–87
Chicago Community Development Corporation, 208
Chicago Dwellings Association, 213n.22
Chicago Housing Authority (CHA): Block Beautiful contest, 160; building in black neighborhoods only, 5, 16, 102, 118, 197; CHA employees prohibited from living at, 23; character building at, 151–77; City Council opposing, 5, 15–16, 24; Clinton on, 39; community fostered by, 41, 193, 198–99; decline of, 3, 6, 34, 38; demolition of projects, 180, 181, 203–4, 205; as dumping ground, 136; as engine for upward mobility, 2, 3, 41–73; as gateway to the American Dream, 75–99; HUD takeover of, 36–37, 180, 183; integration of, 4–6, 20, 101–2; Kean as head of, 16, 22, 25; life in, 68, 75, 82, 86, 89–90, 97–98, 119, 139, 141, 144, 155, 185, 191; maintenance neglected by, 6, 36–37, 182; monthly dinner meetings, 32; as more than housing complexes, 3; neighbors' importance in, 68, 70, 72, 114, 133, 137, 174, 191; new construction as dwindled to a trickle, 197; as "paradise/heaven," 92, 114, 137, 144, 153; Planning Department, 24; political support eroding, 4–6; politicizing of, 16, 118–19; as prestigious for black families, 102; private management of, 36, 77, 194, 200; reasons for early success of, 3–4; a rebirth for, 193–204; renovation recommended for, 180, 186, 188, 203–4; residents who stayed in, 179–92; returning to policies of yesterday, 203–4; screening of applicants at, 4, 6, 22, 69, 75, 76–77, 126, 145, 169, 180, 183, 186, 188, 191, 201; social programs at projects, 22; staff of, 9–40, 199–200; standards set for residents of, 4, 6, 22, 69, 126–27, 145, 169, 179, 180, 182; as stepping-stone, 28, 30, 98, 136, 167, 188; the structure as very difficult to rebuild, 127; Swibel as head of, 180; "vest-pocket" projects, 196; Wood as executive director of, 4, 9–10, 12, 13–14, 16; Wood's ouster from, 6, 9–10, 21–22; working families in, 6, 35, 50, 69, 72, 80, 93, 183, 194, 195, 212n.14; working families leaving, 6, 169, 179, 182, 191; as working well, 2–4, 195. *See also* Altgeld Gardens; Cabrini-Green; Dearborn Homes; Harold Ickes Homes; Henry Horner Homes; Ida B. Wells Homes; Leclaire Courts; Trumbull Park Homes; Wentworth Gardens; *and other projects by name*
Chicago Youth Organization (CYO), 170
child care, 31, 153
Christian Family Movement, 99
church: Austin influenced by, 90; Blocker influenced by, 163–64; in Cabrini-Green neighborhood, 107, 185; Christian Family Movement, 99; Ellis influenced by, 48–49; Farmer on it not reaching out, 127–28; Holy Angels Church, 49, 81; in Ida B. Wells Homes neighborhood, 175; Johnson on importance of, 81; Lewis influenced by, 168; Monumental Baptist Church, 48; in public housing's success, 151, 199; Reed on importance of, 44; St. Thaddeus Catholic Church, 78; Samuel influenced by, 142; storefront churches, 44; Third Baptist Church, 95–96; Townsell influenced by, 173; Trinity United Church of Christ, 164–65; Vernon Park Church of

church (*continued*)
God, 152, 153, 155; Wayman AMC Church, 168; John Wilson influenced by, 83; Melvin Wilson influenced by, 64
Church Federation of Greater Chicago, 27–28
City Colleges of Chicago, 69–70
city-state projects, 15
civil rights, 29, 55, 107
Clinton, Bill, 39, 190, 193
coaches, 151
cocaine, 84, 147
Coffee, Roberta, 36
college education, 69–70, 91–92, 139
Collins, John, 78
Commonwealth Edison, 42, 43
community-building, 41, 48, 193, 198–99
community representatives, 186–87
community standards, 202, 213n.28
Concentrated Employment Program, 187
concentrated poverty, 176
Cook County Hospital, 154
cottage meetings, 157–58
crack cocaine, 147
Crane, Bennie L., 44–47; in Black Belt tenement, 1, 44–45; moves to Ida B. Wells Homes, 2, 45; upward mobility of, 2, 45; and Wilson, 45, 65
Crane, Bill "Butterball," 161–63
crime: in all types of neighborhood, 82; at Altgeld Gardens, 76; as Cabrini Homes, 121; delinquency, 79, 134; lawless teenage boys as hallmark of public housing, 166; as number one issue, 116; vandalism, 76. *See also* gangs
Crowley, Pat and Patti, 99
Cuomo, Andrew, 193
CYO (Chicago Youth Organization), 170

Daley, Richard J.: CHA building in black neighborhoods only, 5, 118; CHA politicized by, 16; and Barbara Jones, 171; loyalists appointed to CHA by, 10, 18, 212n.9
Daley, Richard M., 206
Davis, Dixie, 64
Davis, Maude, 137–38
Dawson, William, 46, 118
Dearborn Homes: Sidney and Bernice Bild as residents of, 103–5; design as not the problem with, 208–9; as engine for upward mobility, 2; Farmer as resident of, 125–27; Frost as resident of, 72; as integrated, 14–15, 23; Henry and Elouise Messiah as residents of, 97–99; in mid 1950s, *see photo essay*; site plan for, 14; *The Tenants Voice* newspaper, 98; Thompson as resident of, 146–47; Women's Organization, 98–99
Defender (newspaper), 2, 64, 84, 102, 117, 206
De LaSalle High School, 147
delinquency, 79, 134
Deloache, Winifred, 130–32
Denive, Dwayne, 174
Denive, Ricky, 174
Dennis family, 160
Department of Housing and Urban Development (HUD), 36–37, 180, 183, 194–96, 213n.26
design, 13, 22, 195–97, 208–9
dinner meetings, 32
discrimination: in employment, 56, 81, 103, 143, 147; for mortgages, 122, 135; restrictive covenants, 101; at University of Illinois at Chicago, 54
displacement, 15, 20
diversity, 43–44, 108, 134
Doolittle Elementary School, 42, 64, 111, 161
Doran, David, 122–24
draconian policies, 4, 202
drugs: at Altgeld Gardens, 35, 138; cocaine, 84, 147; eviction of tenants using, 181; at Henry Horner Homes, 68; heroin, 84, 147; at Ida B. Wells Homes, 84, 87–88, 175; as making it difficult to restore public housing, 127

DuBois, Reginald, 160
Ducey, John, 12–15; later career of, 9, 12; resignation of, 5, 12
Dunbar Vocational High School, 45, 51, 54, 55, 64, 65, 173
Dykeman, Jack, 24

education, 125–49; adult, 69; Algebra Project, 135; as alternative to welfare system, 59; at Altgeld Gardens, 58; Cabrini-Green residents concerned about, 67; Carver High School, 92, 115, 148; City Colleges of Chicago, 69–70; college education as necessary now, 91–92; concerned teachers, 139; Dearborn Homes residents concerned about, 127; De LaSalle High School, 147; Doolittle Elementary School, 42, 64, 111, 161; Dunbar Vocational High School, 45, 51, 54, 55, 64, 65, 173; equal education as the key, 186; G.I. Bill, 120; Gillespie School, 131–32; girls and boys compared in, 80, 138; Grace Lutheran School, 123; Haines Elementary School, 109; Harrison High School, 123–24; Ida B. Wells residents concerned about, 71, 80, 131; integrated schools, 66; Lane Tech, 67; Lighted Schoolhouse program, 28; Lucy Flower High School, 147, 165; Patton Elementary School, 137; private schools, 78–79, 123; public school system as bad, 46; racism in public schools, 37; St. James Grammar School, 147; under segregation, 72, 135; suburban, 37; teacher integration, 172; Tilden Tech, 42–43, 45, 49, 71, 109; Washburne Trade School, 60; Wells High School, 167; Wendell Phillips High School, 42, 172; Williams Elementary School, 98, 147
elderly housing, 37, 70
elevators: adequate number of, 110; children playing in, 146, 180; at Dearborn Homes, 104, 146; exposed, 69, 104; families with children disliking, 186; at Harold Ickes Homes, 110; at Henry Horner Homes, 69; Wood attempts to allow children to avoid, 22
Ellis, Bertrand, 47–52; on community in public housing, 48, 198; at Ida B. Wells Homes, 47–48; as remembering a time with the projects were safe, 204; upward mobility of, 2, 47
employment. *See* work
environmental hazards, 94, 160–61, 190
evictions: *CHA v. Elizabeth Ivory,* 212n.16; community groups blocking, 34; in early 1950s, 26; the law working against, 34, 35, 36; at Long Grove House, 207; present tenants supporting, 177, 180, 181, 186, 202, 213n.28; for public housing rebirth, 202–3

Fairfax, Bob and Bea, 151, 160
families: CHA complexes as like extended, 3, 191; large, 46, 68, 82, 92, 155; two-parent, 42, 53, 58, 67, 70, 90, 121, 123, 145, 165–66. *See also* single-parent families
Farmer, Eugene, 125–28, 152
Farrakhan, Louis, 63, 128, 136, 199
female-headed families. *See* single-parent families
Fernwood Homes, 5
fingerprinting, 19, 20
Fletcher, James, 70–72
flowers: at Altgeld Gardens, 58, 59, 92, 115, 137, 140; at Cabrini Homes, 167; competitions for, 3, 4, 59, 92, 98; at Harold Ickes Homes, 89, 92; at Ida B. Wells Homes, 11, 45, 175
Fowler, Elmer, 95
Frances Cabrini Homes. *See* Cabrini Homes
Frazier, Officer, 86–87
freedom of choice in housing, 102–3, 106, 142, 198
Frost, Wilson, 72–73, 152
Fruchtman, Ed, 9, 15, 18

gangs: boys in, 138; at Cabrini-Green, 67; curtailing by enforcing the rules, 188; eviction of tenants in, 181; guns increasing in, 84; at Harold Ickes Homes, 90, 108; at Ida B. Wells Homes, 45, 48, 84, 142; as making it difficult to restore public housing, 127; as a phase, 45; at Wentworth Gardens, 189
Gans, Herbert, 9, 24
Garcia, Louis, 160
gardens: vegetables, 27, 115, 167. *See also* flowers
Gautreaux program, 37, 50, 103, 197, 212n.17
G.I. Bill, 120
Gillespie School, 131–32
Gingrich, Newt, 181
Glover, William, 117
Grace Lutheran School, 123
Gray, George, 165
Green, William, Homes, 105, 107
Greenhalgh, Ted, 10, 24–26, 33
Greenlee, Andrew, 57–60

Habitat Corporation, 207
Haines Elementary School, 109
Halloween, 137
Hamilton, Leon, 52–57
Hard Times (Terkel), 3
Harold Ickes Homes: annual inspections at, 145; Ashford as resident of, 144–46; Austin as resident of, 89–90; Chadwick working at, 33; decline of, 145; design as not the problem with, 208–9; flowers at, 89, 92; Henry Booth House, 90; as integrated, 109; Thompson as resident of, 108–9
Harris, Acey, 86–89, 174
Harris, Dillard, 86, 174
Harris, Patricia McArthur, 34–35
Harrison Courts, 196
Harrison High School, 123–24
Hayes, Charles, 76
Hazel Crest (Illinois), 50
health services, 4, 11, 48
Henry, Rosita, 187–89
Henry Horner Homes: Brady as resident of, 68, 69; demolition of high-rises at, 205; and Kotlowitz's *There Are No Children Here,* 68
Herald American (newspaper), 2
heroin, 84, 147
Higgins, Ron, 110
high-rises: at Cabrini-Green, 49, 61, 107; demolition of, 194, 205; density at, 69, 84, 146; seen as inappropriate for poor families, 46, 69, 145, 146, 196, 205; successful, 196, 205–9; Wood attempting to influence design of, 22. *See also* elevators
Hirsch, Emil, 19–22
Holden, Alyce Johnson Holmes, 152, 169–70, 171–72
Holmgren, Ed, 15–16, 18, 22, 103
Holy Angels Church, 49, 81
home visits, 23, 32–33, 76
HOPE VI program, 193–95
Horizon House, 31
Horner Homes. *See* Henry Horner Homes
Howard, Betty, 24
HUD, 36–37, 180, 183, 194–96, 213n.26
Hudson, Charles, 160
Hudson, Helen, 160–61
Hudson, Ralph, 161
Hughes, Langston, 136

Ickes Homes. *See* Harold Ickes Homes
Ida B. Wells Homes: Blocker as resident of, 163, 165–66; Brown as manager of, 10–12, 52–53; contact with white people at, 54; Bennie L. Crane as resident of, 45–46; Bill "Butterball" Crane as resident of, 161; DeLoache as resident of, 130–31; drum chorus at, 175; education as concern of residents of, 53; Ellis as resident of, 47–48; as engine for upward mobility, 2, 88, 111, 131; exterior of, *see photo essay*; Fletcher as resident of, 70–72; flowers at, 11, 45, 175; Hamilton as resident of,

52–54; Harris as resident of, 86–89; health services at, 4, 11, *see photo essay*; Johnson as resident of, 79–82; Leon and Barbara Jones as residents of, 168–69; as low-rise, 46, 145; as middle-class black community, 48; opening of, 2; Reed as resident at, 42; resident involvement at, 82; reunion picnics, 88, 198; Phillip and Jeffery Roberts as residents of, 110–11; Samuel as resident of, 140–43; screening applicants for, 75–76, 169; Slaughter as resident of, 116–17; social services at, 48; sports at, 46, 47, 73, 79, 174–75; switchboard operator school at, 11; two-parent families at, 53, 213n.18; Weddington as resident of, 174–75; as "Well Town," 4, 11; John Wilson as resident of, 83–84; Melvin Wilson as resident of, 63–64; in Wiseman's *Public Housing*, 2; Yates as resident of, 94. *See also* Madden Park

Ihlder, John, 201

illegitimacy, 33, 126, 145

Illini Union, 112

Illinois Central Station, 142

income limits: residents forced out by, 93, 98, 120, 140, 154; residents hiding income, 30

industrial economy, 136, 147

integration, 101–24; African American attitude toward, 102; Archer Courts as integrated, 35, 208; Ashburn Homes as integrated, 22–23; black businesses affected by, 107; Cabrini-Green as integrated, 185; Cabrini Homes as integrated, 4–5, 101, 106, 133, 134; Cabrini neighborhood as integrated, 60; of CHA projects, 4–6, 20, 101–2; Dearborn Homes as integrated, 14–15, 23; desegregation contrasted with, 158; Harold Ickes Homes as integrated, 109; integrated schools, 66; Kean ceases to implement, 22, 25; Leclaire Courts as integrated, 27, 38, 101–2, 183, *see photo essay*; managed integration, 27, 102, 120; teacher integration, 172; of Trumbull Park Homes, 24–25; white people moving into black neighborhoods, 108; Wood supporting, 101, 102, 120

Jackson, Everett, 153, 156–59

Jackson, Jesse, Jr., 51

Jackson, Lucille, 167, 168

janitors (maintenance personnel), 30, 64, 68, 70, 80, 191

Johnson, Edgar, 79–82, 204

Johnson, Hazel, 189–90

Johnson, Lyndon, 59

Jones, Barbara, 89, 152, 168–71

Jones, Leon, 168–69

Kean, William B., 16, 22, 25

Keck and Keck (architects), 196

Kelly, Edward, 4, 20

Kemp, Jack, 183

Kennedy, Winston, 4, 26–29, 183

Kennelly, Martin, 5, 6, 10, 20, 212n.9

Kenwood neighborhood, 57, 59

King, Martin Luther, Jr., 46, 65, 66, 128

King, Roscoe, 159–61

"kitchenette" apartments, 1, 101

Klutznick, Philip, 22, 209

Kotlowitz, Alex, 2, 68

Lake Meadows: displacement from site of, 15, 23, 47, 183, 212n.11; Jackson working at, 158; public housing compared with, 82, 127

Lake Parc Place, 50, 110, 204, 207–8

Landry, Mabel, 170

Lane, Vince, 50

Lane Tech High School, 67

Lawndale Christian Development Corporation, 174

Lawndale Gardens, 122–23, 187–89

Lazarra, Phil, 64–65

Leclaire Courts: after-school activities at, 4; Community Center at, 129; consumer cooperative at, 28; as engine for upward mobility, 2; exterior of, *see photo essay*; as ideal

Leclaire Courts (*continued*)
size, 129; as integrated, 27, 38, 101–2, 183, *see photo essay*; interior of, *see photo essay*; as isolated, 27; Kennedy as manager of, 26–28, 183; Lewis-Perry as resident of, 128–29; Mayes as resident of, 121–22; Mendenhall as resident of, 176–77; Preston as resident of, 183–84; resident management at, 38–39, 121, 183, 184, 200; screening of applicants at, 180, 183; social service agency at, 28; Townsell as resident of, 172; vegetable gardens at, 27
Lee, Harold, 89
legal aid, 34, 182
Lemann, Nicholas, 2
Lesser, Reinhart, 14, 24
Lewis, Alvin, 153, 155–56, 159
Lewis, Ramsey, 152, 166–68
Lewis-Perry, Rita, 128–30
libraries, public, 141
Lighted Schoolhouse program, 28
Local Advisory Councils (LACs), 31–32
Loebl, Schlossman and Bennett (architects), 14
Long Grove House, 205–7
Loomis Courts, 13, 196, *see photo essay*
Lowden Homes, 131, *see photo essay*
Lowenberg and Lowenberg (architects), 13, *see photo essay*
Lower North Center, 49
low-income housing: seen as for the poor, 137. *See also* public housing
loyalty oaths, 20, 104, 213n.21
Lucy Flower High School, 147, 165
lung cancer, 94, 160–61, 190

Madden Park: Alyce Holmes Holden as coach at, 152, 169–70, 171–72; Ida B. Wells Homes residents using, 47, 52, 73, 79; Barbara Jones training at, 152, 169–70
maintenance: janitors, 30, 64, 68, 70, 80, 191; neglect of, 6, 36–37, 182; reduced funds for, 179; restoring for rebirth of CHA, 180
Malcolm X, 63, 132
managed integration, 27, 102, 120
management: Brown as manager, 10–12, 52–53; Brumfield as manager, 29–32; Chadwick as manager, 32–34; Greenhalgh as manager, 24–26; Harris as manager, 34–35; as incompetent, 46; Kennedy as manager, 26–28, 183; McDade as manager, 22–24; money squandered by, 182; private management, 36, 77, 194, 200; in private versus public housing, 33. *See also* resident management
Maplewood Courts, 196
"market-rate" families, 194
Martin, Loretta, 171–72
Mayes, Deborah Gilliam, 121–22, 129, 200
McBride, Frank, 87
McCarthyism, 18, 19, 20
McDade, Tom, 22–24
McNeal, Edna, 189
McWhirter, Gerald (Abdul Alkalimat), 133–37, 204
Mendenhall, Larry, 173
Mendenhall, Sam, 173, 176–77
Merriam, Robert, 16
Messiah, Henry and Elouise, 97–99
Messianic Jews, 163
Metropolitan Boys Glee Club, 142
Metropolitan Housing Council, 4, 16
Meyerson, Martin, 9, 24
middle-class blacks: affirmative action and, 52; at Ida B. Wells Homes, 48; at Midway Gardens, 105; as moving out of the old neighborhoods, 72; as one paycheck away from disaster, 135–36; as role models, 44
Midway Gardens, 104–5, 213n.22
Million Man March, 62–63, 128, 136, 143–44, 151, 199
mixed-income housing, 71, 146, 154, 192, 194, 202
Montgomery Ward, 106, 107, 121
Monumental Baptist Church, 48
Moore, Charlotte Young, 92–94
morality, 51, 77, 186

Morrison, Myrtle, 190–92, 200
mortgages, 122, 135
Murrow, Edward R., 17
Museum of Science and Industry, 189
music: Jerry Butler, 60–63, 152; church choirs, 42, 90; drum chorus at Ida B. Wells Homes, 175; Ramsey Lewis, 152, 166–68; Metropolitan Boys Glee Club, 142; structured learning in, 152; VJ Records, 61; Wyatt Choral Ensemble, 139, 152, 153, 155–56, 159
Myerson, Bess, 160

National Press Club, 118
Native Son (Wright), 1
Nedza, Ed, 67
New York City Housing Authority, 200, 201

Offord, Phyllis, 37–40, 200
Ogden Courts, 196
Owens, Jesse, 170

Pacesetter Homes, 137
Paris (France), 200
Park Forest (Illinois), 22
Park Manor neighborhood, 89, 91
Patton Elementary School, 137
Peck, Harvey, 29
People for Community Recovery, 190
Phillips High School, 42
picnics, 88, 92, 198
poker, 47
poverty: concentrated, 176; poverty line, 140. *See also* welfare
Prairie Courts, 196
pregnancy, teenage, 126
Presidential Towers, 82
Preston, Helen, 183–84, 200
Princeton Park, 35, 156
private management, 36, 77, 194, 200
private schools, 78–79, 123
privatization, 136
project management. *See* management
Promised Land, The (Lemann), 2
Pruitt-Igoe (St. Louis), 205
public aid. *See* welfare
public housing: "back-to-basics" approach to, 200; demolition of, 193–94, 195; design and size of, 195–97; as engine for upward mobility, 2, 3; of the future, 71; as gone awry, 71; HOPE VI program, 193–95; as housing of last resort, 69, 80; landlord-tenant model for, 188; lawless teenage boys as hallmark of, 166; McCarthy era opposition to, 20; mix of incomes in, 71, 146, 154, 192, 194, 202; moving to the suburbs, 37, 50, 103, 183, 198, 212n.17; as needed more than ever, 188, 195; private management for, 36, 77, 194, 200; project management requiring strictness, 33; race and location of, 197–98; a rebirth for, 193–204; residents made scapegoats, 39; returning to policies of yesterday, 203–4; scattered-site housing, 122, 177, 183, 196, 197–98, 200; size of project as important, 35, 196–97; staff quality and regulations, 199–200; as transitional, 24, 26, 30, 118, 146–47, 188; as working well, 2–3. *See also* Chicago Housing Authority
Public Housing (Wiseman), 2
Public Housing Association, 20, 212n.10
public libraries, 141
Puckett, Kirby, 175
Pugh, Stephen, 106–8

race, 101–24; and location of public housing, 197–98; in loss of support for CHA, 4–5, 20; racial balance, 27, 102, 120; Wood on, 5. *See also* affirmative action; integration; racism; segregation
racism: the country as built on, 110; on Southwest Side, 37–38; subterranean, 159; Trumbull Park Homes riots, 5–6, 10, 17, 28. *See also* discrimination; segregation
Rainer, Father, 107
redevelopment and slum clearance program, 20

redlining, 122
"Red Squad," 21, 55–56
Reed, Cordell, 42–44; and Acey Harris, 88; at Ida B. Wells Homes, 42; upward mobility of, 2, 42, 48
religion. *See* church
relocation, 32–33, 181
rent parties, 104, 105
rents: seen as too high, 140, 145–46, 182; 30 percent rule, 30, 179, 185, 191, 201, 212n.14
resident management: Amey on, 182, 200; at Ida B. Wells Homes, 82; at Leclaire Courts, 38–39, 121, 183, 184, 200; Offord on problems with, 38–39; people working together compared with, 192; as proving ineffective, 200; Shepherd on problems with, 36
restrictive covenants, 101
reunions, 88, 198
Roberts, Phillip and Jeffery, 110–14
Robert Taylor Homes, 84, 102, 104, 147, 196, 205
Robeson, Paul, 160
Robinson, Mary, 138–40
Rockwell Gardens, 68, 69
role models, 44, 50, 107, 127, 138, 167, 176
Roseland, 159–60
Roseland Hospital, 154
Rotecki, Sally, 23
rules for CHA residents. *See* standards (rules) for CHA residents

Sable, Ruth, 16–19, 199
safety: at Altgeld Gardens, 114, 137; at Cabrini-Green, 66, 181; at Harold Ickes Homes, 109; at Henry Horner Homes, 68; income and, 122; remembering the time when the projects were safe, 204
Saffold, Howard, 62
St. James Grammar School, 147
St. Louis (Missouri), 205
St. Thaddeus Catholic Church, 78
Samuel, Ananias, Jr., 140–44, 152
scattered-site housing, 122, 177, 183, 196, 197–98, 200
School of Social Work (Loyola University), 6
schools. *See* education
screening of tenants: in early CHA, 4, 69, 75, 76–77, 126, 145, 169, 180, 183, 188, 191, 201; elimination in CHA, 6, 22, 186; at Long Grove House, 207; as needing to be revamped, 36; for public housing rebirth, 36, 200–203
Section 8 subsidy, 71, 207, 208
Section 221(d)(3) subsidy, 207, 213n.26
Section 236 subsidy, 213n.26
segregation: blacks living in black neighborhoods, 37, 44, 49–50, 59–60, 82, 83, 102, 116, 118, 121, 134–35, 156, 159, 197–98; CHA building in black neighborhoods only, 5, 16, 102, 118, 197; education under, 135; at Illinois Central Station, 142; in Roseland, 159–60; in the South, 55, 109–10, 142
Shaw, William, 114–16
Shepherd, Beverly, 35–37
Shufro, Milton (Mick): and citizens' organizations, 21; City Council opposing, 5, 18; in keeping CHA free of patronage, 4, 20; as purist, 15; red-baiting of, 18; resignation of, 5, 18; Sable as secretary of, 17–18; and Wallace's visit to CHA, 12
Shuldiner, Joseph, 197
Sing, Erman and Dorothy, 76–79
single-parent families: accountability for, 145; at Altgeld Gardens, 58, 77–78; at Cabrini-Green, 67, 181, 185; at Cabrini Homes, 60–61, 121; at Dearborn Homes, 146; and gangs, 67; at Harold Ickes Homes, 90; at Ida B. Wells Homes, 70, 79, 165–66; illegitimacy as grounds for termination, 33, 145; increase of, 6, 201–2; at Leclaire Courts, 38; at Long Grove House, 206; as not

necessarily bad families, 34; selecting among, 57; at Wentworth Gardens, 191
Skidmore, Owings and Merrill (architects), 196
Slater, Barbara Jones, 89, 152, 168–71
Slaughter, Adolph, 116–19
slavery, 66, 81
slum clearance, 20
Smith, Blanche, 161
Smith, David, 173
Smith, Irene, 39
social work: CHA attempting to provide, 22; home visits, 23, 32–33, 76, 169; at Ida B. Wells Homes, 48, 169; at Leclaire Courts, 28, 39
South Shore Bank, 71
sports: at Altgeld Gardens, 137, 148; as forum for growth and opportunity, 151–52, 199; Frost influenced by, 73; at Ida B. Wells Homes, 46, 47, 73, 79, 174–75; Barbara Jones, 89, 152, 168–71; Townsell influenced by, 173
standards (rules) for CHA residents: ceasing to be enforced, 6, 22, 34, 126, 169, 182; in early CHA, 4, 69, 126–27, 145, 180
Stateway Gardens, 29–31, 46, 93, 102, *see photo essay*
storefront churches, 44
Stracke, Win, 134
Stratton, Samuel, 55
subsidized housing: Section 8, 71, 207, 208; Section 221(d)(3), 207, 213n.26; Section 236, 213n.26. *See also* public housing
suburbs, moving public housing to, 37, 50, 103, 183, 198, 212n.17
Sungro, Harry, 67
Sun-Times (newspaper), 117, 140
Swibel, Charles, 180

Taylor, Robert R., 4, 5
teenage pregnancy, 126
tenant management. *See* resident management
tenant's council, 104
tenant selection. *See* screening of tenants
Tenants Voice, The (newspaper), 98
There Are No Children Here (Kotlowitz), 2, 68
Third Baptist Church, 95–96
30 percent rule (Brooke Amendment), 30, 179, 185, 191, 201, 212n.14
Thomas, Clarence, 85, 135
Thompson, Andrew, 108–9
Thompson, Henry, 173
Thompson, Joe, 146–47
Tilden Tech, 42–43, 45, 49, 71, 109
Townsell, Richard, 152, 172–74
Travis, Dempsey, 56
Tribune (newspaper), 81, 112, 117
trickle-down theory, 168
Trinity United Church of Christ, 164–65
Tronzo, Alfred, 201
Trula, Lewis, 87–88
Trumbull Park (Brown), 25
Trumbull Park Homes: black residents test use of the park, 28–29; federal government building, 12; Greenhalgh as manager of, 24–26; integration of, 24–25; Kennedy as manager of, 28; race riot at, 6, 10, 17, 28

University of Illinois Dental School, 110, 112

vacant land sites, 15–16, 21
vandalism, 76
Vernon Park Church of God, 152, 153, 155
veterans, 5, 20, 22, 101, 120
VJ Records, 61

Wald, John, 160
Waldman, Charlie, 24
Walker, John, 173
Wallace, Dave, 24
Wallace, Henry, 12
Washburne Trade School, 60

Wayman AMC Church, 168
Weddington, Arnold, 152, 174–76
Weese, Harry, 13, 196
welfare: in early CHA, 6, 28; people coming north for, 78; public housing as dumping ground for recipients, 80, 136; recipients in high-rise buildings, 146; single mothers on, 6, 60, 67, 121, 146, 206; the system creating dependency on, 79; work versus, 59, 70, 84
Wellborn, Jean, 29
Wells, Ida B., Homes. *See* Ida B. Wells Homes
Wells High School, 167
Wendell Phillips High School, 42, 172
Wentworth Gardens: Amey as resident of, 182–83; decline of, 191; McNeal as resident of, 189; Morrison as resident of, 190–92; resident management at, 36; reunions at, 198
William Green Homes, 105, 107
Williams, Michael, 173
Williams Elementary School, 98, 147
Willuweit, Angela, 5, 119–21
Wilson, Horace, 53
Wilson, John, 83–86
Wilson, Margaret, 185–87
Wilson, Melvin, 45, 63–66
Wilson, Roosevelt, 155
Winston, Oliver, 201
Wiseman, Frederick, 2
Withers, Enid, 117
Wonder, Stevie, 165
Wood, Elizabeth: background of, 3; as CHA executive director, 4, 9–10, 12, 13–14, 16; in CHA's early success, 3–4, 195; and citizens' organizations, 21; conflict with CHA board, 5–6; design as concern of, 22, 196; feeding a client's baby, 18; flower competitions held by, 4, 98; as inspiring, 13; integration as goal of, 101, 102, 120; as Metropolitan Housing Council director, 4, 16; at monthly dinner meetings, 32; ouster of, 6, 9–10, 21–22; photograph of, *see photo essay*; politics of, 16, 18; on public agencies as catalytic agents, 15; as realist, 3, 15; reporters' attitude toward, 19; residents' gratitude toward, 180; returning to policies of, 203–4; and Shufro, 5, 17, 18; on *The Tenants Voice* newspaper, 98; on vacant land sites, 15; and the Wyatts, 153, 160
work: black women as able to get jobs, 81; discrimination in employment, 56, 81, 103, 143, 147; honorable people wanting to work, 39; versus welfare, 59, 70, 84; working families at CHA, 6, 35, 50, 69, 72, 80, 93, 183, 194, 195, 212n.14; working families leave CHA, 6, 169, 179, 182, 191
"worst-case" housing needs, 195
Wright, Jeremiah, Jr., 164
Wright, Richard, 1
Wuenschel, Daniel, 203
Wyatt, Addie, 152–55; helping people turn their lives around, 151; and Jackson, 153, 157–58; and King, 159, 161; and Lewis, 153, 155–56; sister Maude Davis, 138; Wood and, 160; Wyatt Choral Ensemble, 139, 153, 155–56, 159
Wyatt, Claude, 152–55; helping people turn their lives around, 151; and Jackson, 153, 157–58; and King, 159, 161; and Lewis, 153, 155–56; Wyatt Choral Ensemble, 139, 153, 155–56, 159
Wyatt Choral Ensemble, 139, 152, 153, 155–56, 159

Yates, Sid, 32
Yates, Troy L., Jr., 94–97

About the Authors

J. S. FUERST is now retired but was formerly emeritus Professor of Social Welfare Policy at Loyola University and formerly the Assistant Director of the Graduate Program in Urban Studies. He was Director of Research and Statistics for the Chicago Housing Authority for ten years.

D. BRADFORD HUNT is Assistant Professor of Social Science at Roosevelt University in Chicago.